Lecture Notes in Computer Science 7119

Commenced Publication in 1973
Founding and Former Series Editors:
Gerhard Goos, Juris Hartmanis, and Jan van Leeuwen

T0236057

Zdeněk Kotásek   Jan Bouda
Ivana Černá   Lukáš Sekanina
Tomáš Vojnar   David Antoš (Eds.)

Mathematical and Engineering Methods in Computer Science

7th International Doctoral Workshop, MEMICS 2011
Lednice, Czech Republic, October 14-16, 2011
Revised Selected Papers

 Springer

Volume Editors

Zdeněk Kotásek
Lukáš Sekanina
Tomáš Vojnar
Brno University of Technology, Faculty of Information Technology
Božetěchova 2, 612 66 Brno, Czech Republic
E-mail: {kotasek, sekanina, vojnar}@fit.vutbr.cz

Jan Bouda
Ivana Černá
Masaryk University, Faculty of Informatics
Botanická 68a, 602 00 Brno, Czech Republic
E-mail: {bouda, cerna}@fi.muni.cz

David Antoš
Masaryk University, Institute of Computer Science
Botanická 68a, 602 00 Brno, Czech Republic
E-mail: antos@ics.muni.cz

ISSN 0302-9743   e-ISSN 1611-3349
ISBN 978-3-642-25928-9   e-ISBN 978-3-642-25929-6
DOI 10.1007/978-3-642-25929-6
Springer Heidelberg Dordrecht London New York

Library of Congress Control Number: 2011944974

CR Subject Classification (1998): C.2, D.2, K.6.3, K.6.5, K.4.4, H.4

LNCS Sublibrary: SL 2 – Programming and Software Engineering

Typesetting: Camera-ready by author, data conversion by Scientific Publishing Services, Chennai, India

Printed on acid-free paper

Springer is part of Springer Science+Business Media (www.springer.com)

Preface

MEMICS 2011 was the seventh instance of the international doctoral workshop on Mathematical and Engineering Methods in Computer Science organized in Southern Moravia by the Faculty of Information Technology of the Brno University of Technology and the Faculty of Informatics of the Masaryk University. MEMICS 2011 took place in Lednice, Czech Republic, where it was held during October 14–16, 2011. For the first time in MEMICS's history, the workshop proceedings were published by Springer in the LNCS series.

The MEMICS workshops are intended to provide an opportunity for PhD students to present and discuss their work in an international environment. Their focus on PhD studies instead of a particular narrow scientific area leads to a cross-disciplinary orientation, providing a pleasant environment for an exchange of ideas among researchers in several different fields of computer science and technology.

Submissions are invited especially in the following (though not exclusive) areas: software and hardware dependability, computer security, computer-aided analysis and verification, testing and diagnostics, simulation, parallel and distributed computing, grid computing, computer networks, modern hardware and its design, non-traditional computing architectures, software engineering, computational intelligence, quantum information processing, computer graphics and multimedia, signal, text, speech, and image processing, and theoretical computer science.

As is the tradition in the MEMICS workshops, invited lectures given by internationally recognized researchers complemented the standard program based on papers authored by PhD students. MEMICS 2011 hosted six invited speakers: Saddek Bensalem from VERIMAG, University Joseph Fourier/CNRS/INPG, Grenoble, France, with the talk "Rigorous Component-Based System Design Using the BIP Framework," Peter Bentley from University College London, UK, with a talk on "Modelling Complex Systems—Lessons from the Life Sciences," Krishnendu Chatterjee from IST Austria, with a talk on "Games and Probabilistic Systems with Mean-Payoff, Energy and Parity Objectives," Görschwin Fey from University of Bremen, Germany, with the talk "Assessing System Vulnerability Using Formal Verification Techniques," Renato Renner from ETH Zurich, Switzerland, with a talk on "Security in a Quantum World," and Petr Tůma from Charles University in Prague, Czech Republic, with the talk "Computer Memory: Why We Should Care What Is Under The Hood." Thanks go to all these invited lecturers who found time to participate at the workshop and demonstrated how a top-quality presentation could look.

This post-workshop volume contains 6 papers written by the invited speakers and 13 papers selected from 38 papers submitted by PhD students. Each submitted paper was reviewed by at least three independent reviewers, who provided not only a recommendation to the Program Committee, but also gave an extensive feedback to the authors. The hard work of the Program Committee as well as of the external reviewers is highly appreciated.

All the contributed works were presented by PhD students, who got the opportunity to speak in front of their peers and to receive immediate feedback from participating senior faculty members, including the invited lecturers. All students were encouraged to actively participate in the discussions, to express their opinions, exchange ideas and compare methods, traditions and approaches of groups and institutions whose representatives were participating at the workshop. All these forms of discussions and social networking created a unique environment intended to foster further research collaboration among participants and their institutions.

The MEMICS tradition of best paper awards continued at the MEMICS 2011 workshop. Three student papers were selected at the end of the workshop, taking into account their scientific and technical contribution together with the quality of presentation. The following works were selected for the best paper awards (listed in alphabetical order):

- Jiří Barnat, Ivana Černá and Jana Tůmová, "Timed Automata Approach to Verification of Systems with Degradation"
- Ondrej Moriš and Petr Hliněný, "Generalized Maneuvers in Route Planning"
- Christos Sakellariou and Peter Bentley, "Introducing the FPGA-Based Hardware Architecture of Systemic Computation (HAoS)"

The awards consisted of a diploma for all authors of the selected papers complemented with a financial contribution covered by the sponsoring organizations, Honeywell Czech Republic, IBA CZ, and Red Hat Czech Republic. The sponsorship is highly appreciated.

The MEMICS 2011 workshop was financially supported by the doctoral grant project 102/09/H042 *Mathematical and Engineering Approaches to Developing Reliable and Secure Concurrent and Distributed Computer Systems* from the Czech Science Foundation. This support is highly appreciated. The direct and indirect support and help from the organizing faculties is also highly appreciated.

Last but not least, our appreciation goes to the Organizing Committee of MEMICS 2011 that guaranteed a smooth realization of the MEMICS 2011 workshop, essential to its success. Our thanks go to all members of the Organizing Committee and its Chair, Radek Kočí, for all their efforts and hard work.

The work of the PC of MEMICS 2011, including the preparation of this volume, was greatly aided by the use of the EasyChair system.

October 2011   Zdeněk Kotásek
Brno   Jan Bouda
                                                                  Ivana Černá
                                                               Lukáš Sekanina
                                                                Tomáš Vojnar

Organization

General Chair

Zdeněk Kotásek   Brno University of Technology, Czech Republic

Program Committee Co-chairs

Jan Bouda	Masaryk University, Brno, Czech Republic
Ivana Černá	Masaryk University, Brno, Czech Republic
Lukáš Sekanina	Brno University of Technology, Brno, Czech Republic
Tomáš Vojnar	Brno University of Technology, Brno, Czech Republic

Program Committee

Parosh Aziz Abdulla	Uppsala University, Sweden
Andris Ambainis	University of Latvia, Latvia
Maria Bieliková	Slovak University of Technology in Bratislava, Slovak Republic
Armin Biere	Johannes Kepler University, Linz, Austria
Jan Bouda	Masaryk University, Brno, Czech Republic
Ivana Černá	Masaryk University, Brno, Czech Republic
Pavol Černý	IST Austria, Vienna, Austria
Milan Češka	Brno University of Technology, Czech Republic
Rusins Freivalds	University of Latvia, Latvia
Tomasz Garbolino	Silesian University of Technology, Gliwice, Poland
Elena Gramatová	Slovak University of Technology, Bratislava, Slovak Republic
Jozef Gruska	Masaryk University, Brno, Czech Republic
Peter Habermehl	LIAFA, University Paris Diderot - Paris7, France
Petr Hanáček	Brno University of Technology, Czech Republic
Petr Hliněný	Masaryk University, Brno, Czech Republic
Štefan Hudák	Technical University of Košice, Slovakia
Radu Iosif	VERIMAG, CNRS, Grenoble, France
Petr Jančar	Technical University Ostrava, Czech Republic
Galina Jirásková	Slovak Academy of Sciences in Košice, Slovak Republic

Dušan Kolář   Brno University of Technology, Czech Republic
Zdeněk Kotásek   Brno University of Technology, Czech Republic
Bohuslav Křena   Brno University of Technology, Czech Republic
Mojmír Křetínský   Masaryk University, Brno, Czech Republic
Hana Kubátová   Czech Technical University in Prague,
                             Czech Republic
Paulo Mateus   Instituto Superior Técnico Lisbon, Portugal
Václav Matyáš   Masaryk University, Brno, Czech Republic
Luděk Matyska   Masaryk University, Brno, Czech Republic
Richard Mayr   University of Edinburgh, UK
Felix Moreno   Universidad Politécnica de Madrid, Spain
Daniel Olejár   Comenius University in Bratislava,
                             Slovak Republic
Simon Perdrix   CNRS Grenoble, France
Stanislav Racek   University of West Bohemia, Pilsen,
                             Czech Republic
Hana Rudová   Masaryk University, Brno, Czech Republic
Andrey Rybalchenko   Technical University of Munich, Germany
Zdeněk Říha   Masaryk University, Brno, Czech Republic
Zdeněk Sawa   Technical University of Ostrava,
                             Czech Republic
Lukáš Sekanina   Brno University of Technology, Czech Republic
Jiří Srba   BRICS, Aalborg University, Denmark
Jan Strejček   Masaryk University, Brno, Czech Republic
Giovanni Squillero   Politecnico di Torino, Italy
Andreas Steininger   Vienna University of Technology, Austria
Jiří Šíma   The Academy of Sciences of the
                             Czech Republic, Czech Republic
Jim Torresen   University of Oslo, Norway
Petr Tůma   Charles University in Prague, Czech Republic
Tomáš Vojnar   Brno University of Technology, Czech Republic
Michael Weber   University of Twente, The Netherlands
Pavel Zemčík   Brno University of Technology, Czech Republic

Organizing Committee Chair

Radek Kočí   Brno University of Technology, Czech Republic

Organizing Committee

Pavel Bartoš   Brno University of Technology, Czech Republic
Adam Husár   Brno University of Technology, Czech Republic
Peter Jurnečka   Brno University of Technology, Czech Republic
Filip Konečný   Brno University of Technology, Czech Republic

Pavol Korček	Brno University of Technology, Czech Republic
Zdeněk Letko	Brno University of Technology, Czech Republic
Petr Pospíchal	Brno University of Technology, Czech Republic
Zdenek Prikryl	Brno University of Technology, Czech Republic
Jiří Šimáček	Brno University of Technology, Czech Republic

Steering Committee

Milan Češka	Brno University of Technology, Czech Republic
Zdeněk Kotásek	Brno University of Technology, Czech Republic
Mojmír Křetínský	Masaryk University, Brno, Czech Republic
Antonín Kučera	Masaryk University, Brno, Czech Republic
Luděk Matyska	Masaryk University, Brno, Czech Republic
Tomáš Vojnar	Brno University of Technology, Czech Republic

Additional Reviewers

Gabriela Andrejková	Andrej Podzimek
Andrej Bebjak	Thomas Polzer
Marius Bozga	Karin Quaas
Jonathan Cederberg	Thomas Reinbacher
Florent Garnier	João Rodrigues
Lukáš Holík	Adam Rogalewicz
Martin Hrubý	Václav Šimek
Jozef Janovský	Jiří Šimša
Jiří Jaroš	Jari Stenman
Michal Kajan	David Svoboda
Jan Kaštil	Patrick Totzke
Martin Kot	Varadan Savulimedu Veeravalli
Zbyněk Křivka	Martin Žádník
Markéta Lopatková	

Table of Contents

Rigorous System Design: The BIP Approach

Ananda Basu[1], Saddek Bensalem[1,2], Marius Bozga[1],
Paraskevas Bourgos[1], and Joseph Sifakis[1]

[1] Verimag Laboratory, Université Joseph Fourier Grenoble, CNRS
[2] CEA-Leti, MINATEC Campus, Grenoble France

Abstract. Rigorous system design requires the use of a single powerful component framework allowing the representation of the designed system at different levels of detail, from application software to its implementation. This is essential for ensuring the overall coherency and correctness. The paper introduces a rigorous design flow based on the BIP (Behavior, Interaction, Priority) component framework [1]. This design flow relies on several, tool-supported, source-to-source transformations allowing to progressively and correctly transform high level application software towards efficient implementations for specific platforms.

1 System Design

Traditional engineering disciplines such as civil or mechanical engineering are based on solid theory for building artifacts with predictable behavior over their life-time. In contrast, we lack similar constructivity results for computing engineering: computer science provides only partial answers to particular system design problems. With few exceptions in this domain, predictability is impossible to guarantee at design time and therefore, a posteriori validation remains the only means for ensuring their correct operation.

System design is facing several difficulties, mainly due to our inability to predict the behavior of an application software running on a given platform. Usually, systems are built by reusing and assembling components that are, simpler subsystems. This is the only way to master complexity and to ensure correctness of the overall design, while maintaining or increasing productivity. However, system level integration becomes extremely hard because components are usually highly heterogeneous: they have different characteristics, are often developed using different technologies, and highlight different features from different viewpoints. Other difficulties stem from current design approaches, often empirical and based on expertise and experience of design teams. Naturally, designers attempt to solve new problems by reusing, extending and improving existing solutions proven to be efficient and robust. This favors component reuse and avoids re-inventing and re-discovering designs. Nevertheless, on a longer term perspective, this may also be counter-productive: designers are not always able to adapt in a satisfactory manner to new requirements. Moreover, they a priori exclude better solutions simply because they do not fit their know-how.

Z. Kotásek et al. (Eds.): MEMICS 2011, LNCS 7119, pp. 1–19, 2012.

System design is the process leading to a mixed software/hardware system meeting given specifications. It involves the development of application software taking into account features of an execution platform. The latter is defined by its architecture involving a set of processors equipped with hardware-dependent software such as operating systems as well as primitives for coordination of the computation and interaction with the external environment.

System design radically differs from pure software design in that it should take into account not only functional but also extra-functional specifications regarding the use of resources of the execution platform such as time, memory and energy. Meeting extra-functional specifications is essential for the design of embedded systems. It requires evaluation of the impact of design choices on the overall behavior of the system. It also implies a deep understanding of the interaction between application software and the underlying execution platform. We currently lack approaches for modeling mixed hardware/software systems. There are no rigorous techniques for deriving global models of a given system from models of its application software and its execution platform.

A system design flow consists of steps starting from specifications and leading to an implementation on a given execution platform. It involves the use of methods and tools for progressively deriving the implementation by making adequate design choices.

We consider that a system design flow must meet the following essential requirements:

– *Correctness*: This means that the designed system meets its specifications. Ensuring correctness requires that the design flow relies on models with well-defined semantics. The models should consistently encompass system description at different levels of abstraction from application software to its implementation. Correctness can be achieved by application of verification techniques. It is desirable that if some specifications are met at some step of the design flow, they are preserved in all the subsequent steps.

– *Productivity*: This can be achieved by system design flows

  – providing high level domain-specific languages for ease of expression
  – allowing reuse of components and the development of component-based solutions
  – integrating tools for programming, validation and code generation

– *Performance*: The design flow must allow the satisfaction of extra-functional properties regarding optimal resource management. This means that resources such as memory, time and energy are first class concepts encompassed by formal models. Moreover, it should be possible to analyze and evaluate efficiency in using resources as early as possible along the design flow. Unfortunately, most of the widely used modeling formalisms offer only syntactic sugar for expressing timing constraints and scheduling policies. Lack of adequate semantic models does not allow consistency checking for timing requirements, or meaningful composition of features.

– *Parcimony*: The design flow should not enforce any particular programming or execution model. Very often system designers privilege specific programming models or implementation principles that a priori exclude efficient solutions. They program in low level languages that do not help discover parallelism or non determinism and enforce strictly sequential execution. For instance, programming multimedia applications in plain C may lead to designs obscuring the inherent functional parallelism and involving built-in scheduling mechanisms that are not optimal. It is essential that designers use adequate programming models. Furthermore, design choices should be driven only by system specifications to obtain the best possible implementation.

We call *rigorous* a design flow which allows guaranteeing essential properties of the specifications. Most of the rigorous design flows privilege a unique programming model together with an associated compilation chain adapted for a given execution model. For example, synchronous system design relies on synchronous programming models and usually targets hardware or sequential implementations on single processors [2]. Alternatively, real-time programming based on scheduling theory for periodic tasks, targets dedicated real-time multitasking platforms [3].

A rigorous design flow should be characterized by the following:

– It should be *model-based*, that is all the software and system descriptions used along the design flow should be based on a single semantic model. This is essential for maintaining the overall coherency of the flow by guaranteeing that a description at step n meets essential properties of a description at step $n - 1$. This means in particular that the semantic model is expressive enough to directly encompasses various types of component heterogeneity arising along the design flow [4]:

  – Heterogeneity of computation: The semantic model should encompass both synchronous and asynchronous computation by using adequate coordination mechanisms. This should allow in particular, modeling mixed hardware/software systems.
  – Heterogeneity of interaction: The semantic model should enable natural and direct description of various mechanisms used to coordinate execution of components including semaphores, rendezvous, broadcast, method call, etc.
  – Heterogeneity of abstraction: The semantic model should support the description of a system at different abstraction levels from its application software to its implementation. This makes possible the definition of a clear correspondence between the description of an untimed platform-independent behavior and the corresponding timed and platform-dependent implementation.

– It should be *component-based*, that is it provides primitives for building composite components as the composition of simpler components. Existing theoretical frameworks for composition are based on a single operator e.g., product of automata, function call. Poor expressiveness of these frameworks may lead to complicated designs: achieving a given coordination between components often requires additional components to manage their interaction.

For instance, if the composition is by strong synchronization (rendezvous) modeling broadcast requires an extra component to choose amongst the possible strong synchronizations a maximal one. We need frameworks providing families of composition operators for natural and direct description of coordination mechanisms such as protocols, schedulers and buses.

– It should rely on tractable theory for guaranteeing *correctness by construction* to avoid as much as possible monolithic a posteriori verification. Such a theory is based on two types of rules:

  – Compositionality rules for inferring global properties of composite components from the properties of composed components e.g. if a set of components are deadlock-free then for a certain type of composition the obtained composite components is deadlock-free too. A special and very useful case of compositionality is when a behavioral equivalence relation between components is a congruence [5]. In that case, substituting a component in a system model by a behaviorally equivalent component leads to an equivalent model.
  – Composability rules ensuring that essential properties of a component are preserved when it is used to build composite components.

The paper presents a rigorous design flow based on the BIP (Behavior, Interaction, Priority) component framework [1]. It is organized as follows. Section 2 introduces the underlying modeling framework and the main steps of the design flow. Subsection 2.1 presents the BIP language. Subsection 2.2 explains the principle of translating different programming models into BIP. Subsection 2.3 introduces a method for compositional verification of BIP programs, especially used for checking deadlock-freedom. Subsection 2.4 presents a method for integrating architectural constraints into the BIP model of application software and subsection 2.5 presents a method for generating distributed implementations. The design flow is illustrated through non trivial examples in section 3. In section 4, we conclude and discuss future work directions.

2   The BIP Design Flow

BIP [1] (Behavior, Interaction, Priority) is a general framework encompassing rigorous design. It uses the BIP language and an associated toolset supporting the design flow. The BIP language is a notation which allows building complex systems by coordinating the behavior of a set of atomic components. Behavior is described as a finite-state automaton extended with data and functions described in C. The transitions of the Petri are labelled with guards (conditions on the state of a component and its environment) as well as functions that describe computations on local data. The description of coordination between components is layered. The first layer describes the interactions between components. The second layer describes dynamic priorities between the interactions and is used to express scheduling policies. The combination of interactions and priorities characterizes the overall architecture of a component. It confers BIP strong expressiveness that cannot be matched by other languages [6]. BIP has clean operational semantics that describe the behavior of a composite component as the composition of the behaviors of its atomic components. This allows a direct relation between the underlying semantic model (transition systems) and its implementation.

The BIP design flow uses a single language to ensure consistency between the different design steps. This is mainly achieved by applying source-to-source transformations between refined system models. These transformations are proven correct-by-construction, that means, they preserve observational equivalence and consequently essential safety properties. Functional verification is applied only to high level models for checking safety properties such as invariants and deadlock-freedom. To avoid inherent complexity limitations, the verification method applies compositionality techniques implemented in the D-Finder tool.

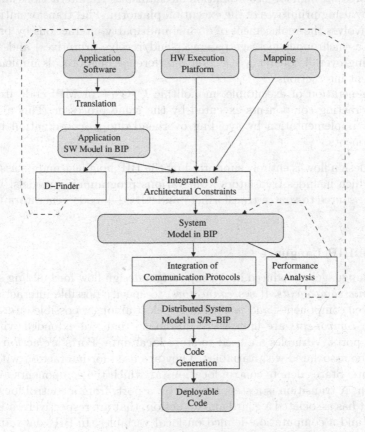

Fig. 1. BIP Design Flow

The design flow involves 4 distinct steps:

1. The translation of the application software into a BIP model. This allows its representation in a rigorous semantic framework. There exist translations of several programming models into BIP including synchronous, data-flow and event driven models.
2. The generation of an abstract system model from the BIP model representing the application software, a model of the target execution platform as well as a mapping of the atomic components of the application software model into processing elements of the platform. The obtained model takes into account hardware architecture constraints and execution times of atomic actions. Architecture constraints include mutual exclusion induced from sharing physical resources such as buses, memories and processors as well as scheduling policies seeking optimal use of these resources.
3. The generation of a concrete system model obtained from the abstract model by expressing high level coordination mechanisms e.g., interactions and priorities by using primitives of the execution platform. This transformation usually involves the replacement of atomic multiparty interactions by protocols using asynchronous message passing (send/receive primitives) and arbiters ensuring overall coherency e.g. non interference of protocols implementing different interactions.
4. The generation of executable, monolithic C/C++ or MPI code from sets of interacting components executed by the same processor. This allows efficient implementation by avoiding overhead due to coordination between components.

The BIP design flow is entirely supported by the BIP language and its associated toolset, which includes translators from various programming models, verification tools, source-to-source transformers and C/C++-code generators for BIP models.

2.1   The BIP Language

The BIP language, introduced in [1], supports a design flow for building systems from *atomic components*. It ses *connectors*, to specify possible interaction patterns etween components, and *priorities*, to select amongst possible interactions.

Atomic components are finite-state automata that are extended with variables and ports. Variables are used to store local data. Ports are action names, and may be associated with variables. They are used for interaction with other components. States denote control locations at which the components await for interaction. A transition is a step, labeled by a port, from a control location to another. It has associated a guard and an action, that are respectively, a Boolean condition and a computation defined on local variables. In BIP, data and their transformations are written in C.

For a given valuation of variables, a transition can be executed if the guard evaluates to true and some *interaction* involving the port is enabled. The execution is an atomic sequence of two microsteps: (i) execution of the interaction involving the port, which is a synchronization between several components, with possible exchange of data, followed by (ii) execution of internal computation associated with the transition.

Composite components are defined by assembling sub-components (atomic or composite) using *connectors*. Connectors relate ports from different subcomponents. They represent sets of interactions, that are, non-empty sets of ports that have to be jointly executed. For every such interaction, the connector provides the guard and the data transfer, that are, respectively, an enabling condition and an exchange of data across the ports involved in the interaction.

Finally, *priorities* provide a mean to coordinate the execution of interactions within a BIP system. They are used to specify scheduling or similar arbitration policies between simultaneously enabled interactions. More concretely, priorities are rules, each consisting of an ordered pair of interactions associated with a condition. When the condition holds and both interactions of the corresponding pair are enabled, only the one with higher-priority can be executed.

Figure 2 shows a graphical representation of an example model in BIP. It consists of atomic components *Sender*, *Receiver1* and *Receiver2*. The behavior of *Sender* is described as an automaton with control locations *Idle* and *Active*. It communicates through port *s* which exports the variable *x*. Components *Receiver1* and *Receiver2* are composed by the connector *C1*, which represents a rendezvous interaction between ports *r1* and *r2*, leading to the composite component *Receivers*. The composite exports *C1* as port *r*. As a result of the data transfer in *C1*, the sum of the local variables *y1* and *y2* is exported as *v* through the port *r*, and *y1*, *y2* eventually receive the value of *v*. The system is the composition of *Sender* and *Receivers* using the connector *C2* which represents a broadcast interaction from the *Sender* to the *Receivers*. When the broadcast occurs, as a result of the composed data transfer, the *Sender* gets the sum of *y1* and *y2*, and each *Receiver* gets the value *x* from the *Sender*.

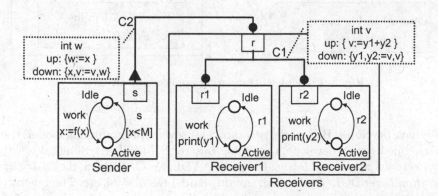

Fig. 2. An example of a BIP system

2.2   Translating Application Software into BIP

The first step in our design flow requires the generation of a BIP model for the application software. We have developed a general method for generating BIP models from languages with well-defined operational semantics. The principle of the method is depicted in Figure 3. It involves the following three steps for a given application software written in a language $\mathcal{L}$:

1. Translation of atomic components of the source language into BIP components. The translation focuses on the definition of adequate interfaces. It encapsulates and reuses data structures and functions of the application software,
2. Translation of coordination between components of the application software into connectors and priorities in the target BIP model,
3. Generation of a BIP component modeling the operational semantics of $\mathcal{L}$. This component plays the role of an engine coordinating the execution of the application software components.

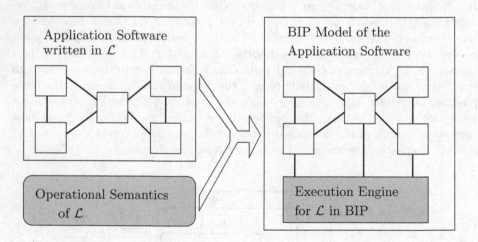

Fig. 3. Principle of translating application software

We have developed BIP model generators for several programming models used by embedded system developers including Lustre [2], MATLAB/Simulink™, the *Architecture Analysis and Design Language* AADL, NesC/TinyOS, the *Distributed Operation Layer* DOL [7], the programming model *GeNoM* [8], etc. The generated models preserve the structure and their size is linear with respect to the size of the initial programs. They are easy to understand by developers in source languages. These facts confirm the adequacy and expressive power of BIP.

2.3   Compositional Verification by Using D-Finder

Monolithic verification of component-based systems often requires computing the product of their atomic components by using interleaving and synchronization. In general, the size of this product is prohibitive and cannot be handled without manual intervention. In a series of recent works, it has been advocated that *compositional techniques* could be used to cope with state explosion in verification of concurrent systems. A key issue is the existence of composition frameworks ensuring *compositionality*, which is, establishing global properties of composite components from properties of their constituent components.

A compositional verification method for BIP based on invariant computation is presented in [9]. This method computes increasingly stronger invariants for composite components as conjunctions of local invariants for atomic components and interaction invariants characterizing the composition glue. Local component invariants are generated by static (and individual) analysis of atomic components. Interaction invariants are generated from abstractions of the composite to be verified.

The method is based on the following rule:

$$\frac{\{B_i < \Phi_i >\}_i,\ \Psi \in II(\|_\gamma \{B_i\}_i, \{\Phi_i\}_i),\ (\bigwedge_i \Phi_i) \wedge \Psi \Rightarrow \Phi}{\|_\gamma \{B_i\}_i < \Phi >}$$

The rule allows to prove invariance of property Φ for systems obtained by using an n-ary composition operation $\|$ parameterized by a set of interactions γ. Φ is implied by the conjunction of invariants Φ_i of components B_i and an *interaction invariant* Ψ. The latter expresses constraints on the global state space induced by interactions. In [9], we have shown that Ψ can be computed automatically from abstractions of the system to be verified. These are the composition of finite state abstractions of the components B_i with respect to their invariants Φ_i.

The method has been recently improved to take advantage of the incrementality of the design process. Incremental system design proceeds by adding new interactions to existing sets of components. Each time an interaction is added, it is possible to verify whether the resulting system violates a given property and discover design errors as soon as they appear. The incremental verification method [10] uses sufficient conditions ensuring the preservation of invariants when new interactions are added along the component construction process. If these conditions are not satisfied, new invariants are generated by reusing invariants of the interacting components. Reusing invariants reduces considerably the verification effort.

The above methods have been implemented in the D-Finder tool [11] for checking deadlock-freedom of systems described in BIP. Experimental results on classical benchmarks (as illustrated in Figure 4) show that D-Finder can be exponentially faster than well-established verification tools. Nonetheless, D-Finder has been also successful for the verification of complex software applications, as illustrated later in section 3.

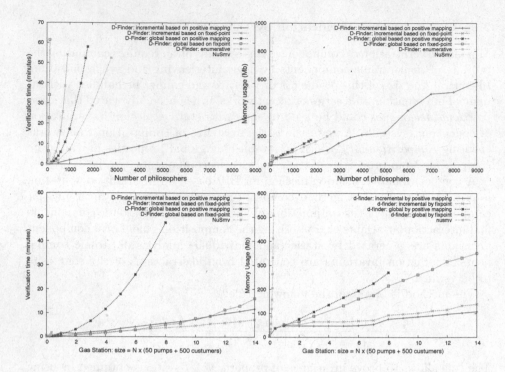

Fig. 4. D-Finder results: time (left) and memory usage (right) as a function of complexity for i) monolithic verification with NuSMV, ii) compositional verification, iii) incremental verification on two benchmarks, dining philosophers (up) and gas station (down)

2.4   Integrating Architectural Constraints in BIP

We developed in [12] a rigorous method for generating a model which faithfully represents the behavior of a mixed hardware/software system from a model of its application software and a model of its underlying hardware architecture. The method takes as input a model of the application software in BIP, a model of the hardware architecture (in XML) and a mapping associating communication operations of the application software with execution/communication paths in the architecture. It builds a model of the corresponding mixed hardware/software system in BIP. This system model can be simulated and analyzed for the verification of functional and extra-functional properties.

The method consists in progressively enriching the application software model by doing:

1. Integration of hardware components used in the system model and,
2. Application of a sequence of source-to-source transformations to synthesize *hardware dependent software routines* implementing communication by using the hardware components.

   The transformations are proved correct-by-construction, that is, they preserve functional properties of the application software.

The system model is parameterized and allows flexible integration of specific target architecture features, such as arbitration policy, throughput, latency for buses and scheduling policy, execution speed, etc. We have defined a library of BIP atomic components that characterize multi-processor tiled architectures, including models for hardware components (e.g., processor, memory) and for hardware-dependent software components (e.g., FIFO channel read/write, bus controllers, schedulers).

The method has been implemented and integrated in the BIP toolset. We used the DOL framework [7] as a frontend to describe the application software, hardware architectures and mapping specifications. The backend of the tool produces the system model in BIP, which can be analyzed by the BIP tool chain for:

- Code generation for simulation/validation on a Linux PC
- Functional correctness using the D-Finder tool, checking for deadlocks
- Performance analysis (e.g. delay computation), based on simulation and statistical model checking

We generated different system models of an MJPEG decoder running on a simplified MPARM platform. The decoder is described in DOL [7], and consists of five processes communicating asynchronously through FIFO channels. The process description consists of about 2500 lines of C. The description is automatically translated into the application software model, which is about 10000 lines of BIP. This model is purely functional and can be analyzed with D-Finder to assess its correctness. It has been mapped on a MPARM platform consisting of three processors, their local memories, and a global shared memory, with all being connected via a global bus. Different mappings were considered, leading to different system models. These models have been used for performance analysis. Using simulation, we measured computation and communication times for relevant parts of the application software. As future work, we intend to use these results in order to build (simpler) statistical abstractions of the system models on which properties can be validated using statistical model-checking.

2.5   Generating Distributed Implementations

To generate distributed implementations from BIP models it is necessary to transform these models into S/R-BIP models. These are a subclass of models where multi-party interaction is replaced by protocols using S/R (Send/Receive) primitives. Then, from S/R-BIP models and a mapping of atomic components into processing elements of a platform it is possible to generate efficient C/C++ or MPI-code.

We developed in [13] a general method for generating distributed implementations from BIP models. The method uses the following sequence of correct-by-construction transformations, that preserve *observational equivalence*:

1. We transform a BIP system model into a S/R-BIP system model such that
   (i) atomicity of transitions in the original model is broken by separating

interaction and computation, and (ii) multi-party interactions of the source model are replaced by protocols using send/receive primitives. Moreover, the target S/R-BIP model is structured in three layers:

(a) The *component layer* consists of a transformation of atomic components in the original model.

(b) The *interaction protocol* layer consists of a set of components, each hosting a user-defined subset of interactions from the original BIP model. This layer detects enabledness of interactions and executes them after resolving conflicts either locally or assisted by the third layer.

(c) The *conflict resolution protocol* layer resolves conflicts requested by the interaction protocol layer. This protocol resolves a *committee coordination problem* [14] using, so far, one distributed algorithm amongst (i) fully centralized, (ii) token-ring, and (iii) dining philosophers [15,14].

2. We generate from the obtained 3-layer S/R-BIP model and a mapping of its atomic components on processors, either a MPI program, or a set of plain C/C++ programs that use TCP/IP communication. The generation consists in statically composing atomic components running on the same processor to obtain a single observationally equivalent component, and consequently reduced coordination overhead at runtime.

The composition operation has been implemented in the BIP2BIP tool, by using three elementary source-to-source transformations:

(a) *Component flattening*, which replaces the hierarchy on components by a set of hierarchically structured connectors applied on atomic components;

(b) *Connector flattening*, which computes for each hierarchically structured connector an equivalent flat connector;

(c) *Component composition*, which composes atomic components to get an atomic component.

We conducted a set of experiments [16,13] to analyze the behavior and performance of the generated code using different scenarios (i.e., different partitioning of interactions, choice of committee coordination algorithm, mapping). Our experiments clearly show that particular configurations are suitable for different topology, size of the distributed system, communication load, and of course, the structure of the initial BIP model.

Table 1 taken from [16] summarizes experimental results obtained for different distributed implementations of a bitonic sorting algorithm [17]. We run experiments for three platform configurations denoted $m \times c$, for m interconnected machines with c cores each. The table provide the total sorting time for arrays of size $k \times 10^4$ elements, and $k = 20, 40, 80, 160$. As can be seen, execution times for handwritten MPI are slightly better than for plain C++ with TCP/IP communication. For example, the execution time for sorting an array of size 80×10^4, for the configuration 2×2 is: 240 seconds for MPI, and 390 seconds for plain C++.

In the case of S/R-BIP models auto-generated as described earlier, it is frequent that some of the atomic components and engines cannot run in parallel.

Table 1. Total sorting time for different implementations of a bitonic sorting algorithm (handwritten or generated, with or without optimisation) deployed on different execution platforms ($m \times c$ denotes m interconnected machines with c cores each) on unsorted arrays of size $k \times 10^4$ elements

	MPI (handwritten)			Plain C++ with TCP/IP			MPI (generated)		
optimised	-			no	no	yes	no	no	yes
$m \times c$	1×1	2×2	4×1	1×1	2×2	2×2	4×1	2×2	2×2
$k = 20$	80	14	14	96	23	24	24	63	24
$k = 40$	327	59	60	375	96	96	100	271	96
$k = 80$	1368	240	240	1504	390	391	397	964	394
$k = 160$	5605	1007	958	6024	1539	1548	1583	4158	1554

Therefore, they can be composed without losing any parallelism. For the bitonic sorting example, the original S/R-BIP model has 7 atomic components (4 atomic components and 3 engines), and can be transformed into a *merged* S/R-BIP model containing only 4 components, while preserving all the parallelism.

The performance gain obtained by using static composition on 2 dual-core machines (2×2 setting) is shown in Table 1. Observe that the performance of the C++ implementation is approximately identical in both cases, with or without optimisation. This is because TCP/IP communication is interrupt-driven. Thus, if a component is waiting for a message, it does not consume CPU time. On the other hand, MPI uses active waiting, which results in CPU time wasting when components are waiting. Since we have four cores for more processes (seven), the MPI code generated from the original S/R-BIP model is much slower than the plain C++ code. Nevertheless, reducing the number of components to one per core by composition allows the MPI code to reach the same speed as the C++ implementation.

3   Case Studies

BIP has been applied to several non trivial case studies. These include the componentization of a MPEG encoder [18] and of the control software of the DALA robot of LAAS [19]. Another case study is modeling TinyOS-based wireless sensor networks [20]. Moreover, BIP has been also used for modeling, verification and performance evaluation of a self-stabilizing distributed reset algorithm [21].

3.1   MJPEG Decoder

The MJPEG decoder application software reads a sequence of MJPEG frames and displays the decompressed video frames. The process network of the application software is illustrated in Figure 5. It contains five processes *SplitStream (SS)*, *SplitFrame (SF)*, *IqzigzagIDCT (IDCT)*, *MergeFrame (MF)* and *MergeStream (MS)*, and nine communication FIFO channels *C1*, ..., *C9*. The total lines of

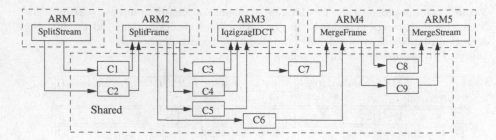

Fig. 5. MJPEG Decoder application software and a mapping

Table 2. Mapping Description of the processes and the FIFOs

	ARM1	ARM2	ARM3	ARM4	ARM5
1	all				
2	SS, SF, IQ	MF, MS			
3	SS, SF	IQ, MF, MS			
4	SS, SF	IQ	MF, MS		
5	SS, MS	SF	IQ	MF	
6	SS	SF	IQ	MF	MS
7	SS, SF	IQ	MF, MS		
8	SS	SF	IQ	MF	MS

	Shared	LM1	LM2	LM3	LM4
1		all			
2	C6, C7	C1, C2, C3, C4, C5	C8, C9		
3	C3, C4, C5, C6	C1, C2	C7, C8, C9		
4	C3, C4, C5, C6, C7	C1, C2		C8, C9	
5	all				
6	all				
7	C6, C7	C1, C2, C3, C4, C5		C8, C9	
8		C1, C2	C3, C4, C5, C6	C7	C8, C9

C code describing the behavior of the application software processes is approximately 1600.

We analyzed the effect of eight different mappings on the total computation and communication delay for decoding a frame. The process and the FIFO mappings are illustrated on Table 2.

For these mappings a system model contains around 50 BIP atomic components and 220 BIP interactions, and consists of approximately 6K lines of BIP code, generating around 19.5K lines of C code for simulation.

The total computation and communication delays for decoding a frame for different mappings are shown in Figure 6. Mapping (1) produces the worst computation delay as all processes are mapped to a single processor. Mapping (2) uses two processors, but still the performance does not improve much. Mapping (3) drastically improves performance as the computation load is balanced. The other mappings cannot further enhance performance as the load cannot be further balanced, even if more processors are used. The communication overhead is

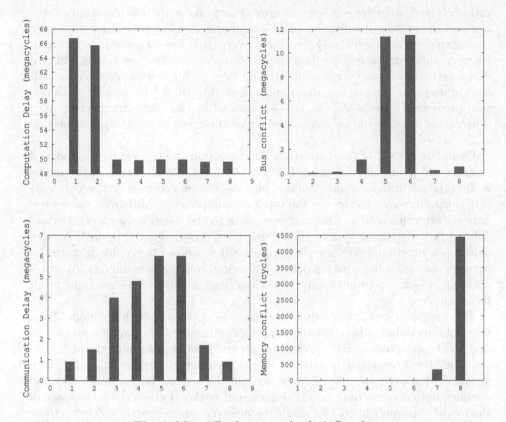

Fig. 6. Mjpeg Performance Analysis Results

reduced if we map more FIFOs to the local memories of the processors. The bus and memory access conflicts are shown in Figure 6. As more FIFOs are mapped to the local memory, the shared bus contention is reduced. However, this might increase the local memory contention, as shown for (8).

3.2   Heterogeneous Communication System

This case study deals with a distributed heterogeneous communication system (HCS) providing an all electronic communication infrastructure, typically for cabin communication in airplanes or for building automation. HCS contains various devices such as sensors (video camera, smoke detectors, temperature, pressure, etc.) and actuators (loudspeakers, light switches, temperature control, signs, etc.) connected through a wired Ethernet network to a central server. The server runs a set of services to monitor the sensors and to control the actuators. The devices are connected to the server using network access controllers.

The architecture and functionality delivered by HCS are highly heterogeneous. The system includes different hardware components, which run different protocols and software services ensuring functions with different characteristics and degree of criticality e.g, audio streaming, clock synchronization, sensor monitoring, video surveillance, etc. Moreover, HCS has to guarantee stringent requirements, such as reliable data transmission, fault tolerance, timing and synchronization constraints. For example, the latency for delivering alarm signals from sensors, or for playing audio announcements should be smaller than certain predefined thresholds. Or, the accuracy of clock synchronization between different devices, should be guaranteed under the given physical implementation of the system.

Complete details of this case study can be found in [22]. We have developed a structural model of HCS using BIP. At top level, the structure of the model follows the natural decomposition into physical elements e.g., server, network access controllers and devices are the top-level components. Moreover, these components are connected and interact according to the wired network connections defined in the original system. Then, one level down, every (physical) component has a functional decomposition. Inner subcomponents provide features for network operation (e.g., packet delivery, filtering, routing, scheduling, ...), protocols (e.g., clock synchronization) or services (e.g., audio/video streaming, event handling, etc.)

The overall complexity of this case study is extremely high. A model for a relevant functional subsystem required approximately 300 atomic components and 1900 connectors in BIP. Almost all atomic components have timed behavior. They totalize approximately 250 clocks variables to express all timing constraints. Moreover, the use of large domain data (e.g., packet numbers) and complex data structures (e.g., FIFO queues of packets) made the state space of the model extremely huge. One single state needs approximately 400 bytes to be represented. Furthermore, the state space has a heterogeneous structure which prevents its compact representation using symbolic techniques based on BDDs.

We have been interested to verify the clock synchronization protocol i.e., the application used to synchronize the clocks of all devices within the system. The challenge is to guarantee that the protocol maintains the difference between a master clock (running on the server) and all the slave clocks (running on devices) under some bound. A first major difficulty is network communication which makes all applications interfering and therefore requires exploration of the whole model. A second difficulty comes from the time granularity i.e., one microsecond, needed to perform faithful observations. These two factors significantly restrict brute-force simulation approaches: 1 second system lifetime needs approximately 10 minutes simulation time with microsecond precision on the BIP model.

To overcome these difficulties, we proposed in [22] a new verification technique which combines random simulation and statistical model checking. We have been able to derive exact bounds on clock synchronization for all devices in the system. We also computed probabilities of clock synchronization for smaller values of the bound. Being able to provide such information is of clear importance, especially when the exact bounds are too high with respect to user's requirements. In particular, we have shown that the bounds strongly depend on the position of the device in the network. We also estimated the average and worst proportion of failures per simulation for smaller bounds i.e., how often the clock synchronization exceeds the given bound on some arbitrary run.

4   Discussion and Future Work

We have shown that the BIP component framework, and the associated design flow and supporting tools allow rigorous and effective system design. A key idea is the application of correctness-preserving source-to-source transformations to progressively refine the application software model by taking into account hardware architecture constraints as well as coordination mechanisms used for the collaboration between processors in a distributed implementation. Verification is used to check essential properties as early as possible in the design flow. To avoid complexity limitations, the verification process is incremental and compositional. When the validity of a property is established for a model, the property will hold for all the models obtained by transformation. The complexity of the transformations is linear with the size of the transformed models. So correctness is ensured at minimal cost and by construction thus overcoming obstacles of design flows involving different and not semantically related languages and models.

The use of a single modeling framework allows to maintain the overall coherency of the design flow by comparing different architectural solutions and their properties. This is a significant advantage of our approach. Semantically related models are used for verification, simulation and performance evaluation. Designers use many different languages e.g. programming languages, UML, SystemC, SES/Workbench. Code generation and deployment is often independent from validation and evaluation.

Clearly, using a single modeling framework does not suffice. An advantage of BIP over other existing frameworks is its expressiveness. It uses a few powerful primitives to express coordination between components. Architecture is a first class concept and can be characterized as the combination of interactions and priorities. It can model in a natural and direct manner both timed and untimed behavior, synchronous and asynchronous. Using less expressive frameworks e.g. based on a single composition operator, would lead to intractable models. For instance, BIP directly encompasses multiparty interaction between components. This type of coordination would require the development of complex coordination mechanisms for frameworks supporting only point-to point interaction. This would lead to models with complicated coordination structure and would make the whole design flow intractable. In particular for such models establishing a clean refinement relation between the different models would be compromised.

Empirical design flows are limited to simple execution models and execution platforms involving a few processing elements. We believe that rigorous and automated design flows are crucial for system development especially when the target architecture is distributed and/or heterogeneous.

References

1. Basu, A., Bozga, M., Sifakis, J.: Modeling Heterogeneous Real-time Systems in BIP. In: Proceedings of Software Engineering and Formal Methods SEFM 2006, pp. 3 –12. IEEE Computer Society Press (2006)
2. Halbwachs, N.: Synchronous Programming of Reactive Systems. Kluwer Academic Publishers (1993)
3. Burns, A., Welling, A.: Real-Time Systems and Programming Languages, 3rd edn. Addison-Wesley (2001)
4. Henzinger, T., Sifakis, J.: The Embedded Systems Design Challenge. In: Misra, J., Nipkow, T., Karakostas, G. (eds.) FM 2006. LNCS, vol. 4085, pp. 1–15. Springer, Heidelberg (2006)
5. Milner, R.: A Calculus of Communication Systems. LNCS, vol. 92. Springer, Heidelberg (1980)
6. Bliudze, S., Sifakis, J.: A Notion of Glue Expressiveness for Component-Based Systems. In: van Breugel, F., Chechik, M. (eds.) CONCUR 2008. LNCS, vol. 5201, pp. 508–522. Springer, Heidelberg (2008)
7. Thiele, L., Bacivarov, I., Haid, W., Huang, K.: Mapping Applications to Tiled Multiprocessor Embedded Systems. In: Proceedings of Application of Concurrency to System Design ACSD 2007, pp. 29–40. IEEE Computer Society (2007)
8. Fleury, S., Herrb, M., Chatila, R.: GenoM: A Tool for the Specification and the Implementation of Operating Modules in a Distributed Robot Architecture. In: IROS 1997, pp. 842–848 (1997)
9. Bensalem, S., Bozga, M., Sifakis, J., Nguyen, T.-H.: Compositional Verification for Component-based Systems and Application. In: Cha, S(S.), Choi, J.-Y., Kim, M., Lee, I., Viswanathan, M. (eds.) ATVA 2008. LNCS, vol. 5311, pp. 64–79. Springer, Heidelberg (2008)
10. Bensalem, S., Bozga, M., Legay, A., Nguyen, T.-H., Sifakis, J., Yan, R.: Incremental Component-based Construction and Verification using Invariants. In: FMCAD 2010, pp. 257–266. IEEE (2010)
11. Bensalem, S., Bozga, M., Nguyen, T.-H., Sifakis, J.: D-Finder: A Tool for Compositional Deadlock Detection and Verification. In: Bouajjani, A., Maler, O. (eds.) CAV 2009. LNCS, vol. 5643, pp. 614–619. Springer, Heidelberg (2009)
12. Bourgos, P., Basu, A., Bozga, M., Bensalem, S., Sifakis, J., Huang, K.: Rigorous system level modeling and analysis of mixed hw/sw systems. In: Proceedings of MEMOCODE, pp. 11–20. IEEE/ACM (2011)
13. Bonakdarpour, B., Bozga, M., Jaber, M., Quilbeuf, J., Sifakis, J.: From high-level component-based models to distributed implementations. In: Proceedings of Embedded Software EMSOFT 2010. ACM (2010)
14. Chandy, K.M., Misra, J.: Parallel Program Design: A Foundation. Addison-Wesley Longman Publishing Co. Inc., Boston (1988)
15. Bagrodia, R.: Process synchronization: Design and performance evaluation of distributed algorithms. IEEE Transactions on Software Engineering 15(9), 1053–1065 (1989)
16. Bonakdarpour, B., Bozga, M., Jaber, M., Quilbeuf, J., Sifakis, J.: Automated Conflict-free Distributed Implementation of Component-Based Models. In: Proceedings of Industrial Embedded Systems SIES 2010. IEEE (2010)
17. Batcher, K.E.: Sorting Networks and Their Applications. In: Proceedings of AFIPS 1968 (Spring), pp. 307–314 (1968)

18. Combaz, J., Fernandez, J.C., Sifakis, J., Strus, L.: Symbolic quality control for multimedia applications. Real-Time Systems 40(1), 1–43 (2008)
19. Basu, A., Gallien, M., Lesire, C., Nguyen, T.-H., Bensalem, S., Ingrand, F., Sifakis, J.: Incremental Component-Based Construction and Verification of a Robotic System. In: ECAI 2008. FAIA, vol. 178, pp. 631–635. IOS Press (2008)
20. Basu, A., Mounier, L., Poulhiès, M., Pulou, J., Sifakis, J.: Using BIP for Modeling and Verification of Networked Systems – A Case Study on TinyOS-based Networks. In: Proceedings of Network Computing and Applications NCA 2007, pp. 257–260. IEEE (2007)
21. Basu, A., Bonakdarpour, B., Bozga, M., Sifakis, J.: Brief Announcement: Incremental Component-Based Modeling, Verification, and Performance Evaluation of Distributed Reset. In: Keidar, I. (ed.) DISC 2009. LNCS, vol. 5805, pp. 174–175. Springer, Heidelberg (2009)
22. Basu, A., Bensalem, S., Bozga, M., Caillaud, B., Delahaye, B., Legay, A.: Statistical Abstraction and Model-Checking of Large Heterogeneous Systems. In: Hatcliff, J., Zucca, E. (eds.) FMOODS 2010. LNCS, vol. 6117, pp. 32–46. Springer, Heidelberg (2010)

Natural Born Computing

Peter J. Bentley

Department of Computer Science, University College of London,
Malet Place, London WC1E 6BT, UK
p.bentley@cs.ucl.ac.uk

Abstract. Nature is not afraid of complexity. Her solutions exploit the unpredictable and messy nature of reality. But our technology seems to be very different. Instead of exploiting its environment it is more frequently damaged by that environment. In this article I describe how we can learn from natural systems and create new technologies that exploit natural principles. I describe our investigations into the technologies of the future – devices that can adapt, be fault tolerant, and even assemble themselves. Examples of a self-repairing robot and physical self-assembling systems are shown, and I describe my systemic computer concept which aims to be the first parallel fault tolerant computer that is based on general biological systems. Through examples such as these, I argue that while we may never be able to predict exactly what a natural system may do, that does not prevent such systems from being extremely useful for us – after all, we are unpredictable natural systems ourselves.

1   Introduction

For several years now I have been troubled by something. I've had a strange feeling of *wrongness*.

It is similar to the uncomfortable feeling you might have if a stranger has come into your home and moved all your belongings around. Maybe they exchanged your favourite appliances with over-complicated alternatives. They also replaced your food with brands and varieties that you don't buy because you find them hard to digest. Despite feeling ill at ease, you continue to live there and most of the time everything seems to work, but now it is clumsy. Inelegant. Awkward. You find certain activities – perhaps operating the satellite TV box or cooking a meal – take much longer than they should. The food is good quality, but you can't make it taste nice. Sometimes you trip over things that shouldn't be there. Or you feel for a light switch, which is somewhere else.

If you have an artistic flair, then it is the same feeling you have when you look at a painting that is unbalanced, or a photograph that is poorly cropped. Perhaps the colours clash or seem ugly. It might be a beautifully executed piece of work; the technical ability of the artist is of a high standard. But somehow you don't like it. The picture looks wrong in your eyes. You see the world differently to the artist and you cannot agree with the interpretation you're looking at.

To begin with, this feeling of wrongness is more of an intuition. You know something could be improved, but you're not quite sure what, or how. But the

Z. Kotásek et al. (Eds.): MEMICS 2011, LNCS 7119, pp. 20–36, 2012.

longer you live with the feeling, the more you begin to pinpoint the things that make you uncomfortable – the reasons for your troubled feeling.

My feeling of wrongness is exactly like this. However I am a scientist, so my feeling is tied up with my perception of science. I'm a computer scientist, so my perceptions are also biased and oriented by an understanding of information processing. I'm also a computer scientist who works with many other scientists of different disciplines, often modelling complex systems, so my views are grounded by the knowledge that it is very difficult to understand, communicate, and exploit the information we gather about our complex world.

It was a grey day some years ago when I was able to crunch my feet in the heart of the issue. I was walking on Hasting Beach in the UK. It was not perhaps the prettiest stretch of beach in the world, with concrete on one side, grey sea on the other, and no sand at all. Just pebbles everywhere. Each wave sighed onto the shore, and hissed as it retreated over the pebbles. On that day I crunched my way over the undulations of the beach, my feet sending small avalanches of stones down the slope towards the latest frothy wave. As I walked, I noticed something fascinating. There was order arising from the chaos on that beach. The pebbles lay in regular stripes, each stripe containing stones of a similar size. But the small stones were not closest to the waves and the largest furthest away. Instead there were actual stripes of large, small, large, small pebbles running parallel to the waves. When I dug down with my hands I found that these strange stripes of order were not just some surface phenomenon – they continued to preserve their ordered sorting as deep as I dug.

I cared about these stones because I recognised the difficulty of duplicating what I was observing. Sorting is not a simple process. If I gave you a few million numbers and asked you to sort them into order, or to cluster them into several groups of most similar numbers, you would have to spend hours and hours comparing each number with a large proportion of the other numbers in order to figure out where it should be placed. Sorting and clustering are very common processes needed for many kinds of computation – any calculation that needs to order, rank or judge values needs this form of process. That includes our financial systems, voting, distribution, medical, telecommunication, betting, examinations... it is a long list. The speed that we can sort or cluster different values also depends on the number of values. When the number reaches a few hundreds of billions, even our fastest computers take some time to complete the task. So looking at a beach containing trillions upon trillions of pebbles – way too many pebbles to even count – but with every pebble carefully sorted and clustered, I was impressed. This was computation on a scale grander than anything I was used to seeing.

To me on that day, the hiss of the retreating wave became the sound of a mechanical computer. As I crunched through the stones I was nothing more than a minor bug in the computer – an unwanted disruption to the computation being performed by the sea and stones. Even now on Hastings Beach, every new wave is performing trillions of new calculations a second as it moves the small and large stones in relation to each other. Every sigh of a new wave brings energy to move larger pebbles, every hiss is the sound of millions of tiny pebbles clicking past each other in the retreating water. Every movement of every stone is as meaningful as the movement of a bead on an abacus. It is a natural computation, a calculation of a new arrangement of pebbles sorted into groups according to their respective sizes. Much more complex than simple arithmetic, these calculations have been carried out on all the pebbled beaches of the world, every second, for billions of years. Waves have been moving stones and sorting them in rows of large and small, large and small, that could not be duplicated by the hands of all the people in the world. Indeed, the sorting and clustering of so many unique objects could not be achieved in the same time by all the computers in the world working together.

But what kind of a technology is made from stones and waves? We can make an abacus with stone beads, but the beach is surely no kind of computer we are used to. This "Hastings Beach device" is huge, it has no software to tell it how to behave, and its data storage system – if you can call it that – comprises different sized pebbles. How do you convert your MP3 file into pebbles? Or how can your MP3 player read a beach of pebbles? There is also no intentionality behind the computation of the waves and pebbles. No-one has assigned this task and no-one is reading the result (at least not until I "read" the beach on that day). So using this conventional way of thinking, then of course Hastings beach is not a computer: it is not designed by anyone to do anything, it doesn't do anything especially useful to us, it is not precise or reliable in its method of storing information (if it can really be said to represent or store any information), and it is largely random in the order in which it "processes" its information.

Something else behaves in a very similar way. Something that has no software to tell it how to behave. Something that does not use the shape of stones, but the shapes of molecules and cells to store information. Something that really can store an (approximation of an) MP3 file in those chemicals and cells, and which can play back that file so that it is recognisable. No-one designed it, or assigned it any of its specific tasks. There is no intentionality behind the specific interactions of those tiny cells and molecules. It is not precise or reliable in its method of storing information, and it is largely random in the order in which it "processes" its information. It is the human brain.

The idea that a beach could process information is perhaps challenging. But our brains? Intuitively most of us feel that our brains are actually quite good at processing information. After all, they can store numbers, perform mathematical operations on them and produce a result. A brain can store music and replay it well enough for its owner to enjoy again a piece of music that they'd heard earlier. It clearly can do many of the same things that a conventional computer can do, and indeed many things that are beyond the abilities of our computers. We have no formal way of describing how and where that information is stored and manipulated, but that does not mean that the human brain does not process information. It just means that at present our understanding and language is not good enough to describe how the brain works.

The human brain is not the only natural "device" that can process information. There are also many other examples in the natural world of living systems that appear to compute. A colony of ants is able to make highly accurate calculations about which paths to take from the nest to a new food source, minimising the energy needed for the colony as a whole. Their ability to find the shortest path emerges from collective intelligence: the ants communicate with each other by laying smelly pheromone trails on the ground, and by following the smelliest paths. The shortest paths are self-reinforcing; in the same amount of time 100 ants running to and from the nest on a long path will leave less concentrated pheromone compared to 100 ants running on a short path, so the shorter path wins. [1]

Like sorting or clustering, finding the shortest path is known to be a complex and time-consuming form of computation. Yet somehow the randomised running of the ants in a physical environment combined with the ability to lay scent and smell scent is sufficient for them to perform this calculation more effectively than our computers can. (Ant colony optimisation algorithms are used to improve the ability of our computers by copying the process used by ants [1].) But where in the living ant colony is the information? When and how is that information processed? Again, these concepts are fuzzy and ill-defined, despite their seeming effectiveness.

There seem to be no end of natural mechanisms that are capable of extraordinary feats of computation. Brains, immune systems, embryogenesis, evolution, crystal growth, swarming insects, flocking birds, bacterial growth, self-replicating systems, chemical reactions, quantum and DNA interactions. The capabilities of all of these have been widely recognised by computer scientists for several decades. In fact, all have their own fields of research in computer science. Thousands of scientists, hundreds of conferences and tens of thousands of scientific papers are all devoted to understanding and exploiting the computational power of natural systems. This tremendous research effort is built on a shared foundation: the belief that nature can teach us important lessons that could improve our human-designed computers. [2]

It turns out that the more you examine the natural world, whether looking at quantum scales, atomic, cellular, organism, species, ecological, planetary or universe scales, you can find more examples that seem to outperform our designs. Natural computation surrounds us, is contained within us and comprises us. All of these systems, regardless of scale, are capable of feats of computation that completely outclass our electronic computers, and all these systems seem to behave in similar ways. Yet *none* of them work in the same way as our computers. Bizarrely, there seem to be more similarities between the working of the human brain and Hastings Beach, than between the way the brain works and the workings of a conventional computer. If we were drawing a family tree showing relatedness, then the human brain would be a far distant cousin to Hastings Beach, and a fairly close relation to an ant colony. Conventional computers (and most current man-made technology) are more like aliens from another planet – it is hard to see how they are related to natural systems at all.

This is what troubles me.

If everything around us appears to be capable of performing natural computation, then why doesn't anything in the natural world resemble our computers? Have we filled the world with technology that all follows the wrong design? Or have we created in a few decades something that is superior to billions of years of physical laws and evolution? If we could understand the differences between natural computation and manmade computers, would we then be able to apply the mathematics and theorems of computer science to everything else? Would we use our understanding of natural systems to change computers, technology or even science itself?

2 Origins

Much of our conventional computer architecture came from the researchers at the Moore School of the University of Pennsylvania [3]. When von Neumann wrote the "First Draft of a Report on the EDVAC" [4] which summarised this work, he scribbled down words that would be used by computer designers for decades to come. The architecture that he described was to form the blueprint of most modern computers. But in addition to the engineering constraints of the time and his mathematics and physics background, von Neumann's words showed just how his thinking was influenced by biology. The key part of the document (where he defines the architecture of a general-purpose computer) is fascinating, for it is full of biological terms:

"In analyzing the functioning of the contemplated device, certain classificatory distinctions suggest themselves immediately.

First: Since the device is primarily a computer, it will have to perform the elementary operations of arithmetics most frequently. These are addition, multiplication and division. It is therefore reasonable that it should contain specialised organs for just these operations... a central arithmetic part of the device will probably have to exist and this constitutes the first specific part: CA.

Second: The logical control of the device, that is the proper sequencing of its operations can be most efficiently carried out by a central control organ... this constitutes the second specific part: CC.

Third: Any device which is to carry out long and complicated sequences of operations (specifically of calculations) must have a considerable memory... this constitutes the third specific part: M.

... The three specific parts CA, CC and M correspond to the associative neurons in the human nervous system. It remains to discuss the equivalents of the sensory or afferent and the motor or efferent neurons. These are the input and the output organs of the device." [4 pp. 3 & 6]

It is no coincidence that many of the other early pioneers in computing also had great interest in biology. Turing actively researched a wide range of biological topics such as neurology, morphogenesis, physiology and intelligence. He regarded biology and human brains as computational devices and according to one writer: *"he became involved in discussions on the contrasts and similarities between machines and brains. Turing's view, expressed with great force and wit, was that it was for those who saw an unbridgeable gap between the two to say just where the difference lay."* [5]

Claude Shannon was also fascinated by the ability of brains to learn and adapt – something difficult to achieve with programmed computers. To investigate learning, he constructed a robot mouse, which could navigate through a maze and learn its path [6]. This was one of the first examples of a learning robot ever created. He also created a simple chess-playing machine. [7]

Shannon's work and students went on to influence the world of computers to an extraordinary degree[1]. Sadly von Neumann and Turing died much younger and were not able to continue their vision of computing. It is fascinating to remind ourselves of the final works of von Neumann, published posthumously as *The Computer and the Brain* [8]. In this short book, von Neumann talks about the future of computing, and discusses both analogue and parallel processing. Other posthumous work appeared as the book: *Theory of self-reproducing automata* [9] where von Neumann introduces cellular automata and advanced ideas such as self-replication. It is perhaps ironic that today the sequential architecture described in the "First Draft of a Report on the EDVAC" has become known as the von Neumann architecture. Given the direction of his work and the fact that the biggest challenges facing today's computer scientists revolve around parallel and distributed computing, perhaps Jonny von Neumann would have preferred to be known for his ideas on parallel and bio-inspired computers.

3   Embodied Computation

Traditional design is all about prediction. We predict what a device or piece of software will be used for, how it will be used, and what problems it might encounter, and then we design a solution accordingly. There are some good reasons why we try to anticipate environmental conditions and design reliable solutions that can survive, whether that environment is made from other programs, computer hardware or the physical world.

Nature also anticipates possible problems in her solutions. Millions of years of trial and error have pushed evolutionary change towards organisms that are adaptable, fault tolerant and tightly coupled to their environments. Nature's approach is one of brute force – try everything possible and exploit whatever works, however bizarre. It turns out that this is a highly effective way to solve problems.

Modeling is one approach we use when designing robots. But modeling the world with any accuracy is difficult. Modeling how an autonomous robot will react in an unseen environment is virtually impossible. Robot controllers that rely on such modeling are brittle and susceptible to catastrophic failure. Experience suggests that the goal of autonomous, self-sustaining robots is unlikely

---

[1] Such as AI (he supervised Marvin Minsky and helped set up the Dartmouth College conference) and graphics (he supervised Ivan Sutherland), in addition to his own works in cryptography and information theory [3].

to be reached by predicting every eventuality and designing solutions for every problem. The complexity of interactions between robot and environment mean that there will always be an unforeseen problem that results in mission failure. Instead, a better way to achieve long-term survival of robots (and potentially other technologies as well) is to learn from nature and make them innately adaptive. Every part of their form and function must enable them to change, to alter themselves. They must learn how to move themselves in unknown environments, whether damaged or not. They must adapt to their environment and increase their ability to transmit or receive signals amongst themselves. They must be embodied in their environments.

Fig. 1. A photograph of the self adaptive snake used for embodied evolution

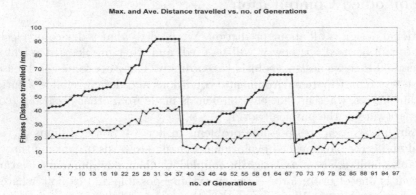

Fig. 2. Maximum fitness (bold) and average fitness plotted at each generation. The robot controller was evolved until maximum fitness remained stable for 7 generations, then was damaged randomly by disabling an actuator. Subsequent evolution shows recovery by the robot. The snake learns to slither using its remaining muscles.

One example of an attempt at such a robot was the self-adaptive snake at UCL [10], [11], [12]. To provide more flexibility in movement, shape memory alloy was exploited for actuation, and in later versions a genetic algorithm was used in combination with a 3D printer to evolve and create a robot snake body with the desired physical properties. A genetic algorithm was also used to evolve the controller for this physical system, under different environmental conditions. Embodied evolution creates and tests controllers in the physical device, in real environments, giving it an innate adaptability. This adaptability was assessed by repeatedly damaging the robot snake and measuring the degree of recovery, see figure 2.

The key feature of the approach is that no simulations are employed. Instead, each evolving control program is uploaded into the actual physical device in its real environment, and performance assessed "in the field". True fitness measures of candidate solutions (in this case corresponding to the distance travelled by the robot) are then used by the evolutionary algorithm to create control programs designed to exploit the actual properties of robot and environment at the time they are occurring. This on-the-spot adaptation is a true example of embodiment – the robot affects its environment by moving in that environment, while the environment plays an immediate and important role in affecting the device and its performance, and thus affecting the subsequent control of the device in the immediate future. It is not necessary for a robot control program to "know" the status of the robot or of the environment – all that is necessary is that the robot be flexible enough to adapt, and some measurable performance metric can be obtained. An evolutionary algorithm is then able to exploit whatever exists and is controllable in order to make the device work.

4   Physical Information

Embodied computation that exploits the true properties of our world as part of its solution is one fundamental difference between natural computation and conventional "von Neumann" computers. Another difference is the "blood" of the computer – information.

Since Claude Shannon's breakthrough in the 1940s [13], [14], we digitise all our data. We turn all our information into long lists of the smallest possible unit of information: the binary digit, made from 1 or 0. There are many advantages for error correction and reproduction of information, but this is the most basic, elementary form of information possible. But imagine if our transport systems worked using the minimal description of matter. They would turn us into long strings of subatomic particles and then move each particle at a time to our destination, reassembling us at the other end. It is the slowest, most inefficient possible way of moving us! We chose to use binary for our information because it is the easiest. There are more accurate ways of storing information (the analogue wiggles of audio on a vinyl record comprise a higher-fidelity recording of audio compared to the digitized audio on a CD). It is just harder to transmit, remove noise from and store analogue information, so we chose the easy option.

Now look at information in natural systems. Nature seems to use the opposite idea – instead of using the minimal description of information, it uses the maximal description. It embeds meaning in morphology, interaction and context. The right shape, interacting in the right way, in the right environment, has a very rich informational content. Use the same principles at all scales, from subatomic to molecular to cellular to organism and upwards, and vast amounts of information can be exploited and manipulated in parallel. The same shapes can mean different things at different times in different environments. Nature also has error correction – bad genes are corrected, bad cells are replaced, bad individuals in societies are corrected or removed. Nature also has a far better ability to store and reproduce information compared to our digital technology. In your body you have 100 trillion cells, each one containing a perfect copy of your genome (except those deliberately designed to be different). Yet nature is not binary.

Fig. 3. Information is mapped to physical components (top) which self-assemble into desired forms (bottom)

To investigate exactly how information can be expressed in morphologies, another ongoing project at UCL and Calgary creates components with morphologies that enable them to self-assemble into a desired form [15], [16], [17]. The method translates self-assembly rule sets into physical objects, which are fabricated using rapid prototyping. The resulting mechanical components are placed in a jar of fluid on an orbital shaker, their environment. The energy and physical properties of the environment, along with the physical properties of the components (including complementary shapes and magnetic-bit patterns, created using permanent magnets to attract and repel components) enable the self-assembly process to create emergent target structures with three-dimensional symmetric and asymmetric features.

The successful results demonstrate how physically encoded information can be programmed by hand or evolved by computer, in order to obtain physical self-assembling systems in three dimensions. They also illustrate a little of how natural information works: we must define the right environments, the right component morphologies and the right adhesive properties for the correct information processing (self-assembly) to take place. Natural information is context sensitive – place the same components in a different environment, and we obtain a different result.

5   Systemic Computation

With these natural processes in mind, and the differences between natural and conventional computations clearly evident, the question arises: what would a "natural computer" look like? What if we had a computer that was parallel, stochastic, distributed? What if its processing was the result of interacting "components" of some abstract type? What if meaning was conditional on the environment or context in which the interactions took place? Could such a computer be built and could we program it?

To address these questions, my research at UCL has resulted in *Systemic Computation* – a model of computation designed to have as many of these natural properties as possible [18], [19]. It is also a language; a way of writing down natural systems in the world around us. It was designed to be as simple as possible.

The first problem is how to represent things. What things exist in the natural world and how do we represent them? Clearly, there appears to be a lot of diverse things around us. Big things, small things. We have a lot of different names for all these things: planet, neuron, virus, water molecule, helium atom, neutron. But it is hard to talk about everything at the same time if it has all got different names. So in Systemic Computation we call everything by the same name. From now on, everything is a "system." It doesn't matter how big or how small, what it is made from, whether it is alive or dead. Everything is a system.

We all know that the things (systems) around us seem to be made from other, smaller things (systems). You are an organism (a system) made from several major organs contained within another organ called the skin (systems within a system). Your organs are made from cells (systems), which are made from molecules (systems), which are made from atoms (systems), which are made from subatomic particles (systems), and so on. There appears to be an embedded hierarchical arrangement of systems. Systems made from systems made from systems.

This hierarchical arrangement is not purely subjective. Each level of scale can be separated from the higher and lower level by degrees of interaction. So planets tend to interact at a planetary scale. While they are ultimately made from subatomic particles, their scale means that they affect vast numbers at a scale similar to them. (At this scale, the combined gravity is more significant compared to many of the smaller and larger scale interactions; at other scales, different interactions predominate.) Animals tend to interact mostly with animals, plants or other features around their scale – one animal is usually not able to modify individual atoms or entire planets in any controlled or significant way. Cells tend to interact mainly with cells; genes and proteins with other genes and proteins, and so on. So systems in the universe seem to form "clumps" at similar scales. These structures are self-organising and appear to be caused by the laws of physics, nothing more or less.

At each level of the hierarchy of organisation, systems are also all limited by boundaries or scopes. So the large bodies in our solar system interact when they are within each others' gravitational fields. If our Moon were ever pushed significantly outside the scope of the Earth's gravitational field, then it could no longer interact with the Earth in any significant way. Species on Earth are often limited by geographical constraints, so if one member of a species was to find itself on another continent with no way of returning, then it would be outside the boundary that contained its species and it would no longer be able to interact with other members of its species. The cells within our bodies can only interact if they remain within our bodies. Remove a cell and it cannot behave as a part of you any more.

If we draw a typical arrangement of systems at just one level of the hierarchy, then it might appear as illustrated in fig. 4.

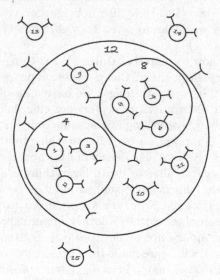

Fig. 4. A hierarchy of systems

Every system is a circle with two little arms. They are numbered for reference, but the numbers are not important. Also, the absolute positions of these systems are not important. Think of them as being like mathematical sets where all that matters is what is inside or outside. So systems 1, 2 and 3 are inside the scope of system 4, which is itself within the scope of system 12. System 9 is outside the scope of system 4, but within 12. System 15 is outside all scopes. The scope of a system is also a system, because that is the first rule: everything is a system.

Perhaps in this picture we are looking at several cells contained within boundaries formed by the organs, which are within the skin of an organism. Or perhaps we are looking at molecules that are within range of each others' electromagnetic charges. Or maybe we're looking at probability distributions of subatomic particles. The exact level doesn't matter – we can use the same language, and see similar structures.

The introduction mentioned some of the important properties of natural systems, so we already know how these systems behave. We know their behaviour has a significant stochastic element – there is randomness in whatever these things do. We know they behave asynchronously – there is no inherent coordination underlying their function. They do things in parallel, so while they may not all exhibit a specific behaviour at the same time (which would then be synchronous), there is nothing to stop them from doing their thing within the same period of time that others do something.

Clearly these hierarchies of systems are autonomous – they need no intelligence to organise them. They also seem to be homeostatic and fault tolerant. They "like" being in their hierarchies and in their scopes so much that they will restore themselves if damaged (even atoms "prefer" to have a certain number of electrons and neutrons and will grab more or discard extra if the number is not in balance). Systems are definitely robust, for example, you don't normally see gravity "crash" or electromagnetism "break. " There are definitely a lot of systems in the universe, with no sign of a central controller, so we can call them distributed. There appears to be almost no limit to the number of hierarchies or the different arrangements of scopes, so our systems are open-ended and complex.

Every system is approximate. Although not shown in fig. 4, every system is usually made from other systems, so you could substitute each system with one or more other systems if they are exactly equivalent. So we could choose to talk about you being a single system, or we could talk about you being a collection of tens of systems (organs), or of trillions of systems (cells). This means whenever we use this language we must choose the level of abstraction (the level of the hierarchy) that we wish to focus upon, and we always recognise that the description is an approximation. There is probably always going to be a different way of expressing each system so each could always be replaced with a different set. The system is a way of talking about and summarising reality while recognising that the words are never absolutely right.[2]

Scopes are a little more complicated than we've discussed so far. Every system can act as a scope, where that scope behaves like a field – other systems may be partially or fully within that scope. Systems should only be able to interact if they are in the same scope as each other. (Or more correctly, the interaction of systems is a function of their membership of the same scope, so they might have a higher probability of interacting the more they share a greater membership.) Intuitively this means that things within the same region or boundary are more likely to interact, while those separated from each other are less likely. While systems are drawn as circles as shown in fig. 4, the field may be any shape or

---

[2] Even the idea that a system is completely separable from other systems may be approximation; like two flowers from one plant, systems may correspond to underlying systems that are shared amongst the higher-level systems.

have any properties. So we may wish to talk about gravitational field systems, or probability distribution systems, or human skin systems. In all cases we're referring to a kind of boundary with some internal properties that affect the internal systems, external properties that effect external systems, and potentially fuzzy edges. This means every system may "overlap" every other system, even if it is to an infinitesimal degree (or to a very large degree), allowing our systems to merge with each other (or have partial memberships of each other). Systems can thus affect each other and be affected by each other to a large degree, making them very embodied. For example if a couple share a house then the scopes of the two people overlap, so they are likely to be able to interact with the same artefacts (that are in both their scopes) and with each other.

It is clear that all systems do something. Maybe they just move. Maybe they pull or distort. Maybe they alter other systems. So in our systems-based language we have to have a notion of behaviour. If two systems interact then they will transform each other at the same time. This means that the first system causes a change to the second and the second causes a change to the first – circular causality. We only need to think about two systems interacting at a time. (Even if more than two interact at precisely the same instant that is the same as multiple sets of two systems interacting in parallel.) When you think about it, that is all behaviour can ever be in the universe: two systems interacting. Nothing can change until some form of interaction occurs, whether we call that interaction a collision, a crash, a conversation, an attraction, or a reaction.

As soon as we have a concept of behaviour causing change, then we have to think about what is being changed. Clearly systems have properties in the universe: they may have specific spatial locations and shapes. These properties may be changing over time so they may have speed, acceleration, compression, stretching or deformation. Looking at higher in the hierarchy and systems corresponding to cells may have considerably more complex properties; systems corresponding to organisms may have massively complex properties. Whatever those properties are, they all derive from and comprise systems.

Their properties also help determine the result arising from interactions. So a baseball moving at 50 mph that hits a stationary glass window will transform the properties of both ball and window. After their interaction, the ball will no longer be travelling at 50 mph and the window may have a rather more complex shape and many types of movement. (After the interaction it may be preferable to move down in the hierarchy of description and talk about the systems that make up the glass, as it may no longer make so much sense to regard it as one system with a very complex broken shape.) But a foam ball moving at 50 mph that hits the same glass window would result in a very different transformation of properties. So in our systems, information appears to be intimately linked with behaviour. Both information and behaviour affect and are affected by all interactions. There is no binary information stored and manipulated in one place, separate from everything else. We cannot separate data and function; we cannot distinguish between message and morphology. Shape, behaviour and information are the same thing.[3]

Returning to the example of the broken window, there is one other factor we need to consider. The environment plays a key part in all interactions. If we were to move our window underwater and then throw the ball at 50 mph towards the window, the resultant interaction would be hugely different. So the result of any interaction depends on the two systems that are interacting, and also upon the context in which that interaction takes place. Since everything is a system, we can express the context as a system as well.

We all intuitively recognise that the real world is context-sensitive. Even the fundamental law in most human societies, "thou shalt not kill," sadly depends on the context in which this interaction occurs. While the context of normal society tries to ensure that the killer is significantly penalised as a result of such a deadly interaction, in the context of warfare the killer may be rewarded after an identical interaction. When children ask, "what will happen?" we may answer, "it depends," because it usually does. The result of any interaction depends on its context.

While it could be argued that there is no need to describe context explicitly as a system (we could replace the context with other interactions occurring in parallel), we are limited by what we can express, so the context is like a summary of those parts of the environment that significantly affect the current interacting pair of systems, allowing us to ensure we do not omit anything important. It also means that now any system can potentially take the role of a context and affect how two other systems interact (that is why we draw systems with two little arms, see fig. 4).[4]

Finally, we should ensure our systems are consistent with existing knowledge. All behaviours should follow those observed in the universe. Systems cannot be destroyed or created from nothing, only transformed. (We may interpret systems differently perhaps by substituting one set of systems with another set, but they would still describe the same feature, so this is not a transformation of any system, just of our representation of it). Any system can be a context, a scope, an interacting system or any combination at once.

---

[3] Its interesting to note that Daniel Tammet, a famous sufferer of Asperger's syndrome, agrees. He believes numbers have colours, shapes, and textures, and by manipulating those features in his imagination he is able to perform extraordinary mental calculations. [20]

[4] The more astute reader will have noticed that if scope and context are both systems, then they must be equivalent. This does indeed appear to be the case: a scope affects the outcome and probability of an interaction just as a context does, and by clustering systems according to their contexts we would organise them just as scopes do. After all, everything is a system. Nevertheless, even if scope and context systems may refer to identical phenomena in some cases, it is often easier and useful to talk of scopes and contexts as though they are different, as they correspond to our everyday experiences more. Scopes are useful when discussing information: position, topology and mutual relationships. Contexts are useful for behaviours, changes, and transformations. In mathematics, they are all, of course, functions.

These notions comprise this new computational language. But what has any of this to do with computation?

The answer comes with the final rule: computation is transformation. At a single stroke, we turn everything imaginable into an entity that can represent information and be instrumental in the manipulation of that information. Everything. We can control how the computation occurs by modifying the nature of the interacting systems, the context in which that interaction occurs, and the scopes that constrain the interactions.

So we can talk about neurons interacting in the context of the chemical and cellular structure of the brain. By interacting, the neurons change each other. Change the properties of the neurons, and the results of their interaction changes. Change the context (introduce a different chemical environment) and the results of their interaction changes. The "wires" that connect the neurons (axons and dendrites) are the scopes – they determine which neuron can interact with which other neuron. Change the scopes and you change the wiring (you alter the organisation of the neural network). Or we can talk about ants interacting in the context of their environment. The scopes of an ant include how far it can sense (see or smell) or move. Two ants may greet each other, help each other carry an object, or many other interactions depending on the current state of the ants and the context of their interaction. Or we can talk about pebbles interacting on Hastings Beach, transforming their relative positions in the context of a wave. The scope of the pebbles is determined by their physical proximity – move them apart and they can no longer interact. Place them adjacent to each other, but change the properties of the pebbles or of the wave and the result of the interaction will be different.

We have a lot of different words for objects, interactions, organisations, and environments, but they can all be expressed using this single overarching language of systems, called Systemic Computation. When we construct a machine that operates according to these systemic computation rules, the resulting systemic computer has all of the natural properties we are interested in mimicking.[5] The right kinds of systems are together also provably Turing Complete.

Our work continues in this area, with a calculus, graph notation, a programming language and compiler [18], [21], Mac and PC simulators [18], [21], a GPU implementation [22], and most recently an FPGA design [23]. We can make a natural computer with the properties of biological systems. We're still learning how to program it.

6   Summary

Our world seems to be capable of astonishing feats of computation. Even a beach of pebbles can do better than our best sorting algorithms. But the best examples of natural computers are inside our own skulls. We are natural born computers. Our brains are superior in most respects to every computer ever

---

[5] Thanks to Dr Erwan Le Martleot who has spent several years of research for his PhD proving this exact point.

made. We may not be perfect at sequential mathematical calculations, but no human designed artefact can beat natural systems like ourselves for parallel, stochastic, distributed computation.

The future of computing, as predicted by von Neumann, will be parallel and distributed. Perhaps by learning lessons from nature we will be able to achieve this future with the efficiency and reliability of a living system. If we could learn to combine the advantages of existing technologies with those of natural systems, our capabilities would be transformed.

References

1. Dorigo, M., Stutzle, T.: Ant Colony Optimization. MIT Press, London (2004)
2. Kari, L., Rozenberg, G.: The many facets of natural computing. Communications of the ACM 51, 72–83 (2008)
3. Bentley, P.J.: Digitized, Oxford, UK (2012)
4. von Neumann, J.: First Draft of a Report on the EDVAC. Moore School of Electrical Engineering, University of Pennsylvania. Developed under contract W-670-ORD-4926 between the United States Army Ordinance Department and the University of Pennsylvania (1945)
5. Obituary on Turing in The Times (1954)
6. Shannon, C.: Presentation of a Maze-Solving Machine. Group Interchange. In: Macy Jr., J. (ed.) Transactions of the Eighth Conference on Cybernetics Foundation, March 15-16, pp. 173–180 (1951)
7. Shannon, C.: Programming a Computer for Playing Chess. Philosophical Magazine, Ser.7 41(314) (March 1950)
8. von Neumann, J.: The Computer and the Brain: 2 edn. (Mrs. Hepsa Ely Silliman Memorial Lectures) (2000)
9. von Neumann, J., Burks, A.W.: Theory of Self-Reproducing Automata. University of Illinois Press, Urbana (1966)
10. Haroun Mahdavi, S., Bentley, P.J.: Innately adaptive robotics through embodied evolution. Journal of Adaptive Robotics (2004)
11. Haroun Mahdavi, S., Bentley, P.J.: Innately adaptive robotics through embodied evolution. In: Proc. of Robosphere 2004, the 2nd Workshop on Self-Sustaining Robotic Systems, November 9-10. NASA Ames Research Center (2004)
12. Mahdavi, S.H., Bentley, P.J.: An Evolutionary Approach to Damage Recovery of Robot Motion With Muscles. In: Banzhaf, W., Ziegler, J., Christaller, T., Dittrich, P., Kim, J.T. (eds.) ECAL 2003. LNCS (LNAI), vol. 2801, pp. 248–255. Springer, Heidelberg (2003)
13. Shannon, C.E.: A Mathematical Theory of Communication. Bell System Technical Journal 27, 379–423, 623–656 (1948)
14. Shannon, C.: Communication Theory of Secrecy Systems. Bell System Technical Journal 28(4), 656–715 (1948)
15. Bhalla, N., Bentley, P.J., Vise, C., Jacob, C.: Programming and Evolving Self-assembling Systems in Three Dimensions. To appear in the Special issue on Engineering Emergence, in the Journal of Natural Computing (2011)
16. Bhalla, N., Bentley, P.J.: Programming Self-assembling Systems Via Physically Encoded Information. In: Doursat, Sayama, Michel (eds.) Morphogenetic Engineering. Springer, Heidelberg (2011)

17. Bhalla, N., Bentley, P.J., Jacob, C.: Mapping Virtual Self-assembly Rules to Physical Systems. In: Proc. of the 2007 Conference on Unconventional Computing, Bristol, July 12-14 (2007)
18. Bentley, P.J.: Systemic computation: A model of interacting systems with natural characteristics. IJPEDS 22, 103–121 (2007)
19. Bentley, P.J.: Methods for Improving Simulations of Biological Systems: Systemic Computation and Fractal Proteins. Special Issue on Synthetic Biology, J R Soc. Interface 2009 6, 451–466 (2009), doi:10.1098/rsif.2008.0505.focus
20. Tammet, D.: Embracing the Wide Sky: A Tour Across the Horizons of the Mind. Hodder & Stoughton (2009)
21. Le Martelot, E., Bentley, P.J., Lotto, R.B.: A Systemic Computation Platform for the Modelling and Analysis of Processes with Natural Characteristics. In: GECCO 2007, pp. 2809–2816. ACM Press (2007)
22. Rouhipour, M., Bentley, P.J., Shayani, H.: Systemic Computation Using Graphics Processors. In: Tempesti, G., Tyrrell, A.M., Miller, J.F. (eds.) ICES 2010. LNCS, vol. 6274, pp. 121–132. Springer, Heidelberg (2010)
23. Sakellariou, C., Bentley, P.J.: Introducing the FPGA-Based Hardware Architecture of Systemic Computation (HAoS). In: Kotásek, Z., et al. (eds.) MEMICS 2011. LNCS, vol. 7119, pp. 179–190. Springer, Heidelberg (2011)

Games and Markov Decision Processes
with Mean-Payoff Parity and Energy Parity Objectives[*]

Krishnendu Chatterjee[1] and Laurent Doyen[2]

[1] IST Austria (Institute of Science and Technology Austria)
[2] LSV, ENS Cachan & CNRS, France

Abstract. In this paper we survey results of two-player games on graphs and Markov decision processes with parity, mean-payoff and energy objectives, and the combination of mean-payoff and energy objectives with parity objectives. These problems have applications in verification and synthesis of reactive systems in resource-constrained environments.

1 Introduction

Two-player games on graphs and Markov decision processes (MDPs) are standard models for reactive systems. In the analysis of reactive systems, the problem may specify a goal as a set of desired traces (such as ω-regular specifications), or as a quantitative optimization objective for a payoff function on the traces. One classical example of quantitative objective is the mean-payoff objective [15,19]. Recently, the energy objectives (corresponding to total-payoff functions) have also been considered in the design of resource-constrained embedded systems such as power-limited systems [2,5], as well as in queueing processes, and gambling models (see also [3] and references therein). The energy objective requires that the sum of the rewards be always nonnegative along a trace. Energy objectives can be expressed in the setting of boundaryless one-counter systems [3]. In recent times, games and MDPs equipped with the combination of a parity objective (which is a canonical way to express the ω-regular conditions [21]), and a quantitative objective specified as either mean-payoff or energy condition have been considered [9,5,6]. Such combination of quantitative and qualitative objectives is crucial in the design of reactive systems with both resource constraints and functional requirements [4,9,2,1]. Also the energy parity objective can be viewed as a natural extension of boundaryless one-counter systems with fairness conditions.

In this paper we summarize the main results about MDPs and games with parity, mean-payoff, energy, mean-payoff parity, and energy parity objectives. We also present an improved algorithm to solve MDPs with mean-payoff parity objectives.

2 Definitions

Probability Distributions. A *probability distribution* over a finite set A is a function $\kappa : A \to [0, 1]$ such that $\sum_{a \in A} \kappa(a) = 1$. The *support* of κ is the set $\mathsf{Supp}(\kappa) = \{a \in A \mid \kappa(a) > 0\}$. We denote by $\mathcal{D}(A)$ the set of probability distributions on A.

---

[*] This work was partially supported by FWF NFN Grant S11407-N23 (RiSE) and a Microsoft faculty fellowship.

Z. Kotásek et al. (Eds.): MEMICS 2011, LNCS 7119, pp. 37–46, 2012.

Markov Decision Processes. A *Markov Decision Process* (MDP) $M = (Q, E, \delta)$ consists of a finite set Q of states partitioned into *player-1 states* Q_1 and *probabilistic states* Q_P (i.e., $Q = Q_1 \cup Q_P$ and $Q_1 \cap Q_P = \emptyset$), a set $E \subseteq Q \times Q$ of edges such that for all $q \in Q$, there exists (at least one) $q' \in Q$ such that $(q, q') \in E$, and a probabilistic transition function $\delta : Q_P \to \mathcal{D}(Q)$ such that for all $q \in Q_P$ and $q' \in Q$, we have $(q, q') \in E$ iff $\delta(q)(q') > 0$. We often write $\delta(q, q')$ for $\delta(q)(q')$. For a state $q \in Q$, we denote by $E(q) = \{q' \in Q \mid (q, q') \in E\}$ the set of possible successors of q. A *Markov chain* is a special case of MDP where $Q_1 = \emptyset$.

Plays. An MDP can be viewed as the arena of a game played for infinitely many rounds from a state $q_0 \in Q$ as follows. If the game is in a player-1 state q, then player 1 chooses a successor state from the set $E(q)$; otherwise the game is in a probabilistic state q, and the successor is chosen according to the probability distribution $\delta(q)$. This game results in a *play* from q_0, i.e., an infinite path $\rho = q_0 q_1 \ldots$ such that $(q_i, q_{i+1}) \in E$ for all $i \geq 0$. The prefix of length n of ρ is denoted by $\rho(n) = q_0 \ldots q_n$, the last state of $\rho(n)$ is $\mathsf{Last}(\rho(n)) = q_n$. We write Ω for the set of all plays.

Strategies. A *strategy* (for player 1) is a function $\sigma : Q^* Q_1 \to Q$ such that for all $\rho \in Q^*$, $q \in Q_1$, and $q' \in Q_P$, if $\sigma(\rho \cdot q) = q'$, then $(q, q') \in E$. We denote by Σ the set of all strategies. An *outcome* of σ from q_0 is a play $q_0 q_1 \ldots$ where $q_{i+1} = \sigma(q_0 \ldots q_i)$ for all $i \geq 0$ such that $q_i \in Q_1$.

Outcomes and Measures. Once a starting state $q \in Q$ and a strategy $\sigma \in \Sigma$ are fixed, the outcome of the game is a random walk ω_q^σ for which the probabilities of every *event* $\mathcal{A} \subseteq \Omega$, which is a measurable set of plays, are uniquely defined [22]. For a state $q \in Q$ and an event $\mathcal{A} \subseteq \Omega$, we denote by $\mathbb{P}_q^\sigma(\mathcal{A})$ the probability that a play belongs to $\mathcal{A}$ if the game starts from the state q and player 1 follows the strategy σ. For a measurable function $f : \Omega \to \mathbb{R}$ we denote by $\mathbb{E}_q^\sigma[f]$ the *expectation* of the function f under the probability measure $\mathbb{P}_q^\sigma(\cdot)$.

Finite-Memory Strategies. A strategy uses *finite-memory* if it can be encoded by a deterministic transducer $\langle \mathsf{Mem}, m_0, \alpha_u, \alpha_n \rangle$ where Mem is a finite set (the memory of the strategy), $m_0 \in \mathsf{Mem}$ is the initial memory value, $\alpha_u : \mathsf{Mem} \times Q \to \mathsf{Mem}$ is an update function, and $\alpha_n : \mathsf{Mem} \times Q_1 \to Q$ is a next-move function. The *size* of the strategy is the number $|\mathsf{Mem}|$ of memory values. If the current state is a player-1 state q, and m is the current memory value, then the strategy chooses the next state q' according to $\alpha_n(m, q)$. If the current state is q, then the memory is updated to $\alpha_u(m, q)$. Formally, $\langle \mathsf{Mem}, m_0, \alpha_u, \alpha_n \rangle$ defines the strategy σ such that $\sigma(\rho \cdot q) = \alpha_n(\hat{\alpha}_u(m_0, \rho), q)$ for all $\rho \in Q^*$ and $q \in Q_1$, where $\hat{\alpha}_u$ extends α_u to sequences of states as expected. A strategy is *memoryless* if $|\mathsf{Mem}| = 1$, and a memoryless strategy $\sigma : Q_1 \to Q$ chooses one edge for every player 1 state. For a finite-memory strategy σ, M_σ denote the Markov chain obtained as the product of M with the transducer defining σ.

Two-Player Games. A *two-player game* is a graph $G = (Q, E)$ with the same assumptions as for MDP, except that the partition of Q is denoted (Q_1, Q_2) where Q_2 is the set of *player-2 states*. Player 2 plays the role of an adversary to player 1. The notions of play, strategies (in particular strategies for player 2), and outcome are analogous to the case of MDP (see [21] for standard definition of games).

Objectives. An *objective* for an MDP M (or game G) is a set $\phi \subseteq \Omega$ of infinite paths. Let $p : Q \rightarrow \mathbb{N}$ be a *priority function* and $w : E \rightarrow \mathbb{Z}$ be a *weight function*[1] where positive numbers represent rewards. We denote by W the largest weight (in absolute value) according to w. The *energy level* of a prefix $\gamma = q_0 q_1 \ldots q_n$ of a play is $\mathsf{EL}(w, \gamma) = \sum_{i=0}^{n-1} w(q_i, q_{i+1})$, and the *mean-payoff value*[2] of a play $\rho = q_0 q_1 \ldots$ is $\mathsf{MP}(w, \rho) = \liminf_{n \rightarrow \infty} \frac{1}{n} \cdot \mathsf{EL}(w, \rho(n))$. In the sequel, when the weight function w is clear from the context we omit it and simply write $\mathsf{EL}(\gamma)$ and $\mathsf{MP}(\rho)$. We denote by $\mathsf{Inf}(\rho)$ the set of states that occur infinitely often in ρ, and we consider the following objectives:

- *Parity objectives.* The *parity* objective $\mathsf{Parity}(p) = \{\rho \in \Omega \mid \min\{p(q) \mid q \in \mathsf{Inf}(\rho)\}$ is even $\}$ requires that the minimum priority visited infinitely often be even. The special cases of *Büchi* and *coBüchi* objectives correspond to the case with two priorities, $p : Q \rightarrow \{0, 1\}$ and $p : Q \rightarrow \{1, 2\}$ respectively.
- *Energy objectives.* Given an initial credit $c_0 \in \mathbb{N}$, the *energy* objective $\mathsf{PosEnergy}(c_0) = \{\rho \in \Omega \mid \forall n \geq 0 : c_0 + \mathsf{EL}(\rho(n)) \geq 0\}$ requires that the energy level be always positive.
- *Mean-payoff objectives.* Given a threshold $\nu \in \mathbb{Q}$, the *mean-payoff* objective $\mathsf{MeanPayoff}^{\geq \nu} = \{\rho \in \Omega \mid \mathsf{MP}(\rho) \geq \nu\}$ (resp. $\mathsf{MeanPayoff}^{>\nu} = \{\rho \in \Omega \mid \mathsf{MP}(\rho) > \nu\}$) requires that the mean-payoff value be at least ν (resp. strictly greater than ν).
- *Combined objectives.* The *energy parity* objective $\mathsf{Parity}(p) \cap \mathsf{PosEnergy}(c_0)$ and the *mean-payoff parity* objective $\mathsf{Parity}(p) \cap \mathsf{MeanPayoff}^{\sim \nu}$ (for $\sim \in \{\geq, >\}$) combine the requirements of parity and energy (resp., mean-payoff) objectives.

Almost-Sure Winning Strategies. For MDPs, we say that a player-1 strategy σ is *almost-sure winning* in a state q for an objective ϕ if $\mathbb{P}_q^\sigma(\phi) = 1$. For two-player games, we say that a player-1 strategy σ is *winning* in a state q for an objective ϕ if all outcomes of σ starting in q belong to ϕ. For energy objectives with unspecified initial credit, we also say that a strategy is (almost-sure) winning if it is (almost-sure) winning for *some* finite initial credit.

Decision Problems. We are interested in the following problems. Given an MDP M with weight function w and priority function p, and a state q_0:

- The *parity problem* asks whether there exists an almost-sure winning strategy for the parity objective from q_0.
- The *mean-payoff problem (resp. mean-payoff parity problem)* asks whether there exists an almost-sure winning strategy for the mean-payoff objective (resp. mean-payoff parity objective) with threshold 0 from q_0. Note that it is not restrictive to consider mean-payoff objectives with threshold 0 because for $\sim \in \{\geq, >\}$, we have $\mathsf{MP}(w, \rho) \sim \nu$ iff $\mathsf{MP}(w - \nu, \rho) \sim 0$, where $w - \nu$ is the weight function that assigns $w(e) - \nu$ to each edge $e \in E$.

---

[1] Sometimes we take the freedom to use rational weights (i.e., $w : E \rightarrow \mathbb{Q}$), while we always assume that weights are integers encoded in binary for complexity results.

[2] The results of this paper hold for the definition of mean-payoff value using $\limsup$ instead of $\liminf$.

- The *energy problem (resp. energy parity problem)* asks whether there exists a finite initial credit $c_0 \in \mathbb{N}$ and an almost-sure winning strategy for the energy objective (resp. energy parity objective) from q_0 with initial credit c_0.

The two-player game versions of these problems are defined analogously, and in two player games we are interested in the existence of winning strategies as compared to almost-sure winning strategies.

3 Games

In this section we summarize the results of games with all the objectives defined in the previous section. We first present the results for parity, mean-payoff and energy objectives, and then present the results for combined objectives.

3.1 Games with Parity, Mean-Payoff, and Energy Objectives

In games with parity, mean-payoff, and energy objectives, memoryless winning strategies exist for both players. The result for parity objectives was established in [14] (also see [23]); for mean-payoff objectives it was shown in [18] (also see [13]); and for energy objectives it follows from [4]. The existence of memoryless optimal strategies, and the fact that the one-player version of the problems can be solved in polynomial time shows that the problems can be decided in NP ∩ coNP. For polynomial time algorithms for the one-player games, see [17] for parity objectives, [16] for mean-payoff objectives, and [4] for energy objectives. A major open question in this area of research is whether games with parity, mean-payoff, and energy objective can be solved in polynomial time. There is a close connection between mean-payoff and energy games, and the equivalence of the decision problems has been established in [2]. The main argument is as follows: by existence of memoryless strategies it follows that if the answer to the mean-payoff objectives with threshold $\nu = 0$ is true, then player 1 can fix a memoryless strategies such that in all cycles the sum of the rewards is non-negative, and this exactly coincides with the finite initial credit problem (where after a prefix, the sum of the rewards in cycles is non-negative). The results are summarized in the following theorem.

Theorem 1. *Memoryless winning strategies exist for both players in two-player games with parity, mean-payoff, and energy objectives, and the decision problems lie in NP ∩ coNP.*

3.2 Games with Mean-Payoff Parity and Energy Parity Objectives

Mean-payoff parity games were first studied in [9] and it was shown that winning strategies for player 1 require infinite memory in general. It follows from the results of [9] that memoryless winning strategies exist for player 2. In [5] games with energy parity objectives were studied and the following results were established: (1) winning strategies for player 1 with energy parity objectives require memory at least $2 \cdot (|Q| - 1) \cdot W + 1$ and memory of size $4 \cdot |Q| \cdot d \cdot W$ is sufficient; (2) memoryless winning strategies exist for player 2; and (3) the decision problem lie in NP ∩ coNP. It was also shown in [5] that the decision problem for mean-payoff parity objectives can be reduced to the decision problem for energy parity objectives, however, as winning strategies require infinite memory for mean-payoff parity objectives, the reduction is more involved than the reduction from mean-payoff to energy objectives. As a consequence it also follows that the decision problem for mean-payoff parity objectives lie in NP ∩ coNP.

Theorem 2. *In games with mean-payoff parity objectives, winning strategies for player 1 (with mean-payoff parity objective) require infinite memory in general, and memoryless winning strategies exist for player 2. In games with energy parity objectives, winning strategies for player 1 (with energy parity objective) require $2 \cdot (|Q| - 1) \cdot W + 1$ memory in general and memory of size $4 \cdot |Q| \cdot d \cdot |W|$ is sufficient, and memoryless winning strategies exist for player 2. The problems of deciding the winner in games with mean-payoff parity and games with energy parity objectives lie in NP ∩ coNP.*

4   Markov Decision Process

In this section we summarize the results for Markov decision processes (MDPs).

4.1   MDPs with Parity, Mean-Payoff and Energy Objectives

As in the case of games, in MDPs memoryless almost-sure winning strategies exist for parity, mean-payoff and energy objectives. The result of existence of memoryless almost-sure winning strategies for MDPs with parity objectives follows from [12] (also see [10] for explicit proofs). The result of existence of memoryless almost-sure winning strategies for mean-payoff objectives follows from the result of [18] (also see [15,19] for details of MDPs with mean-payoff objectives). Almost-sure winning in MDPs with energy objective is equivalent to a two-player energy game (where the probabilistic states are controlled by player 2). Indeed (1) a winning strategy in the game is trivially almost-sure winning in the MDP, and (2) if an almost-sure winning strategy σ in the MDP was not winning in the game, then for all initial credit c_0 there would exist an outcome ρ of σ such that $c_0 + \mathsf{EL}(\rho(i)) < 0$ for some position $i \geq 0$. The prefix $\rho(i)$ has a positive probability in the MDP, in contradiction with the fact that σ is almost-sure winning. As a consequence, it follows that memoryless almost-sure winning strategies exist for MDPs with energy objectives, and it also follows that solving MDPs with energy objectives is as hard as games with energy as well as games with mean-payoff objective. The results of [10] give a polynomial-time algorithm to solve almost-sure winning for MDPs with parity objective. For MDPs with mean-payoff objective, the almost-sure winning problem can be solved through linear programming (see [15,19] for a linear program formulation to solve MDPs with mean-payoff objective). The problem of MDPs with energy objective lies in NP ∩ coNP due to the equivalence with games with energy objective.

Theorem 3. *Memoryless almost-sure winning strategies exist in MDPs with parity, mean-payoff and energy objectives. The decision problems of existence of almost-sure* *winning strategy can be solved in polynomial time for mean-payoff and parity objectives, and for energy objectives it belongs to NP ∩ coNP.*

4.2 MDPs with Mean-Payoff Parity and Energy Parity Objectives

MDPs with mean-payoff parity and energy parity objectives were considered in [6], and the following results were established. For mean-payoff parity objectives, almost-sure winning strategies require infinite memory in general, and the set of almost-sure winning states can be computed in polynomial time. For energy parity objectives, a polynomial time reduction was presented to games with energy Büchi objectives (parity objectives with two priorities), and it follows that the decision problem belongs to NP ∩ coNP.

Theorem 4. *In MDPs with mean-payoff parity objectives, almost-sure winning strategies require infinite memory in general. In MDPs with energy parity objectives, almost-sure winning strategies require $2 \cdot (|Q| - 1) \cdot W + 1$ memory in general and memory of size $2 \cdot |Q| \cdot |W|$ is sufficient. The set of almost-sure winning states can be computed in polynomial time for mean-payoff parity objectives. The decision problem of whether a state is almost-sure winning lies in NP ∩ coNP for energy parity objectives.*

4.3 New Result: Improved Algorithm for Mean-Payoff Parity Objectives

In this section we present an improved polynomial-time algorithm for the computation of the set of almost-sure winning states for mean-payoff parity objectives, using the results of [6] and hierarchical graph decomposition technique. We first define the basic notion of end-component for MDPs.

End-Components. A set $U \subseteq Q$ is δ-*closed* if for all $q \in U \cap Q_P$ we have $\mathsf{Supp}(\delta(q)) \subseteq U$. The sub-MDP induced by a δ-closed set U is $M \upharpoonright U = (U, E \cap (U \times U), \delta)$. Note that $M \upharpoonright U$ is an MDP if for all $q \in U$ there exists $q' \in U$ such that $(q, q') \in E$. A *closed recurrent set* for a Markov chain is a δ-closed set $U \subseteq Q$ which is strongly connected. End-components in MDPs play a role equivalent to closed recurrent sets in Markov chains. Given an MDP $M = (Q, E, \delta)$ with partition (Q_1, Q_P), a set $U \subseteq Q$ of states is an *end-component* if U is δ-closed and the sub-MDP $M \upharpoonright U$ is strongly connected [11,12]. We denote by $\mathcal{E}(M)$ the set of end-components of an MDP M.

End-Component Lemma. We now present an important lemma about end-components from [11,12] that we use in the proofs of our result. It states that for arbitrary strategies (memoryless or not), with probability 1 the set of states visited infinitely often along a play is an end-component. This lemma allows us to derive conclusions on the (infinite) set of plays in an MDP by analyzing the (finite) set of end-components in the MDP.

Lemma 1 ([11,12]). *Given an MDP M, for all states $q \in Q$ and all strategies $\sigma \in \Sigma$, we have $\mathbb{P}_q^\sigma(\{\omega \mid \mathsf{Inf}(\omega) \in \mathcal{E}(M)\}) = 1$.*

We now present the key lemma from [6] where it was shown that for an MDP that is an end-component such that the minimum priority is even, the mean-payoff parity objective $\mathsf{Parity}(p) \cap \mathsf{MeanPayoff}^{\geq \nu}$ is satisfied with probability 1 if the expected mean-payoff value is at least ν at some state (the result also holds for strict inequality). In other words, from the expected mean-payoff value of at least ν we ensure that both the mean-payoff and parity objective is satisfied with probability 1 from all states. For a state q, let $\mathsf{ValMP}(w)(q) = \sup_{\sigma \in \Sigma} \mathbb{E}_q^\sigma[\mathsf{MP}(w)]$ denote the expected mean-payoff value. The following lemma was established in [6].

Lemma 2 ([6]). *Consider an MDP M with state space Q, a priority function p, and weight function w such that (a) M is an end-component (i.e., Q is an end-component) and (b) the smallest priority in Q is even. If there is a state $q \in Q$ such that $\mathsf{ValMP}(w)(q) \geq \nu$ (resp. $\mathsf{ValMP}(w)(q) > \nu$), then there exists a strategy σ^* such that for all states $q \in Q$ we have $\mathbb{P}_q^{\sigma^*}(\mathsf{Parity}(p) \cap \mathsf{MeanPayoff}^{\geq \nu}) = 1$ (resp. $\mathbb{P}_q^{\sigma^*}(\mathsf{Parity}(p) \cap \mathsf{MeanPayoff}^{> \nu}) = 1$).*

Winning End-Component. Given an MDP M with a parity objective $\mathsf{Parity}(p)$ and a mean-payoff objective $\mathsf{MeanPayoff}^{\geq \nu}$ for a weight function w, we call an end-component U *winning* if (a) $\min(p(U))$ is even; and (b) there exists a state with expected mean-payoff value at least ν in the sub-MDP induced by U, i.e., $\max_{q \in U} \mathsf{ValMP}(w)(q) \geq \nu$ in the sub-MDP induced by U. We denote by $\mathcal{W}$ the set of winning end-components, and let $\mathsf{Win} = \bigcup_{U \in \mathcal{W}} U$ be the union of the winning end-components.

Reduction to Reachability of Winning End-Component. By Lemma 2 it follows that in every winning end-component the mean-payoff parity objective is satisfied with probability 1. Conversely, consider an end-component U that is not winning, then either the smallest priority is odd, or the maximal expected mean-payoff value that can be ensured for any state in U by staying in U is less than ν. Hence if only states in U are visited infinitely often, then with probability 1 (i) either the parity objective is not satisfied, or (ii) the mean-payoff objective is not satisfied. In other words, if an end-component that is not winning is visited infinitely often, then the mean-payoff parity objective is satisfied with probability 0. It follows that the almost-sure winning states can be computed by computing the set of almost-sure winning states for reachability objectives with the winning end-components as the target set (i.e., computing almost-sure reachability to the set Win). Since almost-sure winning states for MDPs with reachability objectives can be computed in polynomial time [10], it suffices to present a polynomial-time algorithm to compute Win in order to obtain a polynomial-time algorithm for MDPs with mean-payoff parity objectives.

Computing Winning End-Components. The computation of the winning end-components is done iteratively by computing winning end-components with smallest priority 0, then winning end-components with smallest priority 2, and so on. The computation of Win is as follows:

- For $i \geq 0$, let $\mathcal{W}_{2i}$ be the set of maximal end-components U with states with priority at least $2i$ and that contain at least one state with priority $2i$, i.e., U contains only states with priority at least $2i$, and contains at least one state with priority $2i$. Let $\mathcal{W}'_{2i} \subseteq \mathcal{W}_{2i}$ be the set of maximal end-components $U \in \mathcal{W}_{2i}$ such that there is a state $q \in U$ such that the expected mean-payoff value in the sub-MDP restricted to U is at least ν. Let $\mathsf{Win}_{2i} = \bigcup_{U \in \mathcal{W}'_{2i}} U$.

The set $\text{Win} = \bigcup_{i=0}^{\lfloor d/2 \rfloor} \text{Win}_{2i}$ is the union of the states of the winning end-components (formal pseudo-code in [7]).

Complexity of Computing Winning End-Components. The winning end-component algorithm runs for $O(d)$ iterations and in each iteration requires to compute a maximal end-component decomposition (mec) and compute mean-payoff values of at most n end-components, where n is the number of states of the MDP. We now improve the $O(d)$ iterations to $O(\log d)$ using the hierarchical clustering technique of Tarjan [20].

Given a priority function $p : Q \rightarrow \{0, 1, \ldots, 2d\}$, for $0 \le m \le d$, let $Q_{\le m} = \{q \in Q \mid p(q) \le m\}$ denote the set of states with priority at most m. Given an MDP M, let M_i denote the MDP obtained by removing $Attr_R(Q_{\le 2i-1})$ the set of states with priority less than $2i$ and its random attractor (random attractor denotes the probabilistic alternating reachability, for formal definition of random attractor see [8]). A mec C is a *winning mec* in M_i if there exists $u \in C$ such that $p(u) = 2i$ and there is some state $v \in C$ such that the expected mean-payoff value of v is greater than the given threshold ν. Let WE_i be the union of the vertices of winning mec in M_i, and let $\text{WE} = \cup_{0 \le i \le d} \text{WE}_i$.

Informal Description of the New Algorithm. If two states u, v belong to the same mec in M_i, they also belong to the same mec in M_{i-1}. Thus the mec's of M_i refine the ones of M_{i-1}, which can be exploited using the hierarchical clustering technique. Formally, we will compute WE by the recursive procedure $\text{WINMAXEC}(M, p, i, j)$. The procedure takes an MDP, and two indices i and j, and outputs $\bigcup_{i < 2k \le j} \text{WE}_{2k}$. To obtain WE we invoke $\text{WINMAXEC}(M, p, 0, 2d)$. Given the MDP M, and indices i, j, the procedure first computes the mec's of M_m, where $m = \lceil \frac{i+j}{2} \rceil$. If m is even, then the set WE_m of M_m is computed. Then we recursively call the procedures $\text{WINMAXEC}(M_u, p, m+1, j)$ and $\text{WINMAXEC}(M_\ell, p, i, m-1)$, where M_u is a sub-MDP containing only the edges *inside* the mec's of M_m and the MDP M_ℓ is obtained by collapsing each mec in M_m to a single vertex, thus containing only edges *outside* the mec's of M_m. The formal description of the algorithm is identical to the algorithm of Section 5 of [8] for almost-sure winning of MDPs with parity objectives, and the only change is while determining whether an end-component is winning along with the priority being even, we also check whether there is some state where the expected mean-payoff value is at least the given threshold. The correctness argument is essentially similar to the correctness of [8], and shows that $\text{Win} = \text{WE}$.

Running Time Analysis. Given a MDP M with n states, m edges and a parity objective with d priorities, let us denote by $T(m, n, d)$ the running time of WINMAXEC on M. We observe that in E_u consists of edges with in mec's, and such edges are not present in E_ℓ. Thus we obtain the following recurrence relation for the running time $T(m, n, d)$ of WINMAXEC:

$$T(m, n, d) = T_M(m, n) + T(m_u, n, \lfloor \frac{d-1}{2} \rfloor)$$
$$+ T(m_\ell, n, \lceil \frac{d-1}{2} \rceil),$$

with $m_\ell + m_u \le m$, and $T_M(m, n)$ denotes the time complexity of mec decomposition and MDPs with mean-payoff solving with m edges and n states. It is straightforward to show that $T(m, n, d) = O((\text{MAXEC}(n, m) + \text{MEANPAYOFFSOLVE}(n, m)) \cdot \log(d))$, where MAXEC and MEANPAYOFFSOLVE denote algorithms for computing the maximal end-component decomposition of an MDP and solving MDPs with mean-payoff objectives, respectively. Thus we obtain an improved algorithm to solve MDPs with mean-payoff parity objectives.

5 Conclusion

In this paper we summarized the main results of games and MDPs with parity, mean-payoff, energy, mean-payoff parity, and energy parity objectives. The major open questions are whether games with parity, mean-payoff, and energy objective can be solved in polynomial time.

References

1. Bloem, R., Chatterjee, K., Henzinger, T.A., Jobstmann, B.: Better Quality in Synthesis Through Quantitative Objectives. In: Bouajjani, A., Maler, O. (eds.) CAV 2009. LNCS, vol. 5643, pp. 140–156. Springer, Heidelberg (2009)
2. Bouyer, P., Fahrenberg, U., Larsen, K.G., Markey, N., Srba, J.: Infinite Runs in Weighted Timed Automata With Energy Constraints. In: Cassez, F., Jard, C. (eds.) FORMATS 2008. LNCS, vol. 5215, pp. 33–47. Springer, Heidelberg (2008)
3. Brázdil, T., Brozek, V., Etessami, K., Kucera, A., Wojtczak, D.: One-counter Markov decision processes. In: Proc. of SODA, pp. 863–874. SIAM (2010)
4. Chakrabarti, A., de Alfaro, L., Henzinger, T.A., Stoelinga, M.: Resource Interfaces. In: Alur, R., Lee, I. (eds.) EMSOFT 2003. LNCS, vol. 2855, pp. 117–133. Springer, Heidelberg (2003)
5. Chatterjee, K., Doyen, L.: Energy Parity Games. In: Abramsky, S., Gavoille, C., Kirchner, C., Meyer auf der Heide, F., Spirakis, P.G. (eds.) ICALP 2010. LNCS, vol. 6199, pp. 599–610. Springer, Heidelberg (2010)
6. Chatterjee, K., Doyen, L.: Energy and Mean-Payoff Parity Markov Decision Processes. In: Murlak, F., Sankowski, P. (eds.) MFCS 2011. LNCS, vol. 6907, pp. 206–218. Springer, Heidelberg (2011)
7. Chatterjee, K., Doyen, L.: Energy and mean-payoff parity Markov decision processes. Technical report, IST Austria (February 2011),
   http://pub.ist.ac.at/Pubs/TechRpts/2011/IST-2011-0001.pdf
8. Chatterjee, K., Henzinger, M.: Faster and dynamic algorithms for maximal end-component decomposition and related graph problems in probabilistic verification. In: Proc. of SODA. ACM SIAM (2011)
9. Chatterjee, K., Henzinger, T.A., Jurdziński, M.: Mean-payoff parity games. In: Proc. of LICS, pp. 178–187. IEEE Computer Society (2005)
10. Chatterjee, K., Jurdziński, M., Henzinger, T.A.: Quantitative stochastic parity games. In: Proc. of SODA Symposium on Discrete Algorithms, pp. 114–123 (2004); Technical Report: UCB/CSD-3-1280 (October 2003)
11. Courcoubetis, C., Yannakakis, M.: The complexity of probabilistic verification. J. ACM 42(4), 857–907 (1995)
12. de Alfaro, L.: Formal Verification of Probabilistic Systems. PhD thesis, Stanford University (1997)

13. Ehrenfeucht, A., Mycielski, J.: Positional strategies for mean payoff games. Int. Journal of Game Theory 8(2), 109–113 (1979)
14. Emerson, E.A., Jutla, C.: The complexity of tree automata and logics of programs. In: FOCS, pp. 328–337. IEEE Computer Society Press (1988)
15. Filar, J., Vrieze, K.: Competitive Markov Decision Processes. Springer, Heidelberg (1997)
16. Karp, R.M.: A characterization of the minimum cycle mean in a digraph. Discrete Mathematics 23(3), 309–311 (1978)
17. King, V., Kupferman, O., Vardi, M.Y.: On the Complexity of Parity Word Automata. In: Honsell, F., Miculan, M. (eds.) FOSSACS 2001. LNCS, vol. 2030, pp. 276–286. Springer, Heidelberg (2001)
18. Liggett, T.A., Lippman, S.A.: Stochastic games with perfect information and time average payoff. Siam Review 11, 604–607 (1969)
19. Puterman, M.L.: Markov Decision Processes. John Wiley and Sons (1994)
20. Tarjan, R.E.: A hierarchical clustering algorithm using strong components. Inf. Process. Lett. 14(1), 26–29 (1982)
21. Thomas, W.: Languages, automata, and logic. In: Handbook of Formal Languages. Beyond Words, vol. 3, ch. 7, pp. 389–455. Springer, Heidelberg (1997)
22. Vardi, M.Y.: Automatic verification of probabilistic concurrent finite-state systems. In: FOCS 1985. IEEE Computer Society Press (1985)
23. Zielonka, W.: Infinite games on finitely coloured graphs with applications to automata on infinite trees. Theor. Comput. Sci. 200, 135–183 (1998)

Assessing System Vulnerability
Using Formal Verification Techniques*

Görschwin Fey

Institute of Computer Science, University of Bremen, 28359 Bremen, Germany
fey@informatik.uni-bremen.de

Abstract. Hardware systems are becoming more and more vulnerable to soft errors caused by radiation or process variations. Design techniques to cope with these problems are built into the system. But how to verify that the final system is as resilient as expected? The paper covers modeling issues related to assessing fault tolerance and reliability. Existing approaches are reviewed that analyze transient faults on the electrical as well as the logical level. Trade-offs regarding resource requirements and quality of results are discussed and the individual advantages are highlighted.

1 Introduction

For safety related products ensuring the functionality under all circumstances is mandatory. In certain cases standards apply, e.g., IEC 61508 considering safety-related electronic systems or ISO 26262 which is more specific to the automotive area.

Here, the focus is on hardware-systems implemented as digital integrated circuits where the interest in analyzing the vulnerability to faults has significantly gained momentum in the recent past. Ongoing downscaling of hardware components is the reason due to three main factors. First, smaller hardware components are more sensitive to value changes induced by environmental radiation as smaller amounts of energy are sufficient to change the value of a signal. Second, even though the overall production process is continuously improved the influence of process variations during production increases as, e.g., the relative variation of area, delay etc. increases. Third, aging processes also corrupt the functionality of smaller components more rapidly. Consequently, a designer needs to know the consequence of a fault occurring in the system.

A natural counter-measure is to design systems that are able to tolerate a fault without suffering a system level failure. Such fault tolerant systems have a long tradition and therefore various design practices are known and established. *Triple Modular Redundancy* (TMR) is just one well-known example. A single module is copied for three times and a majority voter selects the output data. By this any single fault of and in one of the three modules can be detected and corrected. Similarly, the Hamming code [Ham50] corrects any single fault in a given data word. Various additional approaches have been proposed more recently.

---

* This work has been supported in part by the German Research Foundation (DFG, grant no. 797/6-1).

Z. Kotásek et al. (Eds.): MEMICS 2011, LNCS 7119, pp. 47–56, 2012.

But any given implementation has to be checked for correctness. If the implementation has bugs, the real system may not be able to tolerate internal faults. Moreover, these bugs cannot be detected without explicitly checking the behavior under faults.

Various approaches have been proposed to analyze whether a given digital circuit is fault tolerant. Approaches based on simulation [KPMH09, TH10] or on emulation [CMR$^+$02, PCZ$^+$08] are predominant to analyze very large systems. But as a disadvantage it is typically impossible to analyze the system completely, i.e., only a subset of the potential input stimuli, the system configurations, or the potential faults can be considered. Thus, fault tolerance cannot be proven but only be established with a certain confidence. Formal approaches fully analyze the state space, the input space and all potential faults.

The present survey concentrates on formal approaches to analyze a hardware system's reaction upon internal malfunctions. Approaches assessing fault tolerance or reliability of a given circuit or system are considered.

This survey is structured as follows: Section 2 introduces basics such as notation, general concepts and modeling issues. A formal model for vulnerability analysis along with a comparison of existing approaches is provided in Section 3. Section 4 concludes.

2 Basics

2.1 Representation of Circuits and Systems

There exist different approaches to represent digital circuits [ABF90]. When the structure of a sequential synchronous circuit C is important graph representations are typically used that describe a Boolean network. Nodes in the graph structure correspond to elements of a library of basic components. The set { AND, OR, NOT, FF } is an example of a typical library where FF denotes a flip-flop. The library may be enriched by parameters of the underlying technology like delay or threshold voltages. When necessary hierarchy may be represented in the graph by introducing nodes referring to modules. Each module is then represented as a Boolean network itself.

The library can be extended to represent primary inputs, primary outputs and memory elements. In the following we assume that a circuit C has n_s memory elements, n_i primary inputs and n_o primary outputs.

When the structure of a digital circuit C is not required, the Boolean function

$$f_C : \mathbb{B}^{n_i} \times \mathbb{B}^{n_s} \to \mathbb{B}^{n_o} \times \mathbb{B}^{n_s}$$

implemented by the Boolean network N_C is an appropriate representation. Given a valuation of inputs and state elements, the combinational logic captured by f_C calculates the valuation of outputs and the new values of state elements of the circuit.

A synchronous sequential circuit corresponds to a finite automaton

$$A_C = (X, Y, S, I, T)$$

where $X = \mathbb{B}^{n_i}$ is the input alphabet, $Y = \mathbb{B}^{n_o}$ is the output alphabet, $S = \mathbb{B}^{n_s}$ is the set of states, $I \subseteq S$ is the set of initial states, and $T \subseteq X \times S \times S \times Y$ is the transition relation. The transition relation is determined by the Boolean function implemented by the circuit: $T_C(x, z, z', y) = f_C(x, z) \equiv (z', y)$, where $x \in \mathbb{B}^{n_i}, z, z' \in \mathbb{B}^{n_s}, y \in \mathbb{B}^{n_o}$ and (z', y) denotes the concatenation of the two vectors z' and y.

Finite automata are often used to model other systems than circuits as well. Therefore, some of the approaches discussed in Section 3 can be applied to other types of systems, too.

One approach to analyze the sequential behavior is *unrolling* as done in formal verification [BCCZ99] also called *time frame expansion* in the testing area [Kub68, PR71]. The result is a combinational representation of the sequential system. An unrolling of a circuit C for t time steps is modeled by the following expression:

$$U_C(t) = I(z_0) \wedge \bigwedge_{i=1}^{t} T_C(x_{i-1}, z_{i-1}, z_i, y_{i-1}) \tag{1}$$

where I is used as a Boolean predicate over state elements, that is 1 exactly when the valuation of the variables corresponds to an initial state.

Any assignment to the variables that yields $U_C(t) = 1$ describes a path in the finite automaton which corresponds to a potential simulation run of the circuit of t times steps.

2.2 Faults and Errors

When considering fault tolerance or reliability of a circuit or a system physical faults are of interest. Typical physical faults induced by particle hits from environmental radiation are voltage pulses in combinational logic, called *Single Event Transients* (SETs), or bit-flips in memory cells, called *Single Event Upsets* (SEUs). Modeling all details like energy and size of potential particles and their impact on the physical structure of the circuit leads to too many parameters for an automated analysis. Therefore the physical faults are abstracted into a fault model to be handled by analysis procedures.

In the following the circuit or system is assumed to be assembled of components that may be gates or larger modules composed of gates. A *fault* ϕ is a malfunction of a component in a circuit that causes one or more signal values to differ from their value during normal operation. Such differing values may propagate to primary outputs of the system. This observation of differing values is then called an *error*. The error may propagate further into a system potentially resulting in a *system failure* or the error may be detected and handled at higher levels of the full system. The universe of all faults in the model for a circuit C is denoted by Φ_C or simply Φ if unambiguous.

A typical fault model known from the testing area is the *Stuck-At Fault Model* (SAFM), where a single line is assumed to be stuck at 0 or 1. Typically, faults in SAFM are considered permanent. A stuck-at fault lasting for one time step only also models a transient fault. This transient fault model only considers *logic masking*, e.g., at an AND-gate with inputs i_1 and i_2 a transient fault at i_1 is masked if i_2 permanently has stores the value 0. Two other masking effects are not considered by this model: timing masking and electrical masking. *Timing masking* happens if the value change induced by a transient fault arrives at a storage value while the new value is not latched. *Electrical masking* is caused by the continuous decrease of a pulse that propagates through subsequent gates and disappear before being observed as an error or being latched in a storage element.

2.3 Fault Tolerance and Reliability

A circuit is *fault tolerant* when none of the faults in Φ leads to an error. By this, analyzing fault tolerance of a system yields a pass/fail result. Multiple faults are modeled by a multiplicity of the universe of faults, i.e., $\phi \in \Phi^n$ where $n \in \mathbb{N}$. Then, fault tolerance may be assessed with respect to multiple faults. If a circuit is not fault tolerant, there exists a *test sequence*, i.e., a sequence of assignments to the primary inputs that leads to an error under the presence of at least one fault.

More elaborate classifications are available, e.g., from the testing area where the notion of self-checking combinational circuits has been introduced [GOSM08].

Reliability and fault tolerance are related but different concepts. A system may be reliable, even though it may be sensitive to internal malfunctions and thus may not always be functional. Reliability is typically measured in *Mean Time To Failure* (MTTF), *Mean Time Between Failures* (MTBF), and *Mean Time To Repair* (MTTR) (e.g., [KK07]). As indicated by the names, these measures estimate how long a system is functional on average.

3 Assessing Vulnerability

Often an abstract model of a circuit or system is used to assess the vulnerability. During this abstraction various choices are made influencing the accuracy of the result and/or the complexity of the computation. Section 3.1 provides a generalized model to provide a common notation for theses choices and their consequences. Based upon that model Section 3.2 evaluates existing approaches and provides a qualitative discussion.

3.1 General Model

The following model is based on unrolling similar to Equation 1. Essentially, the model describes the behavior of the circuit under all input sequences up to a given length and under any fault in a given set of faults $\Psi \subseteq \Phi$.

The analysis is based on a model of the transition relation. The transition relation T describes the normal behavior of the circuit. When modeling a set $\Psi \subseteq \Phi$ of faults, the functionality of the circuit changes leading to a modified transition relation T_Ψ. This fault modeling to create T_Ψ is the first point where different choices are made in different analysis approaches.

Then, based on the formal description of the transitions the temporal behaviors of the circuit with and without faults are compared. The circuit is initialized at first to start from one of the initial states in I at time step 0. The circuit operates normally up to time step $t_{\text{hit}} - 1$ until a fault occurs at time step t_{hit}. At this point normal operation and faulty operation may diverge. The fault(s) may be permanent or transient. Therefore, after t_{ok} time steps the circuit may return to the normal operation described by transition relation T. Afterwards the circuit is observed for another t_{obs} time steps. Starting from time step t_{hit} the behavior is observed. This is denoted by a property P that may, e.g., compare the equality of the primary outputs of the two models with and without fault, respectively. Restrictions R on the primary inputs may or may not be applied depending on the application. These restrictions may be described by a formal property.

Putting these parts into a single formula yields the following model:

$$
\begin{aligned}
M_C(P, R, t_{\text{hit}}, t_{\text{ok}}, t_{\text{obs}}) = \ & I(z_0) \wedge \ N(0, t_{\text{hit}} + t_{\text{ok}} + t_{\text{obs}}) \\
& \wedge \ F(t_{\text{hit}}, t_{\text{hit}} + t_{\text{ok}}) \wedge z(t_{\text{hit}}) \equiv z'(t_{\text{hit}}) \\
& \wedge N'(t_{\text{hit}} + t_{\text{ok}}, t_{\text{hit}} + t_{\text{ok}} + t_{\text{obs}}) \\
& \wedge \neg P \wedge R
\end{aligned}
\tag{2}
$$

where

$I(z_0)$ describes the set of initial states

$N(j, k) = \bigwedge_{i=j}^{k} T(x_{i-1}, z_{i-1}, z_i, y_{i-1})$ describes normal operation between time steps j and k

$F(j, k) = \bigwedge_{i=j}^{k} T_{\Psi}(x'_{i-1}, z'_{i-1}, z'_i, y'_{i-1})$ describes faulty operation with respect to the set $\Psi \subseteq \Phi$ of faults

$N'(j, k) = \bigwedge_{i=j}^{k} T(x'_{i-1}, z'_{i-1}, z'_i, y'_{i-1})$ describes normal operation after the internal fault disappeared

R restrictions on primary inputs

P property comparing faulty and correct behavior

The parameters t_{hit}, t_{ok}, and t_{obs} configure the model. All values of t_{hit} and t_{obs} up to a certain bound and their combinations have to be considered for a complete classification with respect to all faults, states and input sequences. The parameter t_{ok} also relates to the types of faults that are modeled. The creation of T_{Ψ} may be done in different ways, e.g., to model the area affected by a fault, non-deterministic behavior, or stuck-at behavior of gates, components, or modules. The states considered while analyzing the system are determined by I. For example, by setting I to $\underline{1}$ (true) any restriction on the initial state is removed and any state is considered – even states not reachable during normal operation. To analyze only the combinational behavior, one configuration may be $t_{\text{hit}} = 1$, $t_{\text{ok}} = t_{\text{obs}} = 0$, $I = R = 1$, and $P = y_0 \equiv y'_0$.

Any assignment satisfying Equation 2 yields a test sequence, i.e., an input sequence that shows how the behavior under a fault $\phi \in \Psi$ violates property P, e.g., by diverging from normal operation. This is the pass/fail information on the fault tolerance of C with respect to Ψ.

Sometimes it is useful to know which fault causes a violation of P more easily, i.e., to grade the fault sites. The ratio between the number of test sequences over the number of all input sequences yields a probability for the circuit to violate property P under a fault in Ψ under the assumption that all input sequences are equally distributed. Of course, the restriction R has to be taken into account in this process.

If reliability is the focus of the analysis, more information is required. As the modeled faults correspond to physical events, a probability to occur can be assigned to each fault. Taking this probability also into account yields information on the reliability of the circuit.

3.2 Existing Approaches

Existing approaches for assessing vulnerability differ in how parts of the model are configured. Before relating existing approaches to the general model of the previous section, Table 1 gives an overview of the approaches discussed here and their respective characteristics.

The table compares different aspects. The key for the symbols is given below the table. The first column gives a reference for the respective approach. The second column *automaton/circuit* shows whether the approach works on finite automata in general or particularly considers circuits. The third column *area* denotes whether assessing reliability or fault tolerance is the main goal. The fourth column *input* shows which input data is needed besides the system or design. The fifth column *output* shows what output is produced. The sixth column *seq./comb.* informs whether sequential circuits or only combinational circuits are considered. The seventh column *fault model* lists how faults are modeled in the approach and the eighth column *single/multiple* shows whether single or multiple faults are addressed.

One important difference is in the way the approaches create the faulty model of the circuit leading to T_Ψ. The three approaches in [MZM06, MZM10, ZBD07] use a detailed model of transient faults induced by radiation. For this purpose voltage levels and shapes of glitches induced by radiation are modeled and the analysis takes logic masking, timing masking, and electrical masking into account. This requires a large model for T_Ψ. Consequently, the computation is only feasible for small circuits. The propagation of faults manifesting as memory errors through sequential behavior is considered in [MZM10] based on the transition relation.

All other approaches use simple transformations to determine T_Ψ. The fault model is quite coarse for the approaches [BBC$^+$09, BCG$^+$10, BCT07] considering arbitrary systems. The user defines modifications of the system for [BCT07] to check consistency with the non-modified system using a model checker. In [BCG$^+$10] the system properties are given in the form $a \rightarrow g$, where a is an assumption and g is the guarantee to be proven. Now, the approach counts how many guarantees fail, if an increasing number of assumptions are violated by the failing system. Thus, the user indirectly supplies the fault model through the formulation of the properties. The approach is capable of synthesizing "the most robust" system with respect to this fault model. Finally, [BBC$^+$09] assumes faults in state elements and uses theorem proving or model checking techniques to analyze the resulting faulty systems. The outcome of these approaches is a pass/fail information with respect to the user defined properties [BCG$^+$10, BCT07] and grading information given by the number of failing properties [BCG$^+$10] or the influence on the state space [BBC$^+$09].

The fault model of the approaches considering circuits modifies bits in memory and combinational components [FD08, FFD10, FSFD11, HH08, HHC$^+$09, KPJ$^+$06] or memory elements only [HPB07, SLM07].

The analysis may be done for transient faults where $t_{ok} = 1$, or longer lasting faults where $t_{ok} \geq 1$, or even for permanent faults lasting indefinitely where $t_{ok} = \infty$. These approaches mainly differ in the way sequential behavior is handled. Model checking approaches are complete, i.e., all combinations of t_{hit}, t_{ok}, and t_{obs} are considered. These approaches utilize formal tools as a black box and apply transformations to the

Table 1. Overview of the different approaches and their characteristics

reference	automaton/circuit	area	input	output	comb./seq.	fault model	single/multiple	base engine	I	t_{hit}	t_{ok}	t_{obs}
	A/I	F/R	e/l/p	F/G/P	C/S	R/E/L/ T/m/d	s/m	A/B/C/ F/M/S/T				
[BBC$^+$09]	A	F	p	G	S	Rm	s/m	TM	I	free	free	∞
[BCG$^+$10]	A	F	p	G	S	Rm	m	M	I	free	free	∞
[BCT07]	A	F	p	F	S	Rd	m	FM	I	free	free	∞
[CM09]	I	R	e	P	C	Rm	s/m	C	$\underline{1}$	0	1	0
[FD08]	I	F	(p)	G	S	Lm	m	B	$\underline{1}$	0	n	n
[FFD10]	I	F	-	G	S	Lm	(m)	B	$\hat{S}$	free	1	n
[FSFD11]	I	F	-	F	S	Lm	(m)	B	$\hat{S}$	free	1	n
[HH08]	I	F	-	F	C	Lm	s	A	$\underline{1}$	0	1	0
[HHC$^+$09]	I	F	-	G	C	Lm	m	A	$\underline{1}$	0	1	0
[HPB07]	I	F	-	P	S	Lm	s	M	I	free	1	∞
[KPJ$^+$06]	I	F	-	G	S	Ld	(m)	F	I	free	1	∞
[KPMH09]	I	R	p	G	S	Lm	s	S	I	n	n	n
[Lev05]	I	F	p	G	S	Rd	s	F	I	free	n	∞
[MZM06]	I	R	cl	P	C	LETm	s	C	$\underline{1}$	0	1	0
[MZM10]	I	R	el	P	S	LETm	m	C	$\underline{1}$	0	1	0
[SLM07]	I	F	p	F	S	Lm	s	F	I	free	1	∞
[ZBD07]	I	R	el	P	C	LETm	s	C	$\underline{1}$	0	1	0

circuit/system: A →automaton, I →circuit
area: F →fault tolerance, R →reliability
input: e →error probabilities, l →library, p →properties
output: F →pass fail, G →grading, P →probability
circuit model: C →combinational, S →sequential
fault model: R→based on the transition relation,
                    E/L/T→electrical/logic/timing masking,
                    d →user defined, m →embedded
single/multiple: s →single faults, m →multiple faults
base engine: A →ATPG, B →bounded model checking, C →custom model,
                    F →formal tool as a black box, M →model checking,
                    S →simulation, T →theorem proving
I I →initial states of the circuit, $\underline{1}$→any state,
                    $\hat{S}$ →approximation of reachable states
$t_{\text{hit}}, t_{\text{ok}}, t_{\text{obs}}$: free →no restriction, all values, n →an arbitrary fixed value,
                    ∞ →unbounded complete analysis

description of the circuit or system that is passed to the tool [BCT07, KPJ$^+$06, Lev05, SLM07]. Typically, a fixed-point iteration using symbolic representations of the state space is performed. This limits the application to small circuits. The approaches based on *Bounded Model Checking* [FD08, FSFD11] limit the observation t_{obs} to a short window. Moreover, the path to t_{hit} is not explicitly modeled, but uses abstractions of the state space. This further reduces the size of the model. As a consequence, larger circuits can be handled and bounds on the vulnerability are returned instead of a single value. The approach in [FFD10] additionally yields a grading of vulnerable sites.

The ATPG-based approaches [HH08, HHC$^+$09] consider combinational circuits only, i.e., $t_{ok} = t_{obs} = 0$. Initialization of these circuits is not considered, i.e., $t_{hit} = 1$ and $I(z_0) = 1$. As an advantage the model is relatively small.

Simulation is the underlying engine of [KPMH09]. The analysis is incomplete considering only certain values for the parameters. During this analysis process a time frame expansion model is used.

Once the respective parameters for any of these approaches have been determined the subsequent analysis is fully automatic. Nonetheless the user has to interpret the results carefully.

3.3 Potential Pitfalls

Applying these approaches to assess the vulnerability has certain pitfalls a user must be aware of. One issue is complexity of the chosen approach. A full formal analysis is typically limited to small systems or restrictions on state space, observation time etc. are applied. Consequently, incomplete results may be provided hiding problems in the design.

If the analysis finishes without restrictions, only the given universe of faults is taken into account. Typically, there are other sources of faults not modeled and therefore not analyzed. A well-known problem are common-mode failures or common-cause-failures. The system may be immune to any single fault in a component but a certain event may cause a failure in several parts at the same time.

Similarly, the multiplicity of faults is typically restricted to a small number – often to one. If faults occur with higher multiplicity in practice, the analysis is not adequate.

Even though adequate on a certain abstraction level the result of the analysis may not apply to the final implementation. A simple example is a redundant system described, e.g., in a hardware description language undergoing synthesis. A powerful synthesis tool may remove all redundancy if running unconstrained. Similarly, the assessment at a higher abstraction level may not take lower level optimizations into account. For example, a resource may be shared during synthesis while not being shared in the higher level description. Thus, a single fault in the synthesized system corresponds to more than one fault in the higher level description. Such transformations render the analysis done at one abstraction invalid for the implementation at another abstraction level.

These and similar problems are usually handled by obeying a well-defined methodology when assessing a system's vulnerability. Within such a methodology the automated approaches discussed above provide significant support in the assessment.

4   Conclusions

Several powerful formal approaches to assess a circuit's or a system's vulnerability are available. The approaches have individual strength's and differ in the types of faults they consider as well as in the information returned to the user. When applying any of the approaches in practice, a well-defined methodology is required to ensure reliable fault tolerant implementations of the real system.

References

[ABF90]   Abramovici, M., Breuer, M.A., Friedman, A.D.: Digital Systems Testing and Testable Design. Computer Science Press (1990)

[BBC+09]   Baarir, S., Braunstein, C., Clavel, R., Encrenaz, E., Ilie, J.-M., Leveugle, R., Mounier, I., Pierre, L., Poitrenaud, D.: Complementary formal approaches for dependability analysis. In: IEEE International Symposium on Defect and Fault Tolerance in VLSI Systems, pp. 331–339 (2009)

[BCCZ99]   Biere, A., Cimatti, A., Clarke, E., Zhu, Y.: Symbolic Model Checking Without Bdds. In: Cleaveland, W.R. (ed.) TACAS 1999. LNCS, vol. 1579, pp. 193–207. Springer, Heidelberg (1999)

[BCG+10]   Bloem, R., Chatterjee, K., Greimel, K., Henzinger, T.A., Jobstmann, B.: Robustness in the Presence of Liveness. In: Touili, T., Cook, B., Jackson, P. (eds.) CAV 2010. LNCS, vol. 6174, pp. 410–424. Springer, Heidelberg (2010)

[BCT07]   Bozzano, M., Cimatti, A., Tapparo, F.: Symbolic Fault Tree Analysis For Reactive Systems. In: Namjoshi, K.S., Yoneda, T., Higashino, T., Okamura, Y. (eds.) ATVA 2007. LNCS, vol. 4762, pp. 162–176. Springer, Heidelberg (2007)

[CM09]   Choudhury, M.R., Mohanram, K.: Reliability analysis of logic circuits. IEEE Trans. on CAD 28(3), 392–405 (2009)

[CMR+02]   Civera, P., Macchiarulo, L., Rebaudengo, M., Sonza Reorda, M., Violante, M.: An FPGA-based approach for speeding-up fault injection campaigns on safety-critical circuits. Jour. of Electronic Testing: Theory and Applications 18(3), 261–271 (2002)

[FD08]   Fey, G., Drechsler, R.: A basis for formal robustness checking. In: Int'l Symp. on Quality Electronic Design, pp. 784–789 (2008)

[FFD10]   Frehse, S., Fey, G., Drechsler, R.: A better-than-worst-case robustness measure. In: IEEE Symposium on Design and Diagnostics of Electronic Circuits and Systems, pp. 78–83 (2010)

[FSFD11]   Fey, G., Sülflow, A., Frehse, S., Drechsler, R.: Effective robustness analysis using bounded model checking techniques. IEEE Trans. on CAD 30(8), 1239–1252 (2011)

[GOSM08]   Gössel, M., Ocheretny, V., Sogomonyan, E., Marienfeld, D.: New Methods of Concurrent Checking. Frontiers in Electronic Testing, vol. 42. Springer, Heidelberg (2008)

[Ham50]   Hamming, R.W.: Error detecting and error correcting codes. Bell System Technical Jour. 26(2), 147–160 (1950)

[HH08]   Hunger, M., Hellebrand, S.: Verification and analysis of self-checking properties through ATPG. In: IEEE International On-Line Testing Symposium, pp. 25–30 (2008)

[HHC+09]   Hunger, M., Hellebrand, S., Czutro, A., Polian, I., Becker, B.: ATPG-Based grading of strong fault-secureness. In: IEEE International On-Line Testing Symposium (2009)

[HPB07]   Hayes, J.P., Polian, I., Becker, B.: An analysis framework for transient-error toler-ance. In: VLSI Test Symp., pp. 249–255 (2007)

[KK07]   Koren, I., Krishna, C.M.: Fault-Tolerant Systems. Morgan Kaufmann (2007)

[KPJ⁺06]   Krautz, U., Pflanz, M., Jacobi, C., Tast, H.W., Weber, K., Vierhaus, H.T.: Evalu-ating coverage of error detection logic for soft errors using formal methods. In: Design, Automation and Test in Europe, pp. 176–181 (2006)

[KPMH09]   Krishnaswamy, S., Plaza, S., Markov, I.L., Hayes, J.P.: Signature-based SER anal-ysis and design of logic circuits. IEEE Trans. on CAD 28(1), 74–86 (2009)

[Kub68]   Kubo, H.: A procedure for generating test sequences to detect sequential circuit failures. NEC Res. and Dev. 12(3), 69–78 (1968)

[Lev05]   Leveugle, R.: A new approach for early dependability evaluation based on formal property checking and controlled mutations. In: IEEE International On-Line Test-ing Symposium, pp. 260–265 (2005)

[MZM06]   Miskov-Zivanov, M., Marculescu, D.: Circuit reliability analysis using symbolic techniques. IEEE Trans. on CAD 25(12), 2638–2649 (2006)

[MZM10]   Miskov-Zivanov, N., Marculescu, D.: Multiple transient faults in combinational and sequential circuits: A systematic approach. IEEE Trans. on CAD 29(10), 1614–1627 (2010)

[PCZ⁺08]   Pellegrini, A., Constantinides, K., Zhang, D., Sudhakar, S., Bertacco, V., Austin, T.: CrashTest: A fast high-fidelity FPGA-based resiliency analysis framework. In: Int'l Conf. on Comp. Design (2008)

[PR71]   Putzolu, G.R., Roth, J.P.: A heuristic algorithm for the testing of asynchronous circuits. IEEE Trans. on Comp., pp. 639–647 (1971)

[SLM07]   Seshia, S.A., Li, W., Mitra, S.: Verification-guided soft error resilience. In: Design, Automation and Test in Europe, pp. 1442–1447 (2007)

[TH10]   Thompto, B.W., Hoppe, B.: Verification for fault tolerance of the ibm system z microprocessor. In: Design Automation Conf., pp. 525–530 (2010)

[ZBD07]   Zhao, C., Bai, X., Dey, S.: Evaluating transient error effects in digital nanometer circuits. IEEE Transactions on Reliability 56(3), 381–391 (2007)

Information Security in a Quantum World

Renato Renner

Institute for Theoretical Physics, ETH Zurich, Switzerland

Abstract. It is well known that classical computationally-secure cryptosystems may be susceptible to quantum attacks, i.e., attacks by adversaries able to process quantum information. A prominent example is the RSA public key cryptosystem, whose security is based on the hardness of factoring; it can be broken using a quantum computer running Shor's efficient factoring algorithm. In this extended abstract, we review an argument which shows that a similar problem can arise even if a cryptosystem provides information-theoretic security. As long as its security analysis is carried out within classical information theory, attacks by quantum adversaries cannot in general be excluded.

1 Introduction

It is generally impossible to efficiently represent the state of a quantum system using classical information carriers. In fact, the number of *classical bits* required to approximate n *quantum bits (qubits)* grows exponentially in n. It is therefore reasonable to assume (and widely conjectured) that quantum computers cannot in general be efficiently simulated by classical computers. In complexity-theoretic terms, this means that quantum computing is not accurately characterized by the classical model of computation.[1] Therefore, even if a given computational problem was known to be *hard* according to the classical theory, this would not exclude the existence of a quantum algorithm that solves it efficiently. As a consequence, cryptosystems that are based on classical hardness assumptions are not necessarily secure against adversaries equipped with quantum computers. The most prominent example is the RSA public key cryptosystem [RSA78], whose security relies on the hardness of factoring—a problem that a quantum computer can solve efficiently [Sho94].

One may now be tempted to think that this problem is restricted to computational cryptography, where security is based on computational problems whose hardness is anyway only conjectured. This is however not the case. As we shall see, there exist cryptographic systems that are provably secure within the framework of classical information theory, whereas their security can be compromised by adversaries able to process quantum information. Remarkably, these cryptosystems may be purely classical, i.e., the legitimate parties only need to process and exchange classical data.

---

[1] This is equivalent to say that the *Strong Church-Turing Thesis* does not hold in a world where quantum information can be processed (see, e.g., [KLM07]).

Z. Kotásek et al. (Eds.): MEMICS 2011, LNCS 7119, pp. 57–62, 2012.

We start the discussion in Section 2 with the observation that information stored in a quantum memory cannot in general be accurately characterized within classical probability and information theory. In Section 3, we consider, as an example, a (classical) key expansion protocol which is secure in the bounded storage model, i.e., under the assumption that an adversary has only limited storage space. We then argue that this scheme, although provably secure within classical information theory, is vulnerable to quantum attacks.

2   Limitations of Classical Information Theory

Consider a coin that randomly takes one of two values, labelled by 0 and 1, respectively. The coin may be biased, i.e, there may be a value $b \in [-\frac{1}{2}, \frac{1}{2}]$ by which the probability of outcome 1 deviates from $\frac{1}{2}$. We may model the coin as well as the bias by random variables, C and B, respectively. Then, by assumption, we have

$$P_{C|B=b}(1) = \frac{1}{2} + b \,,$$

where $P_{C|B=b}(c)$ denotes the probability that C equals 1 conditioned on the event $B = b$ that the bias takes a specific value b.

Assume now that we know the value of the bias, B, but are ignorant about the outcome of the coin toss, C. The knowledge we have about C is then completely determined by the conditional probability distribution $P_{C|B=b}$. In particular, given $P_{C|B=b}$, we can compute operational quantities such as the probability by which the outcome C can be correctly predicted, or the average number of uniform bits that can be extracted from independent copies of C.

Let us now move to a slightly modified scenario, where the bias B is not available as a classical value, but instead encoded into the state of a qubit, Q. More precisely, we asume that the state of Q is given by a vector of the form

$$|\phi_b\rangle = \cos\frac{\pi b}{2}|e_0\rangle + \sin\frac{\pi b}{2}|e_1\rangle \,, \tag{1}$$

where $\{|e_0\rangle, |e_1\rangle\}$ is an orthonormal basis of the state space. Similarly to the previous example, assume that we do not know the outcome of the coin toss C, but now have access to Q (instead of B). We may then ask whether there is a compact mathematical description of the knowledge we have about C, analogously to the conditional distribution $P_{C|B=b}$ of the previous example. Crucially, however, because of the quantum nature of Q (which now takes the role of B), there is no longer a classical event on which we could condition the probability distribution of the (still classical) value C on.

To be a bit more specific, let us assume that B is uniformly distributed over the interval $[-\frac{1}{2}, \frac{1}{2}]$. Then, using the fact that the classical values of C can without loss of generality be represented by two orthogonal quantum states, denoted $|0\rangle_C$ and $|1\rangle_C$, respectively, the joint state of C and Q is given by[2]

$$\rho_{CQ} = \int_{-\frac{1}{2}}^{\frac{1}{2}} \left[P_{C|B=b}(0)|0\rangle\langle0|_C \otimes |\phi_b\rangle\langle\phi_b| + P_{C|B=b}(1)|1\rangle\langle1|_C \otimes |\phi_b\rangle\langle\phi_b| \right] db \ .$$

A simple calculation shows that this state can be rewritten as

$$\rho_{CQ} = \frac{1}{2}|0\rangle\langle0|_C \otimes \rho_Q^0 + \frac{1}{2}|1\rangle\langle1|_C \otimes \rho_Q^1$$

where the density operators ρ_Q^0 and ρ_Q^1 are given by

$$\rho_Q^0 = \begin{pmatrix} \frac{1}{2} + \frac{1}{\pi} & -\frac{2}{\pi^2} \\ -\frac{2}{\pi^2} & \frac{1}{2} - \frac{1}{\pi} \end{pmatrix} \quad \text{and} \quad \rho_Q^1 = \begin{pmatrix} \frac{1}{2} + \frac{1}{\pi} & \frac{2}{\pi^2} \\ \frac{2}{\pi^2} & \frac{1}{2} - \frac{1}{\pi} \end{pmatrix},$$

respectively. Note that ρ_Q^0 and ρ_Q^1 are not simultaneously diagonalizable. The state of the qubit Q can therefore not be identified with a classical value.

One may now ask whether it is possible to nevertheless define a classical value B' which is equally useful as having access to Q. One possibility could be to set B' equal to the actual bias, B. However, the B' would then be strictly more informative (about C) than Q. To see this, consider for example the case where B and, hence, B' are (almost) equal to $\frac{1}{2}$. Knowing B' then immediately allows us to infer the value of C (which will be 1 with almost certainty). In contrast, since both density operators ρ_Q^0 and ρ_Q^1 have full rank, there is no event (e.g., defined via a measurement of Q) conditioned on which the value of C is fully known.[3] The classical value B' would therefore be strictly more informative than Q.

More generally, it can be shown that it is impossible to define a classical random variable B' which is equivalent to Q, in the sense that any information about C that is extractable from Q can also be obtained from B', and vice versa. Roughly, the argument is that, if B' can be obtained from Q, there must exist a measurement of Q whose result is B'. However, from the measurement outcome B' it is generally impossible to reconstruct the state that Q had before the measurement.[4] Hence, the information Q can no longer be obtained from

---

[2] Note that ρ_{CQ} describes the joint state of a classical and a quantum system, assuming that the values of the classical system are represented by the elements of an orthonormal basis. Such states are sometimes termed *classical-quantum states* or *cq states*.

[3] If the states ρ_Q^0 and ρ_Q^1 have full rank then, for any outcome of a measurement on Q that has strictly positive probability conditioned on $C = 0$, the same outcome also has positive probability when conditioned on $C = 1$, and vice versa. This implies that the measurement outcome does not uniquely determine the value of C.

[4] This is because the *accessible information* between B and Q (which is defined by a maximization of the mutual information over all measurements on Q) can be strictly smaller than the mutual information between B and Q; see [KRBM07] for an example.

B', which means that B' is strictly less informative than Q. We conclude from this that, in a situation where we have access to quantum information Q, our knowledge about C cannot be equivalently described by a classical value B'. In particular, it is not possible to define a conditional probability distribution of C which fully characterizes all information we have about C.

The remarkable feature of this example is that C is classical. This illustrates that, even when we are talking about a classical object such as the outcome of a coin toss, the knowledge we may have about it cannot necessarily be accurately characterized within the classical framework of probability theory. In the next section, we will show that this leads to problems in cryptography, where—even if the data that the legitimate parties are processing and communicating is purely classical—it may be advantageous for an adversary to process her information quantum-mechanically.

3   An Example: The Bounded Storage Model

The bounded storage model, introduced by Maurer [Mau92] (see also [Lu04, Vad04, DM04]) can be seen as an alternative to the standard computational model used in cryptography. Instead of imposing any limitations on the adversary's computing power, one assumes that her storage capacity is limited. This facilitates security proofs that are information theoretic. One of the most prominent examples is a *key expansion protocol* proposed in [Mau92]. It allows two legitimate parties, connected only over an insecure communication channel, to expand an initially short key to an arbitrary long one. The protocol requires in addition that the legitimate parties have access to a large source of randomness (such as cosmic background radiation). The source is assumed to be public (and hence also accessible to an adversary), but the amount of randomness emitted by the source exceeds the adversary's storage capacity.

The idea of the protocol is, roughly, that the legitimate parties use their initial key to decide on positions from which they read the randomness of the large public source in order to form a *raw key*. Since the adversary cannot know these positions, and is furthermore unable to store all randomness of the source, he has large uncertainty about the raw key. Hence, using *privacy amplification* techniques [BBCM95], the legitimate parties can turn their raw keys into highly secure (final) keys.

In the early security proofs for this protocol, the adversary's memory is (implicitly) assumed to be purely classical [Lu04, Vad04, DM04]. Following the discussion in Section 2, we know however that this assumption strictly does not include situations where the adversary can store (parts of her) information in a quantum memory. Consequently, even if the adversary has only *one single* quantum bit available to store data (which, given the recent progress in experimental quantum information science is certainly realistic) the classical security proofs are no longer directly applicable.

So far, we have argued that security proofs referring to a purely classical model of information do not *imply* security of protocols in a quantum world, where adversaries can make use of quantum information processing. This however, does not necessarily imply that cryptographic protocols *are* insecure in the presence of quantum adversaries. One may therefore wonder whether classical security proofs can generally be extended to proofs that include quantum adversaries.

This is however generally not the case. An explicit example can be obtained using a result of Gavinsky, Kempe, Kerenidis, Raz, and de Wolf [GKK+07] on the one-way communication complexity of certain functions. Based on this, it is possible to construct *randomness extractors*, i.e., functions that turn weak randomness into uniform randomness, which have the following property. Whenever the extractor is applied to a uniform classical value C which is correlated to another classical value B consisting of t bits (for some appropriately chosen $t \in \mathbb{N}$), then the extractor output is virtually uniform and uncorrelated to B. However, when the same extractor is applied to a classical value C correlated to a register Q consisting of t quantum bits, then the output may still be strongly correlated to Q. If such an extractor is used for privacy amplification in the key expansion protocol sketched above (so that C takes the role of the weakly secure raw key), the scheme will be secure against classical adversaries (holding information B), while a quantum adversary (holding Q) can break it.

4   Conclusions

The proof that a cryptographic system is secure against any classical adversary does not in general imply that it is also secure in the presence of quantum adversaries. While this is not very surprising for cryptosystems that use quantum communication (such as Quantum Key Distribution schemes), the example shown in Section 3 illustrates that even purely classical cryptosystems may become insecure in the presence of quantum adversaries.

Nevertheless, in various cases the full (quantum) security of a cryptographic scheme may follow generically from its security against classical adversaries (see [Unr10]). Furthermore, in the particular case of key expansion protocols in the bounded storage model, security can be obtained via the use of *quantum-proof* extractors, as shown in [KR11] (see also [DPVR09]). However, it is an open question whether general cryptographic concepts such as privacy amplification schemes based on extractors—for which there is a classical security proof—can in a generic way be shown secure against quantum adversaries.

Acknowledgements. This work was supported by the Swiss National Science Foundation (grant 200020-135048 and through the National Centre of Competence in Research *Quantum Science and Technology*) and the European Research Council (grant 258932).

References

[BBCM95]   Bennett, C.H., Brassard, G., Crépeau, C., Maurer, U.: Generalized privacy amplification. IEEE Transaction on Information Theory 41(6), 1915–1923 (1995)

[DM04]   Dziembowski, S., Maurer, U.: Optimal randomizer efficiency in the bounded-storage model. Journal of Cryptology 17(1), 5–26 (2004)

[DPVR09]   De, A., Portmann, C., Vidick, T., Renner, R.: Trevisan's extractor in the presence of quantum side information. arXiv:0912.5514 (2009)

[GKK+07]   Gavinsky, D., Kempe, J., Kerenidis, I., Raz, R., de Wolf, R.: Exponential separations for one-way quantum communication complexity, with applications to cryptography. In: Proceeding of the 39th Symposium on Theory of Computing, STOC (2007)

[KLM07]   Kaye, P., Laflamme, R., Mosca, M.: An introduction to quantum computing. Oxford University Press (2007)

[KR11]   König, R., Renner, R.: Sampling of min-entropy relative to quantum knowledge. IEEE Transactions on Information Theory 57, 4760–4787 (2011)

[KRBM07]   König, R., Renner, R., Bariska, A., Maurer, U.: Small accessible quantum information does not imply security. Phys. Rev. Lett. 98, 140502 (2007)

[Lu04]   Lu, C.-J.: Encryption against storage-bounded adversaries from on-line strong extractors. Journal of Cryptology 17(1), 27–42 (2004)

[Mau92]   Maurer, U.: Conditionally-perfect secrecy and a provably-secure randomized cipher. Journal of Cryptology 5(1), 53–66 (1992)

[RSA78]   Rivest, R.L., Shamir, A., Adleman, L.: A method for obtaining digital signatures and public-key cryptosystems. Communications of the ACM 21(2), 120–126 (1978)

[Sho94]   Shor, P.W.: Algorithms for quantum computation: Discrete logarithms and factoring. In: Proceedings of the 35nd Annual Symposium on Foundations of Computer Science, pp. 124–134. IEEE Computer Society Press (1994)

[Unr10]   Unruh, D.: Universally Composable Quantum Multi-Party Computation. In: Gilbert, H. (ed.) EUROCRYPT 2010. LNCS, vol. 6110, pp. 486–505. Springer, Heidelberg (2010)

[Vad04]   Vadhan, S.P.: Constructing locally computable extractors and cryptosystems in the bounded-storage model. Journal of Cryptology 17(1), 43–77 (2004)

Computer Memory: Why We Should Care What Is under the Hood

Vlastimil Babka and Petr Tůma

Department of Distributed and Dependable Systems,
Faculty of Mathematics and Physics, Charles University,
Malostranské náměstí 25, 118 00 Prague, Czech Republic
{vlastimil.babka,petr.tuma}@d3s.mff.cuni.cz

Abstract. The memory subsystems of contemporary computer architectures are increasingly complex – in fact, so much so that it becomes difficult to estimate the performance impact of many coding constructs, and some long known coding patterns are even discovered to be principally wrong. In contrast, many researchers still reason about algorithmic complexity in simple terms, where memory operations are sequential and of equal cost. The goal of this talk is to give an overview of some memory subsystem features that violate this assumption significantly, with the ambition to motivate development of algorithms tailored to contemporary computer architectures.

1 Introduction

When we code, we do not try to envision how our code drives the computer in all its complexity. Instead, we hold in our heads a simplified image, free of technical details that are not relevant to the problem at hand. Of course, to do so, we must first know which details can be abstracted away and which details happen to be influential.

It turns out that in the case of memory subsystems of contemporary computer architectures, this distinction is not an easy one to make. Over the past decade, we have witnessed numerous cases where initial judgment lead to ignoring technical details that have turned out to be vital for program correctness or performance. In all fairness, we have to observe that it was not always the initial judgment that was at fault – the technical progress has simply lead to changing conditions and thus changing results.

To help avoid such situations, our goal is to present a compact overview of selected technical details related to the memory subsystems – details that might have not been considered essential knowledge a decade ago, but have grown important since. The choice of the technical details is based mostly on our performance evaluation work [7,8,4,5], where we have analyzed the reasons behind numerous surprising performance anomalies on recent computer architectures of

Z. Kotásek et al. (Eds.): MEMICS 2011, LNCS 7119, pp. 63–75, 2012.

the x86 family. Other articles treat particular issues in more depth and for more platforms, we provide references as appropriate.[1]

2   Motivating Examples

Delving into the details of the memory subsystems can feel like a hunt for the obscure. A computer researcher looking for principal insights will likely wonder whether the details are not just a case of platform specific and short lived knowledge. To convince the reader otherwise, we present two motivating examples, one related to correctness and one to performance.

In the correctness domain, we choose the famous example of the Double Checked Locking pattern. Published in 1996 [24], the pattern deals with the issue of delayed initialization of a shared read only variable. Upon access, the reader checks whether the variable has been initialized, and when that is not the case, the initialization is done:

```
private static SomeRefType var = NULL;
public static getVar () {
  if (var == NULL) var = new SomeType ();
  return (var);
}
```

As listed, the code can fail with multiple concurrent readers. Simply adding a lock to protect the shared variable access can hurt performance, the pattern therefore proposes to first check the variable and only lock and check again when the initialization needs to be done.

The pattern has quickly found its way into the design pattern literature, and it took several years for the community to realize that it would actually fail with many increasingly common memory subsystems [13,19]. In essence, due to the way the memory subsystems work, concurrent readers can see the reference stored in the shared variable before they can see the data the reference points to.

For a performance related example, we choose a recent observation concerning scientific applications in the high performance computing domain, namely the well established code from the Omni Compiler Project [21] that implements the NAS Parallel Benchmark suite [9]. Researchers from the Future Technologies Group of the Oak Ridge National Laboratory have observed that a particular problem happens to increase the execution time of some code by over a half. They add that this is a problem most scientific applications have been considered immune to, going as far as calling the issue insidious [18].

The cited observation is interesting in that fixes to the discovered performance problems often consist of modifying a few lines of code. An example of

---

[1] The exact properties of memory subsystems are highly platform dependent. We have decided to focus on the recent computer architectures of the x86 family, hoping that the reader will find the content general enough to be applicable to their platform, yet specific enough to be useful. It is possible that some generalizations trade precision for brevity.

a more sophisticated refactoring of a three-dimensional stencil kernel shows another significant performance increase, ranging from 40% to 70% depending on the platform. This particular refactoring is based entirely on reflecting memory subsystem features.

In both motivating examples, we see a situation where a relatively detailed knowledge of memory subsystems was required to make seemingly simple code perform efficiently and correctly. The reader can see how similar issues can arise in other work and how knowledge outlined in the following sections can be useful in managing them.

3 Hardware Features

Recent memory subsystems of the x86 family provide shared memory access to multiple cores of multiple processors.[2] Several levels of caches are used to mask memory access latency, coherency protocol is employed to maintain consistent view of memory content across cores and processors. Other latency masking features include speculative reads and buffered writes, which contribute to a specific memory ordering model that differs from the intuitive sequential consistency. Our compact presentation assumes some prior knowledge and focuses on selected properties, we refer the reader to vendor documentation such as [15,16,14,1,2] or comprehensive articles such as [11] for details.

3.1 Caches: Not Just Size

Data in cache is accessed faster than data in main memory. The difference in access latency is expressed as cache miss penalty and depends largely on the cache level where the cache miss occurs. Both vendor documentation and experimental measurements give ranges of values valid for particular platforms and workloads, a general rule is to expect access times in units of processor cycles for first level cache, tens of cycles for second level cache, and hundreds of cycles for memory [7,4]. For an example of how a cache miss penalty can depend on the amount of data accessed and therefore the cache level involved, see Figure 1 (measured on an Intel Xeon processor in [7]).

Cache miss penalty can be accompanied by other penalties related to the same memory access. With write back cache, handling a cache miss may entail not just reading new data from memory, but also writing old data to memory to free space. Also significant are the address translation cache penalty, which can amount to tens of cycles assuming the paging tables are cached, and the coherency protocol overhead, which can amount to hundreds of cycles [7,4]. Finally, some components of a cache miss penalty can be systematic and deterministic, yet difficult to explain from coder perspective. For an example of how a cache miss penalty can differ between odd and even cache lines, see Figure 2 (measured on an Intel Xeon processor in [7]).

---

[2] To improve text flow, we will drop the family designation, but we still refer to the recent computer architectures of the x86 family, even with general statements.

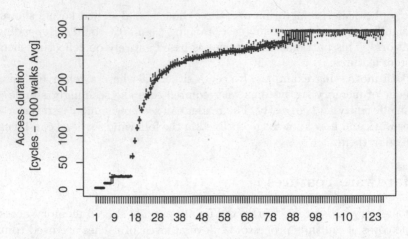

Fig. 1. Dependency of cache miss penalty on amount of data accessed

Cache miss penalties can be partially masked by executing other operations in parallel with the memory access [6]. The availability of other operations to execute depends on both the structure of the code and the architecture of the processor. In [12], the authors show how, for a particular benchmark, up to one quarter of the level one data cache miss penalty can be masked by having a large enough processor instruction window. Even though both processors and compilers perform optimizations to facilitate parallel execution, it makes sense to consider the ratio of memory accesses to other operations in performance sensitive code.

An obvious concern with caches is the size of the cached data. Intuitively, we understand that frequently accessed data should fit in the cache. This need gives rise to techniques such as tiling [28], which splits data into blocks that fit a known cache size, or cache oblivious algorithms [22], which split data in an asymptotically optimal manner even without knowing the cache size.

To tune an algorithm to a particular cache size, the cache size has to be known. Some operating systems can provide detailed information about cache size. Even when such information is not available, techniques to determine cache size by an automated measurement exist [29]. It is important to note that with the common policy of evicting least recently used data, misjudging the effective cache size by mere one line can lead to evicting data just before they are needed – a decidedly wrong thing to do.

There are reasons why the effective cache size that an algorithm uses will be smaller than the determined cache size. Since the unit of cache access is a cache line, any data that is not aligned and sized to fit the cache line exactly will waste some cache space. Also, when fetching a cache line, an adjacent cache line can be fetched by the hardware prefetcher regardless of the access pattern, again potentially limiting cache space utilization.

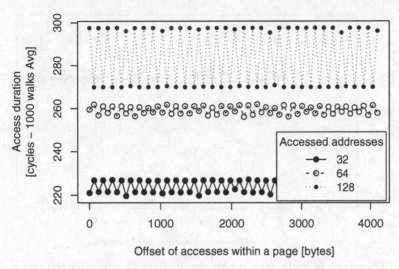

Fig. 2. Dependency of cache miss penalty on offset within a page

Related to cache size is cache organization, specifically the relationship between cache levels and the relationship between multiple caches. Typically, first level caches are separate for code and data, and private to each core. Higher level caches are unified, the last level cache is often shared among cores. The exact impact on effective cache size also depends on whether the caches are inclusive or exclusive.

With inclusive caches, data that resides in lower level caches is also replicated in higher level caches. With exclusive caches, data is not replicated. A cache may also be neither strictly inclusive nor strictly exclusive. Although vendor information in this respect is often scarce, experiments can test inclusivity or exclusivity [4].

Exclusive caches appear more efficient from capacity perspective. Inclusive caches may require less traffic between levels when handling misses or when maintaining coherency. Significant performance effects may depend on the particulars, as illustrated by an example on Figure 3. Figure 3 shows a cache miss penalty spike when accessing data that has just been evicted in an exclusive cache (measured on an AMD Opteron processor in [4]).

A very significant feature of caches is limited associativity. Rather than being a single large cache that serves the entire physical address space, a cache of limited associativity can be viewed as a set of smaller caches, each serving a disjunct subset of the physical address space. When data accesses are not spread evenly across cache sets, this can again limit cache space utilization.

From coder perspective, it is important to realize how cache sets are selected. Starting with the least significant bits, a physical address consists of an offset within a cache line, then a cache set, then a cache key. For example, in a cache with 64 byte lines and 4096 sets, such as an Intel Xeon processor might have [4], bits 6 to 19 of a physical address will determine the cache set used.

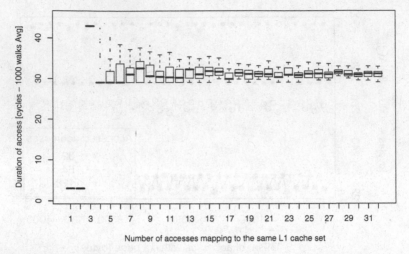

Fig. 3. Dependency of cache miss penalty on amount of data accessed, with visible spike for accessing just evicted data

Typically, code can control virtual address allocation but not physical address allocation. Since a virtual address matches a physical address only in the bits that determine an offset within a page, code has only limited control over cache set choice. Returning to the example, in a system with 4096 byte pages, only bits 0 to 11 of a virtual address necessarily match the corresponding bits of a physical address. In the example, code can therefore easily influence only half of the physical address bits that determine the cache set.

The operating system, which allocates the physical addresses and therefore participates in the choice of the cache sets, does not have sufficient information to assign addresses in an optimal manner. On some platforms, heuristic algorithms are employed to occupy the cache sets evenly, on other platforms, the choice is basically random. As a result, the same code with the same data can execute sometimes with good but sometimes with bad cache space utilization. This has been known to disrupt measurement results significantly [20]. Techniques that can alleviate the issue include using large pages or using special allocation routines [7], there are also statistical methods for correct processing of results [17], Also, some data strides may be discouraged to avoid conflicts in cache [14,2].

3.2   Bandwidth: Far From Peak

Given the differences in clock speeds between processor chips and memory chips, the achievable memory bandwidth is of obvious concern. For various reasons nicely explained in [11], utilizing the memory bandwidth up to the theoretical maximum is not possible, however, some techniques can help get close. In general, the more linear and aligned the memory accesses, the higher the bandwidth.

Besides the memory chips, other parts of the memory subsystem can have properties that translate into apparent bandwidth limitations. Typical are constraints on the maximum number of memory accesses that can be issued per processor clock cycle [14, Section 3.6.1] and constraints on the maximum number of outstanding cache accesses [2, Section 6.5]. Figure 4 shows how a workload that generates outstanding cache misses slows down a concurrent workload that generates outstanding cache hits (measured on an Intel Xeon processor in [4]).

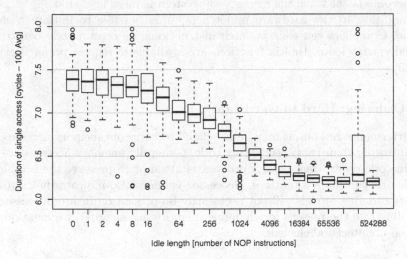

Fig. 4. Dependency of access bandwidth on delay between cache misses, generated by concurrently executing workload

Whenever parts of the memory subsystem are shared by multiple cores or multiple processors, bandwidth is naturally shared as well. Since sharing is often on the first-come first-served basis, more intensive workloads will get larger shares of bandwidth.

3.3 Prefetching: Do Be Linear

Prefetching is utilized to hide the memory access latencies. Starting a memory access well before the data is actually needed in code means that code is likely to find the data in cache rather than in memory, thus executing faster. Hardware typically guesses what data will be needed by assuming linear access patterns.

The access patterns recognized by hardware prefetchers are often fairly simple. Typical is a linear access pattern with a constant stride, or several such patterns anchored to a particular page [14, Section 7.2] or a particular instruction [2, Section 6.5]. The pattern is assumed to be continuous in the virtual address space, and since the hardware prefetcher works in the physical address space, it stops following an access pattern on the page boundary. For typical 4096 byte pages, this limits the useful stride distances to at most hundreds of bytes, since larger stride distances would reach the page boundary too soon.

Other typical features of hardware prefetchers include fetching adjacent cache lines, which may give the impression that cache lines are larger than they actually are.

Memory accesses by hardware prefetchers can be dropped when the memory subsystem is near maximum utilization. Moreover, the behavior of the memory subsystem under cache sharing can exhibit surprising effects, including workloads that become faster when the memory subsystem is more loaded [4,3].

In addition to the hardware prefetchers, it is possible to initiate prefetch in code. Compilers can emit prefetch instructions for certain code constructs, especially array loops. Builtin functions are available to request prefetch explicitly [25].

3.4   Ordering: Hard to Get Right

For performance reasons, it may be beneficial to carry out memory accesses in a different order than that specified by code. Generally, memory accesses are not done in code order, even though processors attempt to preserve the semblance of code order in many situations. Processor vendors also indicate that stronger memory ordering models will not necessarily be present on future processors.

To illustrate the reasons for changing memory access order, we mention two common architectural elements:

- Store buffer. Rather than writing directly to cache or memory, processor can stage writes in a store buffer and only write to cache or memory from there. Writes pending in the store buffer are typically visible to other accesses to the same address, however, certain special memory access operations can bypass the store buffer.
- Write combining buffer. Rather than writing small chunks of data, processor can stage writes in a write combining buffer and only write in larger chunks. Writes pending in the write combining buffer are not necessarily globally visible to other accesses.

Rather than reproducing the exact details of memory access ordering, we only want to impress the reader with the fact that it needs to be considered even in relatively simple situations. For that, we reproduce a short code example from [15, Section 8.2.3]:

```
volatile int x = 0;
volatile int y = 0;

int FunctionOne () {
  x = 1;
  return (y);
}

int FunctionTwo () {
```

```
y = 1;
return (x);
}
```

When the two functions are executed by threads running on two processors, it is possible for both to return zero, which is a result that is not possible on a single processor.

Note that where memory ordering model is concerned, vendor documentation is not always clear and consistent. For example, in a 2008 version of its System Programming Guide, Intel states that "writes to the same location have a total order," but a 2011 version of the same document replaces this with "any two stores are seen in a consistent order by processors other than those performing the stores." Since many of the intricate interactions that can make seemingly reasonable memory ordering models backfire are still only being discovered, we would recommend following recent work on C++ and Java memory models for details [10,23].

3.5   Coherency: Not for Heavy Use

Alongside ordering, coherency is another property where processors generally attempt to present a simple facade over complex internals, where specialized protocols are used to enforce coherent memory view among multiple participants. For all cached data, the participants remember whether the data is also cached elsewhere and whether it was modified since being cached. The participants must also snoop the addresses of all memory accesses and react to certain events:

- An attempt to read data that is cached elsewhere requires indicating the existence of a copy.
- An attempt to write data that is cached elsewhere requires invaliding the copy.
- An attempt to read or write data that is modified elsewhere requires flushing the modifications.

Even though particular variants of the protocol (MESI, MOESI, MESIF) can differ in details, it is important to realize that any memory access, not just access to shared data, can cause coherency protocol activity. Measurements illustrating this effect are available in [6], where a raytracing benchmark is shown to run 21% slower when another workload on another processor accesses memory, even though the raytracing benchmark itself runs almost entirely from cache.

In general, it is recommended that workloads avoid sharing memory. This concerns especially false sharing, where otherwise unrelated data reside close to each other. When workloads require sharing memory, general advice is to place those workloads on cores that share cache, under the assumption that exchanging data through shared cache is faster than exchanging data through memory. Note, however, that there are exceptions to this rule – for example, level one caches can exchange data through main memory even when they are connected to a shared level two cache.

3.6   Controllers: No Longer Uniform

Memory modules are connected to processors through memory controllers. In some multiprocessor architectures, processors share an external memory controller in a symmetrical configuration. Recently, however, processors come equipped with integrated memory controllers. When such processors are used in multiprocessor architectures, each processor has direct access to some memory through its own controller, but only indirect access to other memory through controllers of other processors. Such architectures are necessarily NUMA, since the cost of accessing memory depends on both the accessing processor and the accessed address.

As was the case with associativity, the operating system, which allocates the physical addresses and therefore participates in the choice of the memory controller, does not have sufficient information to assign addresses in an optimal manner. Unlike with associativity, however, there are standard interfaces to direct allocation [11].

Multiprocessor applications that do not provide the operating system with allocation information are known to suffer on NUMA architectures. Since the default policy is to allocate memory close to the processor that first touches it, applications that first initialize their data structures and then fork for computation will most likely have their data placed near the processor that did the initialization rather than near the processors that do the computation. An example analysis of this effect for scientific computing applications is available in [18].

4   Software Techniques

To conclude, we list several examples of software techniques that can help addressing the presented hardware features. In essence, what we look for is designing algorithms and structures with hardware in mind – but since carefully optimized solutions are necessarily algorithm-specific, the examples refer mostly to general coding practice.

To begin with, we should be aware of the requirements our code will place on processor and memory. Even simple calculations will help estimate whether cache occupancy and memory traffic requirements are reasonable. We should also know whether our workload is processor-bound or memory-bound – a handy tool for this purpose are the roofline diagrams [27].

When coding, we should avoid clearly wrong constructs in performance sensitive code:

- Data should be aligned and sized to fit cache lines to avoid incurring both time and space overhead. It is especially important to avoid accessing data on cache line boundaries.
- Iteration steps should be small and constant to facilitate hardware prefetching. Multiple iteration patterns should access different pages, since some architectures recognize one pattern per page.

- Small data distances generally increase the efficiency of the memory subsystem. Address translation caches or memory controller pages are examples where locality matters.
- Data sharing should be avoided to minimize coherency traffic. It is especially important to avoid frequent updates to cache lines accessed from multiple processors.

For specific situations, further optimizations can be considered:

- Code that transforms input data into output data can benefit from modifying data in place rather than working from input buffer into output buffer. That way, outputs will not compete with inputs for cache space.
- When writing data that will not be read, either not soon or not by the same processor, special write operations that bypass cache can be used to conserve cache space.
- Specialized allocators can reduce probability of collisions.
- Inserting prefetch instructions can reduce latencies.

Finally, we should dedicate a special paragraph to experimental measurements. Algorithms in many computing domains perform optimizations based on complex assumptions about their workloads, and the most straightforward way to evaluate such optimizations are experimental measurements. Given the outlined features of memory subsystems – where simple acts of assigning particular address to data or switching two variables can lead to observable performance changes – it is very easy to mistake a performance artifact for a valid result.

We recommend the reader checks some of the documents referenced by the Evaluate Collaboratory [26] to avoid common mistakes in experimental measurements related to the complexities of contemporary computer architectures.

Acknowledgments. The members of the Department of Distributed and Dependable Systems have contributed to the work in performance evaluation, which has provided the necessary backdrop for this paper. The work has been partially funded by project GACR P202/10/J042 and by project SVV-2011-263312.

References

1. AMD: AMD64 Architecture Programmers Manual : System Programming, 3.18 edn. vol. 2 (2011)
2. AMD: Software Optimization Guide for AMD Family 15h Processors, 3.03 edn. (2011)
3. Babka, V.: Cache Sharing Sensitivity of SPEC CPU2006 Benchmarks. Tech. Rep. 2009/3 2.0, Department of Software Engineering, Faculty of Mathematics and Physics, Charles University (2009)
4. Babka, V., Bulej, L., Decky, M., Kraft, J., Libic, P., Marek, L., Seceleanu, C., Tuma, P.: Resource Usage Modeling: Q-ImPrESS Project Deliverable D3.3 (2009), http://www.q-impress.eu

5. Babka, V., Bulej, L., Libic, P., Marek, L., Martinec, T., Podzimek, A., Tuma, P.: Resource Impact Analysis: Q-ImPrESS Project Deliverable D3.4 (2011), http://www.q-impress.eu
6. Babka, V., Marek, L., Tuma, P.: When Misses Differ: Investigating Impact of Cache Misses on Observed Performance. In: Proceedings of ICPADS 2009. IEEE (2009)
7. Babka, V., Tuma, P.: Investigating Cache Parameters of x86 Family Processors. In: Kaeli, D., Sachs, K. (eds.) SPEC Benchmark Workshop 2009. LNCS, vol. 5419, pp. 77–96. Springer, Heidelberg (2009)
8. Babka, V., Tuma, P.: Can Linear Approximation Improve Performance Prediction?. In: Proceedings of EPEW 2011. Springer, Heidelberg (2011)
9. Bailey, D., Barszcz, E., Barton, J., Browning, D., Carter, R., Dagum, L., Fatoohi, R., Fineberg, S., Frederickson, P., Lasinski, T., Schreiber, R., Simon, H.: The NAS Parallel Benchmarks. Tech. Rep. RNR-94-007, RNR (1994)
10. Boehm, H.: Threads and Memory Model for C++, http://www.hpl.hp.com/personal/Hans_Boehm/c++mm
11. Drepper, U.: What Every Programmer Should Know About Memory. Tech. rep., Red Hat (2007)
12. Fields, B.A., Bodik, R., Hill, M.D., Newburn, C.J.: Interaction Cost and Shotgun Profiling. ACM Transactions on Architecture and Code Optimization 1, 272–304 (2004), http://doi.acm.org/10.1145/1022969.1022971
13. Goetz, B.: Double-Checked Locking: Clever, But Broken. JavaWorld (2001)
14. Intel: Intel 64 and IA-32 Architectures Optimization Reference Manual, 248966-025 edn. (2011)
15. Intel: Intel 64 and IA-32 Architectures Software Developers Manual Volume 3A: System Programming Guide, Part 1, 253668-039 edn. (2011)
16. Intel: Intel 64 and IA-32 Architectures Software Developers Manual Volume 3B: System Programming Guide, Part 2, 253669-039 edn. (2011)
17. Kalibera, T., Tuma, P.: Precise Regression Benchmarking with Random Effects: Improving Mono Benchmark Results. In: Horváth, A., Telek, M. (eds.) EPEW 2006. LNCS, vol. 4054, pp. 63–77. Springer, Heidelberg (2006)
18. McCurdy, C., Vetter, J.: Memphis: Finding and Fixing NUMA-Related Performance Problems on Multi-Core Platforms. In: Proceedings of ISPASS 2010. IEEE (2010)
19. Meyers, S., Alexandrescu, A.: C++ and the Perils of Double-Checked Locking. Dr. Dobb's Journal (2004)
20. Mytkowicz, T., Diwan, A., Hauswirth, M., Sweeney, P.F.: Producing Wrong Data Without Doing Anything Obviously Wrong. In: Proceedings of ASPLOS 2009, pp. 265–276. ACM (2009)
21. Omni Compiler Project. High Performance Computing Systems Laboratory, Graduate School of Systems and Information Engineering, University of Tsukuba, http://www.hpcs.cs.tsukuba.ac.jp/omni-openmp/top-en.html
22. Prokop, H.: Cache-Oblivious Algorithms. Master Thesis, Department of Electrical Engineering and Computer Science, Massachusetts Institute of Technology (1999)
23. Pugh, B.: The Java Memory Model, http://www.cs.umd.edu/~pugh/java/memoryModel
24. Schmidt, D.C., Harrison, T.: Double-Checked Locking – An Object Behavioral Pattern for Initializing and Accessing Thread-Safe Objects Efficiently. Presented at PLoP 1996 (1996)
25. Stallman, R.M., et al.: Using the GNU Compiler Collection, 4.6.1 edn.

26. The Evaluate Collaboratory: Experimental Evaluation of Software and Systems in Computer Science, http://evaluate.inf.usi.ch
27. Williams, S.: The Roofline Model. In: Performance Tuning of Scientific Applications. CRC (2010)
28. Wolfe, M.: More Iteration Space Tiling. In: Proceedings of Supercomputing 1989, pp. 655–664. ACM, New York (1989), http://doi.acm.org/10.1145/76263.76337
29. Yotov, K., Pingali, K., Stodghill, P.: Automatic Measurement of Memory Hierarchy Parameters. In: Proceedings of SIGMETRICS 2005. ACM (2005)

Frequency Prediction of Functions*

Kaspars Balodis, Ilja Kucevalovs, and Rūsiņš Freivalds

Faculty of Computing, University of Latvia, Raiņa bulvāris 29, Riga, LV-1459, Latvia

Abstract. Prediction of functions is one of processes considered in inductive inference. There is a "black box" with a given total function f in it. The result of the inductive inference machine $F(< f(0), f(1), \cdots, f(n) >)$ is expected to be $f(n+1)$. Deterministic and probabilistic prediction of functions has been widely studied. Frequency computation is a mechanism used to combine features of deterministic and probabilistic algorithms. Frequency computation has been used for several types of inductive inference, especially, for learning via queries. We study frequency prediction of functions and show that that there exists an interesting hierarchy of predictable classes of functions.

1 Introduction

Physicists are well aware that physical indeterminism is a complicated phenomenon and probabilistical models are merely reasonably good approximations of reality. The problem "What is randomness?" has always been interesting not only for philosophers and physicists but also for computer scientists. The term "nondeterministic algorithm" has been deliberately coined to differ from "indeterminism".

Probabilistic (randomized) algorithms is one of central notions in Theory of Computation. However, since long ago computer scientists have attempted to develop notions and technical implementations of these notions that would be similar to but not equal to randomization.

The notion of frequency computation was introduced by G. Rose [28] as an attempt to have an absolutely deterministic mechanism with properties similar to probabilistic algorithms. The definition was as follows. A function $f: w \to w$ is (m, n)-computable, where $1 \le m \le n$, iff there exists a recursive function $R: w^n \to w^n$ such that, for all n-tuples $(x_1, \cdots, x_n)$ of distinct natural numbers,

$$card\{i : (R(x_1, \cdots, x_n))_i = f(x_i)\} \ge m.$$

R. McNaughton cites in his survey [25] a problem (posed by J. Myhill) whether f has to be recursive if m is close to n. This problem was answered by B.A. Trakhtenbrot [31] by showing that f is recursive whenever $2m > n$. On the other hand, B.A. Trakhtenbrot [31] proved that if $2m = n$ then nonrecursive functions can be

---

* The research was supported by Grant No. 09.1570 from the Latvian Council of Science and by Project 2009/0216/1DP/1.1.1.2.0/09/IPIA/VIA/044 from the European Social Fund.

Z. Kotásek et al. (Eds.): MEMICS 2011, LNCS 7119, pp. 76–83, 2012.
© Springer-Verlag Berlin Heidelberg 2012

(m, n)-computed. E.B. Kinber extended the research by considering frequency enumeration of sets [20]. The class of (m, n)-computable sets equals the class of recursive sets if and only if $2m > n$. The notion of frequency computation can be extended to other models of computation. Frequency computation in polynomial time was discussed in full detail by M. Hinrichs and G. Wechsung [19].

For resource bounded computations, the behavior of frequency computability is completely different: for e.g., whenever $n' - m' > n - m$, it is known that under any reasonable resource bound there are sets (m', n')-computable, but not (m, n)-computable. However, scaling down to finite automata, the analogue of Trakhtenbrot's result holds again: We show here that the class of languages (m, n)-recognizable by deterministic finite automata equals the class of regular languages if and only if $2m > n$. Conversely, for $2m > n$, the class of languages (m, n)-recognizable by deterministic finite automata [3] is uncountable for a two-letter alphabet. When restricted to a one-letter alphabet, then every (m, n)-recognizable language is regular. This was also shown by E.B. Kinber.

Frequency computations became increasingly popular when relation between frequency computation and computation with a small number of queries was discovered [23,18,6,7].

Inductive inference is a process to find an algorithm from sample computations. We restrict ourselves to the case when a total function is to be identified. The first paper in this area was [17], yet (sometimes indirectly) the research was influenced by the theory of experiments with finite automata [24].

In the *prediction of functions* we consider a functional F. We say that F predicts a total function $f : N \to N$ correctly if the result $F(< f(0), \cdots, f(n) >)$ always equals $f(n+1)$. A class U of functions is called predictable if there exists a functional F correctly predicting every function $f \in U$.

This definition of predictability of functions is rather weak because only rather non-interesting classes of functions are predictable. All functions in U are distinguishable using only the value $f(0)$. Hence a more complicated definition is used.

Definition 1. *We say that F predicts a total function $f : N \to N$ in the limit if the result $F(< f(0), \cdots, f(n) >)$ equals $f(n+1)$ for all but a finite number of the values of n. It is not even demanded that $F(< f(0), \cdots, f(n) >)$ is defined for all n. A class U of functions is called predictable if there exists a recursive functional F correctly predicting every function $f \in U$.*

Definition 2. *We say that F (m, n)-predicts a class U of total functions $f : N \to N$ if for arbitrary n-tuple of pairwise distinct functions $f_1, f_2, \cdots, f_n$ from the class U the frequency algorithm works on n inputs receiving $F(< f_j(0), \cdots, f_j(n) >)$ on the j-th input (n being the same on all the inputs) and producing (at different moments!) outputs "$f_j(n + 1) = r$ (the computation is infinitely long and for some j the result can never be produced). It is demanded that there are at least m pairwise distinct functions $g_1, g_2, \cdots, g_m$ such that $\{g_1, g_2, \cdots, g_m\} \subseteq \{f_1, f_2, \cdots, f_n\}$ and for all $i \in \{1, 2, \cdots, m\}$ the correct result on the corresponding output is produced for all but a finite number of n.*

2   Results

Lemma 1. *If a total function f is deterministically predicted in the limit then f is recursive.*

Proof. By the definition of predictability, there exists an n_0 such that for all $n > n_0$ the result $F(< f(0), \cdots, f(n) >)$ equals $f(n+1)$. Whatever the values $< f(0), \cdots, f(n_0) >$, the recursivity of f is implied by the recursivity of F.   □

Nonetheless there is specifics of the frequency computation.

Theorem 1. *There is a class U of total functions containing a non-recursive function g such that for arbitrary positive integer n there is an algorithm $(n, n+1)$-predicting the class U.*

Proof. Let f be a total non-recursive function such that $f(0) = 0$. Let U consist of the function f and all constants c. The frequency algorithm for each f_j predicts the next value as $f_j(0)$. For all the constant functions the prediction is correct. Since the functions are supposed to be distinct, no more than one of the functions is predicted incorrectly.   □

How (m, n)-predictability and (m', n')-predictability is related? Some implications are evident.

Lemma 2. *If U is (m, n)-predictable, then U is also $(m, n+1)$-predictable.*

Lemma 3. *If U is $(m+1, n+1)$-predictable, then U is also (m, n)-predictable.*

Theorem 2. *For arbitrary positive integer k there is a class U_k of total functions such that:*
1) for arbitrary positive integer n the class U_k is $(n, n+k)$-predictable,
2) for no positive integer n the class U_k is $(n, n+k-1)$-predictable.

Proof. The class U_k consists of all the constants and k distinct non-recursive functions. If at any tuple of distinct target functions at least k errors are allowed, then the frequency algorithm can predict the functions as they were constants. If less than k errors are allowed then existence of a frequency predicting algorithm is supposed to predict in the limit at least one non-recursive function. This contradicts an easy modification of Lemma 1.   □

The proofs of Theorems 1 and 2 used essentially the property of the class U to contain non-recursive functions. This raises a natural question: does $(n, n+k)$-predictability depend on the parameters (n, k) if all the functions in U are recursive?

Theorem 3. *For arbitrary positive integer k there is a class U_k of total recursive functions such that:*
1) for arbitrary positive integer n the class U_k is $(n, n+k)$-predictable,
2) for no positive integer n the class U_k is $(n, n+k-1)$-predictable.

The main idea of the proof is to construct U_k as a set of total recursive functions f_{ab} where $a \in N$ and $b \in \{1, 2, \cdots, k\}$. Each $f_{ab}(0)$ contains information about the value of a involved and complete information about the programs for all the functions $f_{0b}, f_{1b}, \cdots, f_{(a-1)b}$ but not the information about the programs for any of the functions f_{ab}. This way, if a is the largest first index of the target functions of the frequency algorithm, there is no need for an error on all the target functions with exception of $f_{a1}, f_{a2}, \cdots, f_{ak}$. On the other hand, the functions $f_{a1}, f_{a2}, \cdots, f_{ak}$ are constructed to ensure that the frequency algorithm F computed by Turing machine φ_a working on these k functions cannot predict correctly all but a finite number of values $f_{aj}(n)$ for at least one of the functions f_{aj}. (In our paper φ is a Gödel numbering of all one argument partial recursive functions such that φ_0 is the nowhere defined function. For instance, any standard numbering of Turing machines can be used for this purpose.)

Formally, we use Smullyan's double recursion theorem [30]:

Smullyan's Double Recursion Theorem. [27,30] For any recursive functions g and h, there exist m and n such that

$$\varphi_m = \varphi_{g(<m,n>)}, \text{ and } \varphi_n = \varphi_{h(<m,n>)}.$$

This theorem can easily be generalized:

Lemma 4. *[30] For any s-tuple of total recursive functions* $(h_1, h_2, \cdots, h_s)$ *there exists an s-tuple of natural numbers* $< y_1, y_2, \cdots, y_s >$ *such that*

$$\varphi_{y_1} = \varphi_{h_1(<y_1, y_2, \cdots, y_s>)}, \cdots, \varphi_{y_s} = \varphi_{h_s(<y_1, y_2, \cdots, y_s>)}.$$

Proof of Theorem 3. We define $f_{ab} \in U_k$ by induction. There cannot be a universal 3-argument recursive function $U(a, b, x) = f_{ab}(x)$ because otherwise U would be deterministically predictable in the limit. We define $f_{a1}, \cdots, f_{ak}$ only after $f_{a'b}$ have been defined for all $a' < a$. Lemma 4 will be used to prove that φ_a cannot be a frequency algorithm predicting the k-tuple of functions $f_{a1}, \cdots, f_{ak}$.

Basis. We define $f_{01}, \cdots, f_{0k}$ as constant functions equal to zero. We define every number among $n_{01}, \cdots, n_{0k}$ as an integer v such that φ_v is constant zero (every number n_{ab} will be a correct φ-program for the function f_{ab}). We define every number among $z_{01}, \cdots, z_{0k}$ as 0 (every number z_{ab} will be a correct information about all φ-programs for all the functions $f_{a'b'}$, where $a' < a$ and $b' \in \{1, 2, \cdots, k\}$).

Since we define the functions $h_1, h_2, \cdots, h_k$ by a common procedure, we use infinite injury priority method to establish temporal priorities among the numbers $\{1, 2, \cdots, k\}$. These priorities are needed to describe the construction of the functions. We start with the "natural" priority $(1, 2, \cdots, k)$.

Inductive step. Assume that all the functions $f_{a'b}$ where $a' < a$ have already been defined. Let $t_1, t_2, \cdots, t_k$ be arbitrary natural numbers. For each $b \in \{1, 2, \cdots, k\}$ we construct a k-tuple of functions as follows. For all $b \in \{1, 2, \cdots, k\}$ we define the functions $\varphi_{h_b(<t_1, t_2, \cdots, t_s>)}$ stepwise. First, we define

$$\varphi_{h_b(<t_1,t_2,\cdots,t_s>)}(0) = < f_{a-1}(0), n_{a-1} > .$$

This value does not depend on b.

Assume, by a new induction, that each of the functions $\varphi_{h_b(<t_1,t_2,\cdots,t_s>)}$ is already defined on some $(0,1,\cdots,d_b)$ and the priority among the numbers $\{1,2,\cdots,k\}$ is now $\{w_1,w_2,\cdots,w_k\}$. For each $j \in \{1,2,\cdots,k\}$, we define $b(j)$ as the value p such that $w_p = j$. Assume, by induction, that priority is coordinated with the number of values of the arguments where the functions are defined, i.e., $d_{b(1)} \leq d_{b(2)} \leq \cdots \leq d_{b(k)}$.

In a way to serialize the parallel processing of computing predictions by the frequency algorithm φ_a the k-tuple of functions to be constructed (where the values of the functions already constructed are taken as they are but the new values of the target functions are taken equal to zero), we compute (in this order) $\cdots$ q steps of φ_a on all the functions up to the length $d_{b(1)}$, then q steps of φ_a on all the functions up to the length $d_{b(2)}$, $\cdots$, then q steps of φ_a on all the functions up to the length $d_{b(k)}$, then $q+1$ steps of φ_a on all the functions up to the length $d_{b(1)}$, then $q+1$ steps of φ_a on all the functions up to the length $d_{b(2)}$, $\cdots$, then $q+1$ steps of φ_a on all the functions up to the length $d_{b(k)}$, $\cdots$, then $q+1$ steps of φ_a on all the functions up to the length $d_{b(1)}+1$, then $q+1$ steps of φ_a on all the functions up to the length $d_{b(2)}+1$, $\cdots$, then $q+1$ steps of φ_a on all the functions up to the length $d_{b(k)}+1$, then $q+2$ steps of φ_a on all the functions up to the length $d_{b(1)}$, then $q+2$ steps of φ_a on all the functions up to the length $d_{b(2)}$, $\cdots$, then $q+2$ steps of φ_a on all the functions up to the length $d_{b(k)}$, then then $q+3$ steps of φ_a on all the functions up to the length $d_{b(1)+1}$, then $q+3$ steps of φ_a on all the functions up to the length $d_{b(2)+1}$, $\cdots$, then $q+3$ steps of φ_a on all the functions up to the length $d_{b(k)+1}$, $\cdots$, then then $q+4$ steps of φ_a on all the functions up to the length $d_{b(1)+2}$, then $q+4$ steps of φ_a on all the functions up to the length $d_{b(2)+2}$, $\cdots$, then $q+4$ steps of φ_a on all the functions up to the length $d_{b(k)+2}$, $\cdots$ till the first new prediction on one of the functions is found. Say, the prediction for $f_j(m+1) = e$ is found. Then we define $\varphi_{h_j(<t_1,t_2,\cdots,t_s>)}(d_b+1) = \varphi_{h_j(<t_1,t_2,\cdots,t_s>)}(d_b+2) = \cdots = \varphi_{h_j(<t_1,t_2,\cdots,t_s>)}(m) = 0$ and $\varphi_{h_j(<t_1,t_2,\cdots,t_s>)}(m+1) = e+1$, (the prediction by φ_a is made wrong). Additionally, we extend the definition domains for all the functions whose priority comes after j, i.e., using the notation $w_p = j$, for all the functions $\varphi_{h_{w_p}(<t_1,t_2,\cdots,t_s>)}, \cdots, \varphi_{h_{w_k}(<t_1,t_2,\cdots,t_s>)}$.

By Lemma 4, there exists an s-tuple of natural numbers $< y_1, y_2, \cdots, y_s >$ such that

$$\varphi_{y_1} = \varphi_{h_1(<y_1,y_2,\cdots,y_s>)}, \cdots, \varphi_{y_s} = \varphi_{h_s(<y_1,y_2,\cdots,y_s>)}.$$

However, these functions may be not total. We define f_{ab} as φ_{y_b} if it is total, and as

$$f_{ab}(x) = \begin{cases} \varphi_{y_b}(x) & \text{, if } \varphi_{y_b} \text{ is defined on } [0,d] \text{ and } x \in [0,d], \\ 0 & \text{, if } \varphi_{y_b} \text{ is defined on } [0,d] \text{ and } x \geq d. \end{cases}$$

It is easy to see that f_{ab} either is equal to φ_{y_b} and the frequency algorithm φ_a makes infinitely many incorrect predictions on this function or φ_{y_b} is a function defined on a finite segment $[0, d]$ and f_{ab} is a total function extending φ_{y_b} but φ_a produces no predictions after the segment $[0, d]$.

Nonetheless, U_k is $(n, n+k)$-predictable for arbitrary natural n. Indeed, from the values $g_1(0), g_2(0), \cdots, g_{n+k}(0)$ the frequency algorithm can find the maximum value of a such that the target functions are $f_{ab} \in U_k$. The programs for all functions with $a' < a$ can be computed knowing $f_{ab}(0)$. No more than k distinct target functions can correspond to the maximum value of a. $\square$

Theorem 4. *There are two classes U_1 and U_2 of total recursive functions such that:*
1) U_1 is deterministically predictable,
2) U_2 is deterministically predictable,
3) If $U_1 \cup U_2$ is (m, n)-predictable then $m = 0$.

Proof. Following example of [4], we define U_1 as the class of all total recursive functions f such that for all but a finite number of values of x it is true that $f(x) = 0$, and U_2 is the class of all total recursive functions f such that $\forall x (\varphi_{f(0)}(x) = f(x))$.

Now we prove that $U_1 \cup U_2$ is not (m, n)-predictable with $m > 0$. Assume from the contrary that it is (m, n)-predictable by a frequency algorithm φ_a. In order to use Lemma 4 we define an n-tuple of recursive functions $(h_1, h_2, \cdots, h_n)$. The functions take values $\varphi_{h_1(t_1, \cdots, t_n)}(0) = t_1, \cdots, \varphi_{h_n(t_1, \cdots, t_n)}(0) = t_n$, $\varphi_{h_1(t_1, \cdots, t_n)}(1) = 1, \cdots, \varphi_{h_n(t_1, \cdots, t_n)}(1) = n$.

To define the values of these functions for $x > 1$ we compute predictions made by φ_a initial fragments of these functions of length 2, 3, $\cdots$ supposing that the subsequent values of the functions are zeros (but we do not add any new values to these functions) till for at least one of these predictions equal zero.

Copying the method used in the proof of Theorem 3 we get that all the constructed functions are either defined on a finite initial fragment of the sequence of natural numbers (and then the algorithm φ_a has produced only a finite number of predictions for this function) or the algorithm φ_a has produced infinitely many wrong predictions for this function. $\square$

It was proved in [2] that Theorem 4 cannot be generalized to 3 classes U_1, U_2 and U_3. More precisely, it was proved in [2] that deterministic predictability of $U_1 \cup U_2, U_2 \cup U_3$ and $U_1 \cup U_3$ implies deterministic predictability of $U_1 \cup U_2 \cup U_3$.

Theorem 5. *Let n be a natural number such that $n \geq 7$, $m > \frac{n}{2}$ and $U_1, U_2, \cdots,$ U_n be classes of total recursive functions such that:*
1) $U_1 \cup U_2 \cup \cdots \cup U_{n-1}$ is (m, n)-predictable,
2) $U_1 \cup U_2 \cup \cdots \cup U_{n-2} \cup U_n$ is (m, n)-predictable,
3) $U_1 \cup U_2 \cup \cdots \cup U_{n-3} \cup U_{n-1} \cup U_n$ is (m, n)-predictable,
$\cdots$
n) $U_2 \cup U_3 \cup \cdots \cup U_n$ is (m, n)-predictable.
Then $U_1 \cup U_2 \cup \cdots \cup U_n$ is $(2m, 2n)$-predictable.

Proof. We describe the processing by the $(2m, 2n)$-algorithm the $2n$-tuple of functions $f_1, \cdots, f_{2n}$ from the class $U_1 \cup U_2 \cup \cdots \cup U_n$. The new frequency algorithm A has $2n$ distinct functions $f_1, \cdots, f_{2n}$ as the input. The old n algorithms $A_1, A_2, \cdots, A_n$ have only n functions as the input. The new algorithm A uses all possible $(2n)!/n!$ copies of each of algorithms $A_1, A_2, \cdots, A_n$ by choosing n functions out of $f_1, \cdots, f_{2n}$. To predict the next value of any function $f_i \in \{f_1, \cdots, f_n\}$ the algorithm A considers predictions of all old frequency algorithms on all n-tuples such that the tuple contains f_i. This restriction removes $\frac{n.(2n-1)!}{n!}$ for every old algorithm leaving $n(\frac{(2n)!}{n!} - \frac{n.(2n-1)!}{n!})$ predictions in total for the current value of f_i.

Our frequency algorithm A for $U_1 \cup U_2 \cup \cdots \cup U_n$ always considers the set of the pairs (algorithm A_j, n-tuple of inputs f_i) having made the least number of wrong number predictions for the function f_i under question. Since $n \geq 7$, and $m > \frac{n}{2}$, most of these pairs allow only a finite number of wrong predictions. When a pair has made a wrong prediction, this pair is removed from the set. When the first (!) prediction is made by one of the pair in the set, this prediction is output as the result of the new frequency algorithm for $U_1 \cup U_2 \cup \cdots \cup U_n$. Since $n \geq 7$ and $m > \frac{n}{2}$, at least $2m$ of the functions f_i get only finite number of wrong predictions.   □

References

1. Farid, M.: Why Sometimes Probabilistic Algorithms Can Be More Effective. In: Wiedermann, J., Gruska, J., Rovan, B. (eds.) MFCS 1986. LNCS, vol. 233, pp. 1–14. Springer, Heidelberg (1986)
2. Apsītis, K., Freivalds, R., Kriķis, M., Simanovskis, R., Smotrovs, J.: Unions of Identifiable Classes of Total Recursive Functions. In: Jantke, K.P. (ed.) AII 1992. LNCS, vol. 642, pp. 99–107. Springer, Heidelberg (1992)
3. Austinat, H., Diekert, V., Hertrampf, U., Petersen, H.: Regular frequency computations. Theoretical Computer Science 330(1), 15–20 (2005)
4. Bārzdiņš, J., Barzdin, Y.M.: Two theorems on limiting synthesis of functions. Theory of algorithms and programs 1, 82–88 (1974) (in Russian)
5. Bārzdiņš, J., Freivalds, R.: On the prediction of general recursive functions. Soviet Mathematics Doklady 13, 1224–1228 (1972)
6. Beigel, R., Gasarch, W.I., Kinber, E.B.: Frequency computation and bounded queries. Theoretical Computer Science 163(1/2), 177–192 (1996)
7. Case, J., Kaufmann, S., Kinber, E.B., Kummer, M.: Learning recursive functions from approximations. Journal of Computer and System Sciences 55(1), 183–196 (1997)
8. Degtev, A.N.: On (m,n)-computable sets. In: Moldavanskij, D.I., Gos, I. (eds.) Algebraic Systems, pp. 88–99. Universitet (1981)
9. Freivalds, R.: On the growth of the number of states in result of the determinization of probabilistic finite automata. Avtomatika i Vichislitel'naya Tekhnika (3), 39–42 (1982) (Russian)
10. Freivalds, R., Karpinski, M.: Lower Space Bounds for Randomized Computation. In: Shamir, E., Abiteboul, S. (eds.) ICALP 1994. LNCS, vol. 820, pp. 580–592. Springer, Heidelberg (1994)
11. Freivalds, R.: Complexity of Probabilistic Versus Deterministic Automata. In: Barzdins, J., Bjorner, D. (eds.) Baltic Computer Science. LNCS, vol. 502, pp. 565–613. Springer, Heidelberg (1991)

12. Freivalds, R.: Inductive Inference of Recursive Functions: Qualitative Theory. In: Barzdins, J., Bjorner, D. (eds.) Baltic Computer Science. LNCS, vol. 502, pp. 77–110. Springer, Heidelberg (1991)

13. Freivalds, R., Bārzdiņš, J., Podnieks, K.: Inductive Inference of Recursive Functions: Complexity Bounds. In: Barzdins, J., Bjorner, D. (eds.) Baltic Computer Science. LNCS, vol. 502, pp. 111–155. Springer, Heidelberg (1991)

14. Freivalds, R.: Models of Computation, Riemann Hypothesis, and Classical Mathematics. In: Rovan, B. (ed.) SOFSEM 1998. LNCS, vol. 1521, pp. 89–106. Springer, Heidelberg (1998)

15. Freivalds, R.: Non-constructive methods for finite probabilistic automata. International Journal of Foundations of Computer Science 19(3), 565–580 (2008)

16. Freivalds, R.: Amount of nonconstructivity in finite automata. Theoretical Computer Science 411(38-39), 3436–3443 (2010)

17. Gold, E.M.: Language identification in the limit. Information and Control 10(5), 447–474 (1967)

18. Harizanova, V., Kummer, M., Owings, J.: Frequency computations and the cardinality theorem. The Journal of Symbolic Logic 57(2), 682–687 (1992)

19. Hinrichs, M., Wechsung, G.: Time bounded frequency computations. Information and Computation 139, 234–257 (1997)

20. Kinber, E.B.: Frequency calculations of general recursive predicates and frequency enumeration of sets. Soviet Mathematics Doklady 13, 873–876 (1972)

21. Kinber, E.B.: On frequency real-time computations. In: Barzdin, Y.M. (ed.) Teoriya Algoritmov i Programm, vol. 2, pp. 174–182 (1973) (Russian)

22. Kinber, E.B.: Frequency computations in finite automata. Kibernetika 2, 7–15 (1976); Russian; English translation in Cybernetics 12, 179–187 (1976)

23. Kummer, M.: A proof of Beigel's Cardinality Conjecture. The Journal of Symbolic Logic 57(2), 677–681 (1992)

24. Moore, E.F.: Gedanken-experiments on sequential machines. Automata Studies Ann. of Math. Studies (34), 129–153 (1956)

25. McNaughton, R.: The Theory of Automata, a Survey. Advances in Computers 2, 379–421 (1961)

26. Rabin, M.O., Scott, D.: Finite automata and their decision problems. IBM Journal of Research and Development 3(2), 115–125 (1959)

27. Rogers Jr., H.: Theory of Recursive Functions and Effective Computability. MIT Press (1987)

28. Rose, G.F.: An extended notion of computability. In: Abstracts of International Congress for Logic, Methodology and Philosophy of Science, p. 14 (1960)

29. Rose, G.F., Ullian, J.S.: Approximations of functions on the integers. Pacific Journal of Mathematics 13(2), 693–701 (1963)

30. Smullyan, R.M.: Theory of Formal Systems, Annals of Mathematics Studies, vol. (47), Princeton, NJ (1961)

31. Trakhtenbrot, B.A.: On the frequency computation of functions. Algebra i Logika 2, 25–32 (1964)

Timed Automata Approach to Verification of Systems with Degradation

Jiří Barnat*, Ivana Černá**, and Jana Tůmová***

Masaryk University, Faculty of Informatics,
Botanicka 68a, 602 00, Brno, Czech Republic
{barnat,cerna,xtumova}@fi.muni.cz

Abstract. We focus on systems that naturally incorporate a degrading quality, such as electronic devices with degrading electric charge or broadcasting networks with decreasing power or quality of a transmitted signal. For such systems, we introduce an extension of linear temporal logic with quantitative constraints (Linear Temporal Logic with Degradation Constraints, or DLTL for short) that provides a user-friendly formalism for specifying properties involving quantitative requirements on the level of degradation. The syntax of DLTL resembles syntax of Metric Interval Temporal Logic (MITL) designed for reasoning about timed systems. Thus, we investigate their relation and a possibility of translating DLTL verification problem for systems with degradation into previously solved MITL verification problem for timed automata. We show, that through the mentioned translation, the DLTL model checking problem can be solved with limited, yet arbitrary, precision.

Further, we show that probability in Markov Decision Processes can be viewed as a degrading quality and DLTL as a probabilistic linear temporal logic with quantitative operators. We discuss expressiveness of DLTL as compared with expressiveness of probabilistic temporal logics.

1 Introduction

Model checking [4] has been recognized as one of the successful formal verification techniques that if employed during the software development cycle, may bring significant reduction in total development cost or time-to-market [9,8]. Recently, we have shown how the automata-based verification procedure as used for model checking of non-deterministic systems may be extended to systems with *degradation* [5]. Degradation is a natural phenomenon present in many systems we encounter regularly in our everyday life, for example, value of money degrades with time due to inflation, signal strength degrades with the distance from the transmitter, capacity of a recharging battery pack degrades with every charging cycle, and many others. There is no doubt that a number of software systems produced must take the degradation phenomenon into account. Verification of

---

* The author has been partially supported by grant number LH11065.
** The author has been partially supported by grant number GAP202/11/0312.
*** The author has been partially supported by grant number GD102/09/H042.

Z. Kotásek et al. (Eds.): MEMICS 2011, LNCS 7119, pp. 84–93, 2012.

worst-case degradation scenarios that a software system under development must survive or designing a strategy to avoid degradation below a given threshold are examples of problems that can be addressed with the model checking approach.

In our previous work, we have introduced two formalisms to capture the verification problem for systems with degradation [5]. These were *Transition Systems with Degradation* (TSD) used to describe the degradation aspects in the behavior of the system under development, and *Büchi Automata with Degradation Constraints* (BADC) used to capture degradation properties. Given a TSD and a BADC specification of undesired system behavior we have shown how to decide whether the system exhibits the undesired behavior or not.

A drawback of the designed verification framework is the necessity to express the undesired behavior of the system with use of an automaton. According to our experiences, constructing a BADC from a natural language description of a property is far more complicated than in standard non-degradation case, let alone the necessity of negation of the degradation specification. We address this issue in this paper by introducing an easy-to-use specification formalism.

We present *Linear Temporal Logic with Degradation Constraints* (DLTL) that is capable of expressing quantitative properties of systems with degradation. To our best knowledge, so far none of the existing temporal logics has focused on systems with a quality that degrades relatively, not absolutely, along a run of a system. We show, that DLTL verification problem can be translated into a verification problem for real-time systems. In particular, we show how a system with degradation can be interpreted as a *Timed Automaton* (TA) and a DLTL formula as a formula of *Metric Interval Temporal Logic* (MITL) [1]. Using this approach, the verification problem for systems with degradation and DLTL fomulas can be solved up to chosen precision. Furthermore, we show that with DLTL we can distinguish discrete time Markov decision processes that are indistinguishable by standard probabilistic logics such as PLTL or PCTL, which is an extension to our previous result that BADCs can do that.

The rest of the paper is organized as follows. Section 2 reviews timed automata and MITL. In Section 3, we review transition systems with degradation, introduce DLTL, and focus on verification of DLTL formulas. In Section 3.3, we focus on interpretation of probability in Markov decision processes as a degrading phenomenon. Finally, in Section 5 we conclude and outline possible future directions.

2   Preliminaries

A timed automaton is an automaton equipped with a finite set of real-valued clock variables (*clocks*) that can be intuitivelly viewed as stopwatches allowing us to reason about timed properties of real-time systems.

A *clock constraint* γ over finite set of clocks X is a finite expression constructed according to the grammar $\gamma ::= x \bowtie c \mid \gamma \wedge \gamma$, where $\bowtie \in \{<, \leq, >, \geq\}$, $x \in X$, and $c \in \mathbb{N}$. Let $CC(X)$ denote the set of all clock constraints over X. A *clock valuation* ν is a function $\nu : X \to \mathbb{R}_{\geq 0}$ assigning to each clock $x \in X$ its current value $\nu(x)$. We use $\nu + d$ to denote valuation ν', where $\nu'(x) = \nu(x) + d$ for each $x \in X$.

Definition 1 (Timed Automaton). *A* timed automaton *(TA) is a tuple* $\mathcal{A} = (Q, \Sigma, X, \delta, Q_{init}, Inv, AP, L)$, *where*

- *Q is a finite set of states,*
- *Σ is a finite set of actions,*
- *X is a finite set of clocks,*
- *$\delta \subseteq Q \times CC(X) \times \Sigma \times 2^X \times Q$ is a transition relation,*
- *$Q_{init} \subseteq Q$ is a set of initial states,*
- *$Inv : Q \to CC(C)$ is an invariant-assignment function,*
- *AP is a set of atomic propositions,*
- *$L : Q \to 2^{AP}$ is a labeling function.*

A 5-tuple $(q_1, \gamma, \sigma, R, q_2) \in \delta$ corresponds to a transition from state q_1 to q_2 labeled with σ that is enabled if constraint γ is satisfied. R denotes the subset of clock variables that are reset to zero when the transition is executed. Time can progress (*i.e.* the value of clock can increase) in states, whereas transitions between states always take zero time. Function Inv assigns to each state an invariant that gives a limit on how much time can be spent in that state. There are two possible ways how a TA can evolve: via *discrete* transitions *i.e.*, those between states, and *delay* transition, *i.e.*, staying in a state with letting time pass.

A run of a timed automaton is a sequence $\rho = (q_0, \nu_0) \xrightarrow{d_0} (q_0, \nu_0') \xrightarrow{\sigma_0} (q_1, \nu_1) \xrightarrow{d_1} (q_1, \nu_1') \xrightarrow{\sigma_1} (q_2, \nu_2) \ldots$, such that $q_0 \in Q_{init}$, $\forall x \in X : \nu_0(x) = 0$, and $\forall i \in \mathbb{N}$:

- $((q_i, \nu_i), d_i, (q_i, \nu_i'))$ if and only if $d_i \in \mathbb{R}_{\geq 0}$, $\nu_i'(x) = \nu_i(x) + d_i$ for all $x \in X$, and ν_i' satisfies $Inv(q_i)$, and
- $((q_i, \nu_i'), \sigma_i, (q_{i+1}, \nu_{i+1}))$ if and only if there exists $(q_i, \gamma_i, \sigma_i, R_i, q_{i+1}) \in \delta$, such that $\nu_i' \models \gamma_i$, $\nu_{i+1}(x) = \nu_i'(x)$ for all $x \in X \setminus R_i$, $\nu_{i+1}(x) = 0$ for all $x \in X \cap R_i$, and ν_{i+1} satisfies $Inv(q_{i+1})$.

A *position* on the run ρ is defined as any state that may appear during the run, *i.e.*, a tuple (q_i, ν), where $\nu = \nu_i + d$, and $d \leq d_i$. A *time duration* $\mathbb{T}_\rho(q_i, \nu)$ up to position (q_i, ν) is the sum of the delays up to this position $\mathbb{T}_\rho(q_i, \nu) = \sum_{j=0}^{i-1} d_j + d$. We denote by $\rho(t)$ and ρ^t a position (q, ν) on ρ, such that $\mathbb{T}_\rho(q, \nu) = t$ and suffix of run ρ initialized in $\rho(t)$, respectively. Run ρ produces a *word* $w = (L(q_0), \mathbb{T}_\rho(q_0, \nu_0'))(L(q_1), \mathbb{T}_\rho(q_1, \nu_1')) \ldots$. A *language* of a timed automaton $\mathcal{A}$, denoted by $\mathcal{L}(\mathcal{A})$ is a set of all words produced by all runs of $\mathcal{A}$.

Metric Interval Temporal Logic (MITL) is a specification logic for real-time systems. MITL formulas are interpreted over runs of timed automata.

Definition 2 (MITL Syntax). *The syntax of a MITL formula over the set of atomic propositions AP is given as follows:* $\varphi ::= tt \mid \alpha \mid \neg\varphi \mid \varphi \wedge \varphi \mid \varphi \mathsf{U}_I \varphi$, *where* $\alpha \in AP$, *and I is a non-singular[1] interval with integer end-points (I may be also unbounded).*

---

[1] Singular intervals are those of form $[t, t]$.

Definition 3 (MITL Semantics). *Given a MITL formula φ and a run ρ of a timed automaton $\mathcal{A}$, the satisfaction relation $\rho \models \varphi$ is for formulas φ of form $tt \mid \alpha \mid \neg\varphi \mid \varphi \wedge \varphi$ given analogously as for LTL [1,4]. Furthermore, $\rho \models \phi \, U_I \, \psi \Leftrightarrow \exists t \in \mathbb{R}_{\geq 0}$, such that $(\rho^t \models \psi \wedge t \in I \wedge \forall 0 \leq t' < t.(\rho^{t'} \models \phi))$.*

Each MITL formula φ defines a language $\mathcal{L}(\varphi)$ of all words produced by all runs satisfying φ. Note, that MITL formulas do not contain next operator, because the time domain is dense. Boolean operators $\vee$, and $\Rightarrow$ are defined in the usual way. Besides that, we define temporal operators $F_I \, \varphi \equiv tt \, U_I \, \varphi$ (eventually) and $G_I \, \varphi \equiv \neg F_I \, \neg\varphi$ (globally), and $\phi \, R_I \, \varphi \equiv \neg(\neg\phi \, U_I \, \neg\varphi)$ (release).

Given a timed automaton $\mathcal{A}$ and a MITL formula φ, the model checking question whether $\mathcal{L}(\mathcal{A}) \subseteq \mathcal{L}(\varphi)$ can be solved using automata-based approach. First, φ is negated and translated into a timed automaton $\mathcal{B}_{\neg\varphi}$. Then, a product timed automaton $\mathcal{A} \times \mathcal{B}_{\neg\phi}$ is built, such that $\mathcal{L}(\mathcal{A} \times \mathcal{B}_{\neg\varphi}) = \mathcal{L}(\mathcal{A}) \cap \mathcal{L}(\mathcal{B}_{\neg\varphi})$. Finally, by checking emptiness of $\mathcal{L}(\mathcal{A} \times \mathcal{B}_{\neg\varphi})$, the answer to model-checking problem is obtained. MITL model checking is EXPSPACE-complete [1].

The translation process from a MITL formula $\neg\varphi$ into timed automaton $\mathcal{B}_{\neg\varphi}$ requires the intervals appearing in $\neg\varphi$ to have integer bounds. Although this might seem quite restrictive, there is a simple way how to extend the results to deal with intervals with rational bounds as well. The "trick" is to pick a suitable constant $p \in \mathbb{Q}_{>0}$ and multiply all the interval bounds appearing in $\neg\varphi$ with p in order to get integer interval bounds. All the constants that appear in the model-checked timed automaton $\mathcal{A}$ have to be multiplied with p as well.

3 Verification of Systems with Degradation

3.1 Modeling Systems with Degradation

In this section we review a modeling formalism for systems with degradation that we introduced in our previous work [5]. A *Transition System with Degradation* (TSD) is a labeled transition system that is enhanced with a rational degradation constant associated with every transition.

Definition 4 (Transition System with Degradation). *A transition system with degradation is a tuple $\mathcal{T} = (S, Act, T, D, S_{init}, AP, L)$, where*

- *S is a finite set of states,*
- *Act is a finite set of actions,*
- *$T \subseteq S \times Act \times S$ is a transition relation,*
- *$D : T \rightarrow (0, 1]$ is a degradation relation,*
- *$S_{init} \subseteq S$ is a set of initial states,*
- *AP is a set of atomic propositions,*
- *$L : S \rightarrow 2^{AP}$ is a labeling function.*

Transition $t = (s_1, a, s_2) \in T$ represents that the system can make a transition from state s_1 to state s_2 under action a. The degradation constant $D(t)$ determines to what fraction the level of quality degrades when the transition t is executed. If $D(t) = 1$ the level of quality is unchanged, if $D(t) = 0.75$ the level of quality is decreased to 75% of the level of quality at the moment before the transition was executed. In other words, if the level of degradation is l at state s_1, then after the execution t, the level of degradation at state s_2 is $l \cdot D(t)$.

A *run* of a TSD $\mathcal{T} = (S, Act, T, D, S_{init}, AP, L)$ is an infinite sequence $\pi = s_0 \xrightarrow{t_0} s_1 \xrightarrow{t_1} \ldots$ where $s_i \in S$ and $t_i = (s_i, a_i, s_{i+1}) \in T$ for all $i \geq 0$. We denote by $\pi(i)$ and π^i the (i-1)-st state of the run π (*i.e.*, s_i) and the suffix beginning in $\pi(i)$, respectively. A *level of degradation* $\mathbb{D}_\pi(i)$ on run π up to state $\pi(i)$ is defined as a product of all degradation constants associated with transitions along this state $\mathbb{D}_\pi(i) = \prod_{j=1}^{i-1} D(t_j)$.

3.2   Temporal Logic for Systems with Degradation

In our previous work [5], we have shown that systems with degradation may be model checked if the property to be verified (its negation to be more precise) is described by a so-called Büchi automaton with degradation constraints (BADC). This is however, the major drawback of the method as specifying properties (or their negations) directly as BADCs is not a user-friendly process. On the other hand, expressing properties by means of a temporal logic can be viewed as quite intuitive with some resemblance to the natural language.

We propose *Linear Temporal Logic with Degradation Constraints* (DLTL) that allows for specification of quantitative properties of systems with degradation. The syntax of DLTL resembles syntax of MITL, however the logics differ in their semantics as they are interpreted over significantly different models.

Definition 5 (DLTL Syntax). *Let $\alpha \in AP$, and I be an interval within $(0, 1]$. The syntax of a DLTL formula over the set of atomic propositions AP is given according to the following rules:*

$$\varphi ::= tt \mid \alpha \mid \neg\varphi \mid \varphi \wedge \varphi \mid \mathsf{X}_I\, \varphi \mid \varphi\, \mathsf{U}_I\, \varphi$$

Definition 6 (DLTL Semantics). *Let π a run of a TSD $\mathcal{T}$. DLTL semantics is defined through the satisfaction relation $\models$.*

- $\pi \models tt$ *always*
- $\pi \models a \iff a \in L(s_0)$
- $\pi \models \neg\varphi \iff \pi \not\models \varphi$
- $\pi \models \varphi \wedge \psi \iff \pi \models \varphi \wedge \pi \models \psi$
- $\pi \models \mathsf{X}_I\varphi \iff \pi(1) \models \varphi \wedge \mathbb{D}_\pi(1) \in I$
- $\pi \models \varphi\, \mathsf{U}_I\, \psi \iff \exists j.(\pi^j \models \psi \wedge \mathbb{D}_\pi(j) \in I \wedge \forall 0 \leq i < j.(\pi^i \models \varphi))$

The standard LTL operators X, and U are included in DLTL as $\mathsf{X}_{(0,1]}$, and $\mathsf{U}_{(0,1]}$, respectively. Other boolean operators such as $\vee$ (disjunction), and $\Rightarrow$ (implication) are defined in expected way. In addition to that, we also define three useful temporal operators $\mathsf{F}_I\, \varphi \equiv tt\, \mathsf{U}_I\, \varphi$ (eventually), $\mathsf{G}_I\, \varphi \equiv \neg\mathsf{F}_I\, \neg\varphi$ (globally), and $\phi\, \mathsf{R}_I\, \psi \equiv \neg(\neg\phi\, \mathsf{U}_I\, \neg\psi)$ (release). Similarly as LTL formulas, DLTL formulas can be *normalized, i.e.* transformed into a form, where all negations are applied only directly to atomic propositions.

An example of a system with degradation is given in Figure 1.

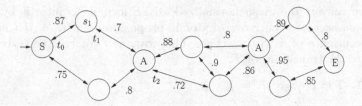

Fig. 1. An example of a signal coverage map. States of the systems represent geographical places and transition between them are labelled with constants determining how much the signal degrades between the places. For instance, signal degrades to 87% of its quality between states S and s_1. A starting point (sender) is labelled with S and an end point (receiver) is labelled with E. The signal is fully restored in amplifiers, which are labelled with A. An example of a run in such a system is $\pi = S \xrightarrow{t_0} s_1 \xrightarrow{t_1} A \xrightarrow{t_2} \ldots$. The level of degradation up to state A on this run is $\mathbb{D}_\pi(2) = 0.87 \cdot 0.7 = 0.609$, meaning that the signal quality in A will be 60.9% of its quality in S. An example of a DLTL formula for this system is $\mathsf{F}E \wedge \mathsf{G}\big((S \vee A) \Rightarrow \mathsf{F}_{[0.9,1]}(A \vee E)\big)$ saying that on a run satisfying the formula the signal eventually reaches E while its quality does not decrease under 90% of its full strength.

3.3   DLTL Model Checking

The verification question we would like to answer is, whether all runs of a given TSD satisfy a given DLTL formula. We approach this problem via its conversion into verification problem for timed automata and MITL formulas. During the conversion process, two major differences have to be overcome: (1) in systems with degradation, the degradation decreases along the *transitions*, whereas in timed systems, the time passes in the *states*, and (2) the degradation constants are meant to be *multiplied*, whereas time passes in *additive* fashion. We address the first one by modelling transitions of a TSD as states of a timed automaton and the second one by applying logarithm to the degradation constants. We build on the fact that $\log a \cdot b = \log a + \log b$.

Assume that the given DLTL formula φ sastisfies two additional assumptions: (1) the intervals that appear in φ are non-singular, and (2) φ does not contain next operator. These restrictions allow us to translate φ into a MITL formula. We discuss how to deal with full DLTL later.

First, we preprocess the given TSD $\mathcal{T} = (S, Act, T, D, S_{init}, AP, L)$ into a TSD $\mathcal{T}' = (S', Act', T', D', S_{init}, AP', L')$ this way:

- $S' = S \cup S \times T \cup T \times S$,
- $Act' = Act \cup \{\epsilon\}$, where $\epsilon \notin Act$,
- $T' = \{(s_1, \sigma, (s_1, t)), ((s_1, t), \epsilon, (t, s_2)), ((t, s_2), \epsilon, s_2) \mid t = (s_1, \sigma, s_2) \in T\}$,
- $D'(t) = 1$ for all transitions leading from and to some $s \in S$, and
  $D'\big((s_1, t), \epsilon, (t, s_2)\big) = D(t)$ for the rest of the transitions,
- $AP' = AP \cup \{\alpha_\epsilon\}$, where $\alpha_\epsilon \notin AP$,
- $L'(s) = L(s)$ for all $s \in S$, and $L'(s) = \{\alpha_\epsilon\}$ for all $s \in S' \setminus S$.

Second, we convert the given normalized DLTL formula φ into φ' by replacing each *non-negated* occurrence of atomic proposition α with $\alpha_\epsilon \cup \alpha$ and each *negated* occurrence of α with $\alpha_\epsilon \cup \neg\alpha$. This way, we "ignore" the states corresponding to the transitions of $\mathcal{T}$.

Lemma 1. $\mathcal{T} \models \varphi \iff \mathcal{T}' \models \varphi'$

Proof: (Sketch.) Each run π producing word $\alpha_0\alpha_1\alpha_2 \dots$ in $\mathcal{T}$ maps to a single run π' producing word $\alpha_0\alpha_\epsilon\alpha_\epsilon\alpha_1\alpha_\epsilon\alpha_\epsilon\alpha_2 \dots$ in $\mathcal{T}'$. It is easy to show by induction, that for all $i \geq 2$ it holds that $\pi^i \models \varphi$ if and only if $\pi'^{3i-4} \models \varphi' \wedge \pi'^{3i-3} \models \varphi' \wedge \pi'^{3i-2} \models \varphi'$. Finally, we get that $\pi \models \varphi \iff \pi' \models \varphi'$.

Given TSD $\mathcal{T}$ and the corresponding TSD $\mathcal{T}'$, we build a timed automaton $\mathcal{A} = (S \cup T, Act', \{x\}, \delta, S_{init}, Inv, AP', L_\mathcal{A})$, where

- $\delta = \{(s_1, x = 0, \sigma, \emptyset, t), (t, x = \log D(t), \epsilon, \{x\}, s_2) \mid t = (s_1, \sigma, s_2) \in T\}$,
- $Inv(s) = x \leq 0$ for all $s \in S$, and $Inv(t) = x \leq \log D(t)$ for all $t \in T$,
- $L_\mathcal{A}(s) = L(s)$ for all $s \in S$, and $L_\mathcal{A}(t) = \{\alpha_\epsilon\}$ for all $t \in T$.

A DLTL formula φ' is transformed into a MITL formula ϑ as follows: Each occurrence of interval (a, b) is replaced with $(\log b, \log a)$, and analogously, each occurrence of $(a, b]$, $[a, b]$, and $[a, b)$ is replaced with $[\log b, \log a)$, $[\log b, \log a]$, and $(\log b, \log a]$, respectively. In case $a = 0$, we use ∞ instead of $\log a$. The rest of the formula remains the same.

Lemma 2. $\mathcal{T}' \models \varphi' \iff \mathcal{A} \models \vartheta$

Proof: Follows directly from the structure of $\mathcal{T}'$, construction of $\mathcal{A}$, and the fact, that $log(a \cdot b) = \log a + \log b$, and $0 < a \leq c \leq b \leq 1 \Rightarrow 0 \leq \log b \leq \log c \leq \log a < 1$.

Corollary 1. $\mathcal{T} \models \varphi \iff \mathcal{A} \models \vartheta$

The remaining task is to check emptiness of $\mathcal{L}(\mathcal{A}) \cap \mathcal{L}(\neg\vartheta)$. Without loss of generality, assume that $\neg\vartheta$ is normalized from now on. Let us assume that $\log c$ is a rational number for all constants c that appear in formula $\neg\vartheta$. We will discuss the remaining cases shortly. First, we pick a suitable constant $p \in \mathbb{Q}_{>0}$ and multiply all the constants both in $\mathcal{A}$ and $\neg\vartheta$ with p in order to make all the interval bounds appearing in formula $\neg\vartheta$ integer. Now, $\neg\vartheta$ can be translated into a timed automaton $\mathcal{B}_{\neg\vartheta}$. The rest is just well-known checking language emptiness for timed automaton $\mathcal{A} \times \mathcal{B}_{\neg\vartheta}$.

Of course, it is not always the case that $\log c$ is a rational number for each constant c that appears in $\neg\vartheta$. Furthermore, in a number of cases it is not even possible to find n, such that $\log_n c$ is rational. Therefore, necessarily, some kind of approximation is needed.

Lemma 3. *Consider intervals I and I', such that interval I' is within I. For any run ρ, it holds that $\rho \models \varphi \cup_{I'} \psi \Rightarrow \varphi \cup_I \psi$, and dually, $\rho \models \varphi R_I \psi \Rightarrow \varphi R_{I'} \psi$.*

Proof: Directly from expanding definition of $\cup_I$ and R_I, respectively.

Based on Corollary 1 and Lemma 3, the model checking procedure can be summarized as follows:

1. Transform TSD $\mathcal{T}$ into timed automaton $\mathcal{A}$ and DLTL formula φ into MITL formula ϑ. Obtain $\neg\vartheta$ as normalized negation of ϑ.
2. Pick a precision constant $p \in \mathbb{Q}_{>0}$, and multiply all constants both in $\mathcal{A}$ and in $\neg\vartheta$ with p.
3. In each U_I operator in $\neg\vartheta$ replace left bound a and right bound b of interval I with $\lceil a \rceil$ and $\lfloor b \rfloor$, respectively. Dually for each R_I operator.
4. Translate $\neg\vartheta$ into $\mathcal{B}_{\neg\vartheta}$ and check, whether $\mathcal{L}(\mathcal{A}) \cap \mathcal{L}(\mathcal{B}_{\neg\vartheta}) = \emptyset$. If yes, then $\mathcal{T} \models \varphi$, otherwise continue on line 5.
5. In each U_I operator in of $\neg\vartheta$ replace left bound a and right bound b of interval I with $\lfloor a \rfloor$ and $\lceil b \rceil$, respectively. Dually for each R_I ope.
6. Translate $\neg\vartheta$ into $\mathcal{B}_{\neg\vartheta}$ and check, whether $\mathcal{L}(\mathcal{A}) \cap \mathcal{L}(\mathcal{B}_{\neg\vartheta}) = \emptyset$. If no, then $\mathcal{T} \not\models \varphi$, otherwise pick a precision constant $p' > p$ and repeat the procedure from line 3.

If the outlined procedure provides an answer, the answer is correct. On the other hand, the termination is not guaranteed and thus we can only answer model checking question with limited, although arbitrary precision. The price paid for increasing precision is rapidly increasing computational demands. The size of timed automaton $\mathcal{B}_{\neg\vartheta}$ is $O(2^{N \cdot K})$ with $N \cdot K$ clocks, where N is the number of atomic propositions, boolean, and temporal operators in $\neg\vartheta$ and $K - 1$ is the largest integer constant in $\neg\vartheta$ [1]. Higher precision causes increase of the constant K, and therefore also significant increase of the size of $\mathcal{B}_{\neg\vartheta}$.

Remark 1. For the sake of presentation simplicity, we assumed continuous semantics of timed automata and MITL, although the dynamics of a TSD is purely discrete. Therefore we had to restrict DLTL formulas not to contain next operators and singular intervals. In order to solve the model checking problem for full DLTL, we have to consider discrete semantics of timed automata and Metric Temporal Logic (which is MITL including singular intervals). The approach is analogous to the one we presented above, but approximation is needed not only in the formulas, but in the timed automaton as well. The complexity of emptiness checking of $\mathcal{L}(\mathcal{A}) \cap \mathcal{L}(\neg\vartheta)$ remains EXPSPACE-complete and dependent on the size of constants appearing in $\neg\vartheta$ [2].

4   DLTL Viewed as a Probabilistic Logic

In this section we focus on probability viewed as a degrading quality. In [5] we showed that Markov Decision Processes (MDPs, [6], [11]) are a specialized form of transition systems with degradation and that there exist two MDPs that are indistinguishable by any LTL ([10]), PCTL ([7]), or PCTL* ([3]) formula, but are distinguishable by a BADC. The question is, whether there exist two LTL, PLTL, and PCTL indistinguishable MDPs that can be distinguished with a DLTL formula. In this section we show that this is the case, which proves the incomparable expressiveness of DLTL with respect to LTL, PCTL, and PCTL*.

Markov Decision Processes. Let $\mathcal{T} = (S, Act, T, D, S_{init}, AP, L)$ be a transition system with degradation extended with the following restriction on the transition relation T:

$$\forall s_1 \in S, \forall a \in Act : \sum_{t=(s_1,a,s_2)\in T} D(t) = 1 \text{ or } 0.$$

When we think of probability as of a system quality that degrades in time, the transition systems with degradation restricted as above are syntactically equivalent to Markov decision processes.

We showed in [5] that two MDPs given in Figure 2 are indistinguishable by any LTL, PCTL or even PCTL* formula. However, a DLTL formula

$$\varphi = \neg(a \, \mathsf{U}_{[0,0.7]} \, \neg a)$$

is satisfied for $\mathcal{M}$, but not for $\mathcal{M}'$. In $\mathcal{M}$, there exists no run satisfying $a \, \mathsf{U}_{[0,0.7]} \, \neg a$, because the level of degradation between $\pi(1)$ and $\pi(2)$ is 1 for all runs π. On the other hand, there is a run $\pi' = s_0' \xrightarrow{\gamma} s_1' \ldots$ in $\mathcal{M}'$ satisfying $a \, \mathsf{U}_{[0,0.7]} \, \neg a$. The level of degradation between $\pi'(1)$ and $\pi'(2)$ is 0.5.

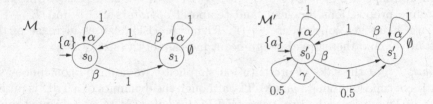

Fig. 2. Two MDPs indistinguishable by any LTL, PCTL, or PCTL* formula

DLTL allows us to capture quite different aspects than the usual probabilistic logics. Whereas there, we look for probability of a whole set of runs that satisfy a given property, in DLTL approach we aim at prefixes of individual runs and measure how much the probability degrades if the prefix is extended with a transition. In other words, with DLTL we are able to express the amount of contribution to the target probability of a set of runs that is brought by the set of runs exhibiting the same finite prefix. Furthermore, unlike in probabilistic LTL, the requirements on the level of degradation can be nested in DLTL formulas.

5   Conclusions and Future Work

In this paper we aimed at quantitative properties of systems with degradation. We introduced a new version of linear temporal logic that allows for specification of requirements on the level of degradation of individual system runs. We showed a connection between systems with degradation and timed automata and used MITL model checking algorithm to solve DLTL model checking problem.

The solution suffers from two major drawbacks. First, the verification problem can be answered only with limited precision, and second, higher precision causes rapidly higher computational demands. In our future work, we plan to overcome these issues by introducing a direct translation process from DLTL formulas into BADCs. Another future focus of ours is on control strategy synthesis for systems with degradation from DLTL specifications, on continuous and hybrid systems with degradation, and also on a case study.

References

1. Alur, R., Feder, T., Henzinger, T.A.: The benefits of relaxing punctuality. Journal of the ACM 43, 116–146 (1996)
2. Alur, R., Henzinger, T.A.: Real-time logics: complexity and expressiveness. In: Information and Computation – Special issue: selections from 1990 IEEE Symposium on Logic in Computer Science, vol. 104, pp. 35–77 (1993), doi:10.1006/inco.1993.1025
3. Aziz, A., Singhal, V., Balarin, F., Brayton, R.K., Sangiovanni-Vincentelli, A.L.: It Usually Works: The Temporal Logic of Stochastic Systems. In: Wolper, P. (ed.) CAV 1995. LNCS, vol. 939, pp. 155–165. Springer, Heidelberg (1995)
4. Baier, C., Katoen, J.P.: Principles of Model Checking. The MIT Press (2008)
5. Barnat, J., Černá, I., Tůmová, J.: Quantitative model checking of systems with degradation. In: QEST 2009, pp. 21–30 (2009)
6. Derman, C.: Finite State Markovian Decision Processes. Academic Press, Inc., Orlando (1970)
7. Hansson, H., Jonsson, B.: A Framework for Reasoning about Time and Reliability. In: IEEE Real-Time Systems Symposium, pp. 102–111 (1989)
8. iFEST homepage (August 2011), http://www.artemis-ifest.eu
9. Kaivola, R., Ghughal, R., Narasimhan, N., Telfer, A., Whittemore, J., Pandav, S., Slobodová, A., Taylor, C., Frolov, V., Reeber, E., Naik, A.: Replacing Testing with Formal Verification in Intel ® Coretm i7 Processor Execution Engine Validation. In: Bouajjani, A., Maler, O. (eds.) CAV 2009. LNCS, vol. 5643, pp. 414–429. Springer, Heidelberg (2009)
10. Pnueli, A.: The temporal logic of programs. In: Proceedings of the 18th IEEE Symposium on the Foundations of Computer Science, pp. 46–57. IEEE Computer Society Press (1977)
11. Puterman, M.L.: Markov Decision Processes-Discrete Stochastic Dynamic Programming. John Wiley &Sons, New York (1994)

Basic Operations
on Binary Suffix-Free Languages[*]

Roland Cmorik[1] and Galina Jirásková[2]

[1] Institute of Computer Science, P.J. Šafárik University,
Jesenná 5, 041 54 Košice, Slovakia
roland.cmorik@gmail.com
[2] Mathematical Institute, Slovak Academy of Sciences,
Grešákova 6, 040 01 Košice, Slovakia
jiraskov@saske.sk

Abstract. We give a characterization of nondeterministic automata accepting suffix-free languages, and a sufficient condition on deterministic automata to accept suffix-free languages. Then we investigate the state complexity of basic operations on binary suffix-free regular languages. In particular, we show that the upper bounds on the state complexity of all the boolean operations as well as of Kleene star are tight in the binary case. On the other hand, we prove that the bound for reversal cannot be met by binary languages. This solves several open questions stated by Han and Salomaa (Theoret. Comput. Sci. 410, 2537-2548, 2009).

1 Introduction

A language is suffix-free if it does not contain two strings, one of which is a proper suffix of the other. Motivating by suffix-freeness property of some codes used in information processing and data compression, Han and Salomaa [8] examined state complexity of basic operations on suffix-free regular languages. This is a part of research devoted to investigation of the state complexity of regular operations in various subclasses of the class of regular languages [1,3,4,5,7,9,10].

Here we continue this research, and study the class of suffix-free languages in more detail. We first give a characterization of nondeterministic finite automata recognizing suffix-free languages. Using this characterization we state a sufficient condition on a deterministic finite automaton to accept a suffix-free language. This allows us to avoid proofs of suffix-freeness of languages throughout the paper. Then we study the state complexity of operations in the class of binary suffix-free languages. In particular, we show that the bounds for all the boolean operations as well as for Kleene star are tight in the binary case. On the other hand, the bound for reversal, that is tight in the ternary case [8], cannot be met by binary languages. We provide lower and upper bounds on the state complexity of reversal of binary suffix-free languages. In the case of concatenation, where witness languages in [8] are defined over a four-letter alphabet, we give ternary worst-case languages. We conclude the paper with several open problems.

[*] Supported by VEGA grants 1/0035/09 and 2/0183/11, and grant APVV-0035-10.

Z. Kotásek et al. (Eds.): MEMICS 2011, LNCS 7119, pp. 94–102, 2012.

2   Suffix-Free Languages and Suffix-Free Automata

We assume that the reader is familiar with basic notions of formal languages and automata theory, and for all unexplained notions, we refer to [13,14]. State complexity of a regular language L, $\mathrm{sc}(L)$, is the smallest number of states in any *complete* deterministic finite automaton (dfa) recognizing language L. Non-deterministic finite automata (nfa's) throughout the paper are ε-free.

If $w = uv$, then v is a *suffix* of w, and if, moreover, $v \neq w$, then v is a *proper suffix* of w. A language L is *suffix-free* if for every string w in L, no proper suffix of w is in L. An automaton is *suffix-free* if it accepts a suffix-free language.

If an automaton accepts a non-empty suffix-free language, then it is *non-returning*, that is, no transition goes to the initial state [8]. A suffix-free minimal dfa must have a *dead state*, that is, a rejecting state that goes to itself on every symbol [8]. Our first theorem provides a characterization of suffix-free nfa's. Then, a lemma providing a sufficient condition for a dfa to be suffix-free follows. We use the lemma several times to prove the suffix-freeness of automata.

Theorem 1 (Characterization of Suffix-Free NFA's). *Consider a non-returning nfa without unreachable states and with the initial state s. Let L_q be the set of strings accepted by the nfa from state q. The nfa accepts a suffix-free language if and only if for each state q with $q \neq s$, the language $L_s \cap L_q$ is empty.*

Proof. Let a non-returning nfa accept a suffix-free language. Assume for a contradiction that there is a state q with $q \neq s$ such that $L_s \cap L_q \neq \emptyset$. Then there exists a string w that is accepted by the nfa from both s and q. Since state q is reachable, the initial state s goes to state q by a non-empty string u. Then the nfa accepts both strings w and uw, which is a contradiction. The converse can be proved by contradiction in a similar way. $\square$

Lemma 1. *Consider a non-returning dfa without unreachable states and with the sole final state. If there do not exist two distinct states that go to the same useful state by the same symbol of the input alphabet, then the dfa accepts a suffix-free language.*

Proof. By Theorem 1, if the dfa is not suffix-free, then there exists a string w accepted from the initial state and also from some other state. The two accepting paths end in the sole final state. So these paths must meet in some useful state q. The two predecessors of q on the two paths go to q by the same symbol. $\square$

3   Basic Operations on Binary Suffix-Free Languages

Han and Salomaa investigated the upper bounds for complexity of Kleene star, reversal and concatenation in [8]. They also presented witness languages for these bounds, however, the problem of tightness for small alphabets remained open. Here we investigate the complexity of mentioned operations on small alphabets.

First, we study the complexity of difference $(K \setminus L)$ and symmetric difference $(K \oplus L)$ that were not considered in [8]. Here we use the same witness binary languages as Olejár has used in [9] for union and intersection.

Theorem 2 (Boolean Operations). *Let K and L be suffix-free languages over an alphabet Σ with $\mathrm{sc}(K) = m$ and $\mathrm{sc}(L) = n$, where $m, n \geq 4$. Then*

1. $\mathrm{sc}(K \cap L) \leq mn - 2(m + n - 3)$;
2. $\mathrm{sc}(K \cup L), \mathrm{sc}(K \oplus L) \leq mn - (m + n - 2)$;
3. $\mathrm{sc}(K \setminus L) \leq mn - (m + 2n - 4)$.

All the bounds are tight if $|\Sigma| \geq 2$.

Proof. The cases of intersection and union hold according to [9]. Let Q_K, Q_L, F_K, F_L, s_K, s_L and d_K, d_L denote the sets of states, final states, the initial states, and the dead states of suffix-free dfa's for K and L, respectively. Consider the cross-product automaton for difference and symmetric difference, respectively. They differ only in final states. The set of final states is $(F_K \times Q_L) \setminus (F_K \times F_L)$ for difference and $(F_K \times Q_L \cup Q_K \times F_L) \setminus (F_K \times F_L)$ for symmetric difference. No pair (s_K, q) with $q \neq s_L$ and (p, s_L) with $p \neq s_K$ is reachable in the cross-product automaton since the two dfa's are non-returning. So we can remove these $m + n - 2$ unreachable states. Moreover, in the case of difference, there is no string accepted from a state, the first component of which is d_K. We can replace all such $n - 2$ states with one dead state. Therefore, the minimal dfa for difference has at most $mn - (m + n - 2) - (n - 2)$ states, and for symmetric difference at most $mn - (m + n - 2)$ states.

For tightness, consider the languages K and L accepted by dfa's A and B from [9], shown in Fig. 1, where dead states m and n, as well as all the transitions to dead states, are omitted. By Lemma 1, both languages are suffix-free.

Consider the cross-product automaton for the language $K - L$, where the set of final states is $\{(m - 1, j) \mid j \neq n - 1\}$. In the proofs of Lemma 6 and Lemma 7 in [9], it is shown that states (i, j) for $i = 2, \ldots, m$ and $j = 2, \ldots, n$, and the initial state $(1, 1)$ are reachable. We show that these states are pairwise distinguishable. State (m, n) is the only dead state. State $(1, 1)$ is distinguished from any other state by a string starting with b. Consider two distinct states (i, j) and (k, ℓ), where $2 \leq i, k \leq m - 1$, and $2 \leq j, \ell \leq n$. If $i < k$, then the string $a^n b^{m-1-k}$ is accepted from (k, ℓ) and rejected from (i, j). If $i = k$, then we can move the two states into two distinct states $(m - 1, j')$ and $(m - 1, \ell')$ in row $m - 1$ by a word in b^*. If $j' < \ell'$, then the string $a^{n-1-j'}$ is rejected from state $(m - 1, j')$ and accepted from state $(m - 1, \ell')$. This proves distinguishability of all the $mn - (m + 2n - 4)$ states.

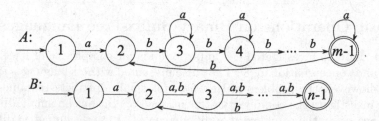

Fig. 1. Binary suffix-free dfa's meeting the upper bounds for Boolean operations

In the case of symmetric difference $K \oplus L$, the set of final states of the cross-product automaton is $\{(i,j) \mid i = m-1 \text{ or } j = n-1\} - \{(m-1, n-1)\}$. The proof of reachability is the same as above. State (m,n) is the only dead state, and state $(1,1)$ is distinguished from any other state by a string starting with b. State $(m-1, n-1)$ is distinguished from any other rejecting state by string a^m. Consider two distinct rejecting states (i,j) and (k,ℓ), both different from $(m-1, n-1)$. If $i = k$ and $j < \ell$, then they can be distinguished by a^{n-1-j}. If $i < k$, then string $b^{m-1-i}a^m$ distinguishes them. Now consider two distinct accepting states. States $(m-1, n-2)$ and $(m-2, n-1)$ can be distinguished by aa. Every other pair of accepting states can be distinguished by b since either one state of the pair goes to an accepting state and the second one to a rejecting state, or both go to different rejecting and, as shown above, distinguishable states. This concludes our proof. $\square$

The next theorem shows that the upper bound $2^{n-2}+1$ for Kleene star, shown to be tight for a four-letter alphabet [8], is tight even in the binary case.

Theorem 3 (Star). *Let L be a suffix-free language over an alphabet Σ with $sc(L) = n$, where $n \geq 6$. Then $sc(L^*) \leq 2^{n-2}+1$. The bound is tight if $|\Sigma| \geq 2$.*

Proof. The upper bound is from [8]. For tightness, consider the binary dfa A depicted in Fig. 2, where $n \geq 6$. By Lemma 1, automaton A is suffix-free.

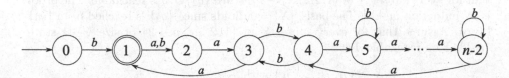

Fig. 2. Binary suffix-free dfa meeting the bound $2^{n-2}+1$ for star

According to [8], we can obtain an nfa for $L(A)^*$ from automaton A by adding a new transition from state 1 to itself by b, and making the initial state final. Furthermore we can omit the dead state. Let us denote the obtained $(n-1)$-state nfa for $L(A)^*$ by A'. If we omit the initial state of nfa A', and consider state 1 as the initial state, then we get an $(n-2)$-state nfa which is isomorphic to the reverse of the $(n-2)$-state Šebej's automaton [12] meeting the upper bound 2^{n-2} for reversal. This means that in the subset automaton corresponding to nfa A', all the subsets of $\{1, 2, \ldots, n-2\}$ are reachable and pairwise distinguishable. The initial state of the subset automaton is state $\{0\}$, which is final. The string a^3 distinguishes state $\{0\}$ from any other final state. $\square$

Now we investigate the state complexity of concatenation of two suffix-free languages. The upper bound is $(m-1)2^{n-2}+1$ by [8], where its tightness for a four-letter alphabet is also proved. We start with the ternary case.

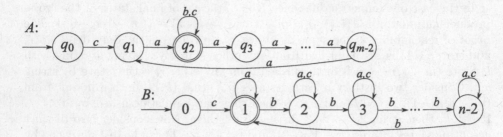

Fig. 3. Suffix-free dfa's meeting the bound $(m-1)2^{n-2}+1$ for concatenation

Theorem 4 (Concatenation: Ternary Case). *Let K and L be suffix-free languages over an alphabet Σ with $\mathrm{sc}(K) = m$ and $\mathrm{sc}(L) = n$, where $m \geq 4$, $n \geq 3$. Then $\mathrm{sc}(KL) \leq (m-1)2^{n-2}+1$, and the bound is tight if $|\Sigma| \geq 3$.*

Proof. The upper bound is from [8]. For tightness, consider ternary regular languages K and L accepted by the dfa's A and B shown in Fig. 3; to keep the figure transparent, we omit the dead states q_{m-1} and $n-1$, and all the transitions to the dead states. By Lemma 1, languages K and L are suffix-free.

Construct an nfa for language KL from dfa's A and B by adding the transition on c from state q_2 to state 1 and by declaring q_2 as a rejecting state.

The initial state of the corresponding subset automaton is $\{q_0\}$. We first show that for every subset X of $\{1, 2, \ldots, n-2\}$, state $\{q_2\} \cup X$ is reachable. The proof is by induction on $|X|$. The basis, $|X| = 0$, holds since $\{q_2\}$ is reached from $\{q_0\}$ by ca. Assume that for every subset Y of $\{1, 2, \ldots, n-2\}$ of size $k-1$ state $\{q_2\} \cup Y$ is reachable. Let

$$X = \{j_1, j_2, \ldots, j_k\} \text{ with } j_1 < j_2 < \cdots < j_k$$

be a subset of $\{1, 2, \ldots, n-2\}$ of size k. Let

$$Y = \{j_2 - j_1 + 1, \ldots, j_k - j_1 + 1\}.$$

Then state $\{q_2\} \cup Y$ is reachable by the induction hypothesis. Next, state $\{q_2\} \cup Y$ goes to $\{q_2\} \cup X$ by cb^{j_1-1}. Now if $i \in \{1, \ldots, m-2\}$, then state $\{q_i\} \cup X$ is reached from state $\{q_2\} \cup X$ by string a^{m-4+i}. State $\{q_{m-1}\} \cup X$ is reached from state $\{q_2\} \cup X$ by $b^{n-3}ab$. This proves the reachability of $(m-1)2^{n-2}+1$ states.

It remains to show that these states are pairwise distinguishable. Since string cac is accepted by the nfa only from state q_0, the initial state $\{q_0\}$ of the subset automaton is distinguishable from any other state. States $\{q_i\} \cup X$ and $\{q_j\} \cup Y$ with $i < j$ are distinguished by $a^{m-i}c$. Finally, two states $\{q_i\} \cup X$ and $\{q_i\} \cup Y$ with $X \neq Y$ differ in a state j in $\{1, 2, \ldots, n-2\}$, and so the string b^{n-j-1} distinguishes the two states. $\square$

Next we investigate the binary case. We present an m-state dfa and an n-state dfa such that the state complexity of $L(A)L(B)$ is $(m-1)2^{n-2}$ providing that $m-2$ and $n-2$ are relatively prime numbers.

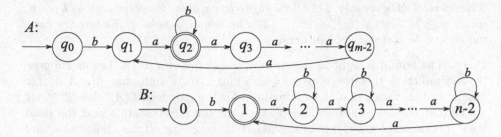

Fig. 4. Suffix-free dfa's A and B on binary alphabet

Theorem 5 (Concatenation: Binary Case). *Let $m \geq 4$, $n \geq 3$, and let $m-2$ and $n-2$ be relatively prime. There exist binary suffix-free regular languages K and L with $\mathrm{sc}(K) = m$ and $\mathrm{sc}(L) = n$ such that $\mathrm{sc}(KL) \geq (m-1)2^{n-2}$.*

Proof. Let K and L be the languages accepted by dfa's A and B shown in Fig. 4. By Lemma 1, languages K and L are suffix-free. Construct an nfa for KL from dfa's A and B by adding the transition on b from state q_2 to state 1, and by declaring q_2 as a rejecting state.

The lengths of the cycles in A and B are $m-2$ and $n-2$, respectively. Since $m-2$ and $n-2$ are relatively prime, there exist integers y and x such that $(m-2)y \equiv 1 \pmod{n-2}$ and $(n-2)x \equiv 1 \pmod{m-2}$.

The initial state of the subset automaton is $\{q_0\}$. We first show that for every subset X of $\{1, 2, \ldots, n-2\}$, state $\{q_2\} \cup X$ is reachable. The proof is by induction on $|X|$. The basis, $|X| = 0$, holds since $\{q_2\}$ is reached from the initial state $\{q_0\}$ by ba. Let $X = \{j_1, j_2, \ldots, j_k\}$ with $j_1 < j_2 < \cdots < j_k$ be a subset of $\{1, 2, \ldots, n-2\}$ of size k. State $\{q_2\} \cup X$ is reached from state $\{q_2\} \cup \{j_2 - j_1 + 1, \ldots, j_k - j_1 + 1\}$ by $ba^{(m-2)y(j_1-1)}$. Now if $i \in \{1, \ldots, m-2\}$, then state $\{q_i\} \cup X$ is reached from state $\{q_2\} \cup X$ by string $a^{(n-2)x(m-4+i)}$. If $i = m-1$ and $X \neq \{1, \ldots, n-2\}$, then there exists some $z \in \{1, \ldots, n-2\}$ such that $z \notin X$. By string $a^{(m-2)y(n-2-z)+1}$, state $\{q_3\} \cup X'$ is reached from $\{q_2\} \cup X$, where X' is a rotation of X such that $1 \notin X'$. Then from this state, we can reach $\{q_{m-1}\} \cup X'$ by reading b. Then we can reach the desired state $\{q_{m-1}\} \cup X$ by reading a^{z-1}. This proves the reachability of $(m-1)2^{n-2}$ states.

It remains to show that these states are pairwise distinguishable. Since string bab is accepted by the nfa only from state q_0, the initial state $\{q_0\}$ of the subset automaton is distinguishable from any other state. States $\{q_i\} \cup X$ and $\{q_j\} \cup Y$ with $i < j$ are distinguished by $a^{m-i}b$. Finally, states $\{q_i\} \cup X$ and $\{q_i\} \cup Y$ with $X \neq Y$ differ in a state j in $\{1, 2, \ldots, n-2\}$, and so string a^{n-j-1} distinguishes the two states.   □

Han and Salomaa [8] proved that $2^{n-2} + 1$ states are sufficient for reversal of suffix-free languages. They met this bound using a ternary alphabet. Theorem 6 shows that this upper bound cannot be met in the binary case.

Theorem 6 (Reversal). *Let L be a suffix-free regular language with $\mathrm{sc}(L) = n$, where $n \geq 3$. Then $\mathrm{sc}(L^R) \leq 2^{n-2} + 1$. The bound is tight in the ternary case, but cannot be met in the binary case.*

Proof. The bound is tight in the ternary case as shown in [8]. Let us suppose by contradiction that there exists a minimal n-state suffix-free dfa A over a binary alphabet such that the minimal dfa for the language $L(A)^R$ has $2^{n-2} + 1$ states. Let the set of states of A be Q, with the initial state s and the dead state d. Construct nfa A^R from the dfa A by reversing all the transitions, and by swapping the role of the initial and final states. The dead state d becomes unreachable in A^R, so we can omit it. The subset automaton corresponding to nfa A^R, after removing unreachable states, is a minimal dfa for $L(A)^R$ [2].

No subset X of Q such that $s \in X$ and $\{s\} \neq X$ is reachable in the subset automaton [8, Lemma 6]. It follows that the state set of the subset automaton consists of all the subsets of $Q - \{s, d\}$ and state $\{s\}$, that is, $2^{n-2} + 1$ states in total. This means that the set $Z = Q - \{s, d\}$ is reachable in the subset automaton. Since in dfa A there is a transition from state s to some state q in $Q - \{s, d\}$ on some letter a, in the subset automaton there is a transition on a from Z to a subset Y such that $s \in Y$. If there are some states p, p' in $Q - \{s, d\}$ such that p' goes to p by a in dfa A, then $p' \in Y$. Thus $\{s, p'\} \subseteq Y$. This is a contradiction since such a state cannot be reachable in the subset automaton.

There remains the case when there are no states p, p' in $Q - \{s, d\}$ such that p' goes to p by a in dfa A. Then there are just transitions on b among the states in $Q - \{s, d\}$. The determinization of $(n - 2)$-state nfa over a unary alphabet requires $e^{\Theta(\sqrt{(n-2)\ln(n-2)})} = o(2^{n-2} + 1)$ states [6]. $\qquad\square$

The next theorem provides upper and lower bounds on the state complexity of the reversal of suffix-free languages in the binary case.

Theorem 7 (Reversal: Binary Case). *Let $f_2(n)$ be the state complexity of reversal of binary suffix-free languages. Then $2^{n/2-2} + 1 \leq f_2(n) \leq 2^{n-4} + 2^{n-3} + 1$ for every integer n with $n \geq 12$.*

Proof. Let us prove the upper bound. We will continue our considerations from the proof of previous Theorem 6. Let K be a language over $\{a, b\}$ accepted by an n-state suffix-free minimal dfa A with the state set $Q = \{s, d, 1, 2, \ldots n - 2\}$, the initial state s, and the dead state d. Without loss of generality, state s goes to a state q in $\{1, 2, \ldots, n - 2\}$ by a. Construct nfa A^R as in the previous proof.

First consider the case when there are two states p and p' in $\{1, 2, \ldots, n - 2\}$ such that p goes to p' by a in dfa A. We have shown in the previous proof that we cannot reach the subset $Q - \{s, d\}$. Moreover, we cannot reach any subset containing both p and q due to the same argument. There are 2^{n-4} subsets of $Q - \{s, d\}$ that did not contain neither p nor q. And there are 2^{n-3} subsets that contain at least one but not both of them. So, including the final state $\{s\}$, there are at most $2^{n-4} + 2^{n-3} + 1$ states in the corresponding subset automaton. If among the states in $\{1, 2, \ldots, n - 2\}$, there are just transitions on symbol b, then the state complexity of K^R is asymptotically equal to $1 + e^{\sqrt{(n-2)\ln(n-2)}}$.

Now we prove the lower bound. Consider the language $\#L_{m-2}$, where L_{m-2} is the language over $\{a, b\}$ accepted by the $(m-2)$-state Šebej's dfa [12] meeting the upper bound 2^{m-2} for reversal. The minimal dfa $B_\#$ for $\#L_{m-2}$ has m states. Language $\#L_{m-2}$ is suffix-free. Now, we can construct an automaton C over a binary alphabet by encoding the three alphabet symbols of $B_\#$ with two symbols 0 and 1 as follows. For symbol $\#$ we use code 00, for symbol a code 10, and for b we use 11. For every state q in $B_\#$, we add two special states q' and q'', and replace the transitions from q as follows. The transition from q to some $q_\#$ by $\#$ is replaced with two transitions: The first one goes from q to q' by 0, and the second one from q' to $q_\#$ by 0. The transition from q to some q_a by a is replaced with transitions from q to q'' by 1 and from q'' to q_a by 0. The transition from q to some q_b by b is replaced with transitions from q to q'' by 1 and from q'' to q_b by 1. All the transitions not defined above go to the dead state. The number of states in C is $3m$. However, there are $m + 1$ states that are equivalent to the dead state: For the initial state s, state s'' goes to the dead state d by both 0 and 1. For all states q except for s, q' goes to d by both 0 and 1, and in the case of d, also state d'' goes to d by 0 and 1. So we can replace all the mentioned special states with d. After removing these equivalent states, there remains $2m - 1$ states in C. Automaton C is deterministic. Let us prove that it is suffix-free. Suppose by contradiction that C accepts a string w and also its proper suffix v. Both are of even length, since strings of odd length are not accepted by C. So they can be decoded as w' and v', respectively, where v' is a suffix of w' and both are accepted by $B_\#$, which is a contradiction.

Now we prove that C accepts the encoded language of $B_\#$. If the length of a string w in $\{0, 1\}^*$ is odd, then it is rejected in C since it ends in a special state or in d. If the length is even, then w can be decoded and it is accepted in C if and only if the decoded w is accepted in $B_\#$. We construct nfa C' for language $L(C)^R$ by reversing all the transitions in C. In the corresponding subset automaton, we can reach all the $2^{m-2} + 1$ states which are pairwise distinguishable, as in the subset automaton for $L(B_\#)^R$. So if n is the size of the minimal dfa for the encoded language, then $L(C)^R$ requires at least $2^{n/2-2} + 1$ states.   □

4 Conclusions

We gave a characterization of suffix-free nfa's and a sufficient condition on a dfa to accept a suffix-free language. This allowed us to avoid proofs of suffix-freeness of all the languages we have used throughout the paper. Then we investigated the operational state complexity of suffix-free regular languages. We solved completely the case of difference, symmetric difference, and Kleene star since we proved that the general upper bounds for these operations can be met in the binary case.

In the case of concatenation, we provided ternary witness languages. For the binary case, we presented an example that almost meets the upper bound in infinitely many cases. It remains open whether the bound for concatenation can be met in the binary case.

Then we showed that the upper bound for reversal cannot be met in the binary case, and we also gave lower and upper bounds for that case. The exact value of the state complexity of reversal in the binary case remains open.

References

1. Bordihn, H., Holzer, M., Kutrib, M.: Determinization of finite automata accepting subregular languages. Theoret. Comput. Sci. 410, 3209–3222 (2009)
2. Brzozowski, J.: Canonical regular expressions and minimal state graphs for definite events. In: Mathematical Theory of Automata. MRI Symposia Series, vol. 12, pp. 529–561. Polytechnic Press, Polytechnic Institute of Brooklyn, NY (1962)
3. Brzozowski, J., Jirásková, G., Li, B.: Quotient complexity of ideal languages. In: López-Ortiz, A. (ed.) LATIN 2010. LNCS, vol. 6034, pp. 208–221. Springer, Heidelberg (2010)
4. Brzozowski, J., Jirásková, G., Zou, C.: Quotient complexity of closed languages. In: Ablayev, F., Mayr, E.W. (eds.) CSR 2010. LNCS, vol. 6072, pp. 84–95. Springer, Heidelberg (2010)
5. Câmpeanu, C., Salomaa, K., Culik II, K., Yu, S.: State complexity of basic operations on finite languages. In: Boldt, O., Jürgensen, H. (eds.) WIA 1999. LNCS, vol. 2214, pp. 60–70. Springer, Heidelberg (2001)
6. Chrobak, M.: Finite automata and unary languages. Theoret. Comput. Sci. 47, 149–158 (1986); Erratum: Theoret. Comput. Sci. 302, 497–498 (2003)
7. Han, Y.-S., Salomaa, K., Wood, D.: Operational state complexity of prefix-free regular languages. In: Automata, Formal Languages, and Related Topics, pp. 99–115. University of Szeged, Hungary (2009)
8. Han, Y.-S., Salomaa, K.: State complexity of basic operations on suffix-free regular languages. Theoret. Comput. Sci. 410, 2537–2548 (2009)
9. Jirásková, G., Olejár, P.: State complexity of intersection and union suffix-free languages and descriptional complexity. In: Bordihn, H., Freund, R., Holzer, M., Kutrib, M., Otto, F. (eds.) NCMA 2009, pp. 151–166. Osterreichische Computer Gesellschaft (2009)
10. Jirásková, G., Masopust, T.: Complexity in union-free regular languages. In: Gao, Y., Lu, H., Seki, S., Yu, S. (eds.) DLT 2010. LNCS, vol. 6224, pp. 255–266. Springer, Heidelberg (2010)
11. Rabin, M., Scott, D.: Finite automata and their decision problems. IBM Res. Develop. 3, 114–129 (1959)
12. Šebej, J.: Reversal of regular languages and state complexity. In: Pardubská, D. (ed.) ITAT 2010, pp. 47–54. P. J. Šafárik University of Košice, Slovakia (2010)
13. Sipser, M.: Introduction to the theory of computation. PWS Publishing Company, Boston (1997)
14. Yu, S.: Regular languages. In: Rozenberg, G., Salomaa, A. (eds.) Handbook of Formal Languages, vol. I, ch. 2, pp. 41–110. Springer, Heidelberg (1997)

Efficient Data Representation
of Large Job Schedules

Dalibor Klusáček and Hana Rudová

Faculty of Informatics, Masaryk University, Czech Republic
{xklusac,hanka}@fi.muni.cz

Abstract. The increasing popularity of advanced schedule-based techniques designed to solve Grid scheduling problems requires the use of efficient data structures to represent the constructed job schedules. Based on our previous research in the area of advanced scheduling algorithms we have developed data representation designed to maintain large job schedules. We provide new details of the applied representation, especially about the binary heap data structure. The heap guarantees good efficiency of the crucial schedule update procedure which is used to keep the schedule consistent and up-to-date subject to dynamically changing state of the system. We prove the time complexity related to the use of such a structure and — using an experimental evaluation — we demonstrate the performance of this structure even for very large job schedules.

1 Introduction

The *Grid* technology allows to build large and powerful computing infrastructures using relatively cheap hardware [5]. To guarantee good performance, efficient scheduling techniques are necessary. From this point of view, techniques using *schedule* become very important, as they allow to plan job execution ahead, predict the behavior of the system, guarantee job start time [11,6] or establish reservations [7,14]. Moreover, the use of schedule allows to easily *evaluate* the quality of constructed schedule using selected objective functions [9,15]. Then, its quality can be improved through the application of optimization algorithms, e.g., metaheuristics, as was shown in our earlier works [9,10] as well as by other researchers [18,16,1].

On the other hand, the use of schedule requires much more complicated data representation with respect to the common queue-based solutions that are widely applied in existing production schedulers. Such a data representation must guarantee good performance and scalability with respect to the size of the system. As the Grid scheduling is an on-line problem, the schedule is created subject to dynamically changing environment [13,9]. Typically, the number of jobs or the number of available machines are changing through the time. In order to remain consistent with the actual state of the system, the schedule must be *updated* according to the current situation. The *update procedure* is used to repair all information stored in the schedule when a dynamic event causes that previously computed values are no longer valid. There are several events that may cause

Z. Kotásek et al. (Eds.): MEMICS 2011, LNCS 7119, pp. 103–113, 2012.

such inconsistencies. For example, when a *machine failure* appears the schedule must be updated such that no job in the schedule is planned on that failed machine [8]. Another frequent event is an *early job completion*. When a job finishes earlier than expected the schedule must be updated. Typically, some jobs can be shifted to earlier time slots due to the premature job termination [11]. Last but not least, iterative optimization routines often *modify existing schedule* to improve the quality of the initial schedule. Each such modification requires an update so that the effect of this modification can be correctly evaluated using up-to-date data. Typically, it is necessary to compute some objective function to evaluate the modification. Here the update is always performed prior the evaluation so that the objective function is computed using correct data that reflect the "effect" of the recently performed modification [8]. Moreover, as the situation can change frequently, updates must be performed efficiently so that there is enough time left for the optimization phase. From this point of view, the most crucial goal is to use an *efficient update procedure*, which assures that all information concerning planned job execution are up-to-date in the schedule.

The update procedure shall not be confused with methods that are used to create or optimize the schedule. While these methods frequently use updates, the update procedure itself is not responsible for the creation or the optimization of the schedule. It only guarantees that the dynamic changes are correctly propagated into the schedule data structure. An overview of scheduling techniques that can be used to build and optimize the initial schedule can be found in [18,16,8].

In this work we closely describe an efficient schedule update procedure that uses data representation designed to successfully represent schedules of large Grid systems [9,8]. A binary heap structure [3] is applied to speed up the update routine, keeping the runtime in a decent level. Next, the asymptotic time-complexity of such procedure is analyzed. Finally, an experimental evaluation is presented proving the good scalability and low memory and runtime requirements of the applied solution.

2   Problem Description

Let us formally describe the requirements concerning the schedule data representation. We consider a Grid system that consists of m CPUs and n jobs. Each job j is characterized by its processing time p_j and by the number of requested CPUs $usage_j$. Intuitively, the schedule defines *when and where* jobs will be executed, introducing a two dimensional rectangular representation such that for each job the set of assigned CPUs and the time interval is specified. Here the x-axis represents the time and the y-axis represents the CPUs of the system. An example of such a schedule is shown in Fig. 1 (top left). Formally, the schedule assigns each job j a set of CPUs ($\mathcal{CPU}_j$) it will use, where the size of $\mathcal{CPU}_j$ is equal to $usage_j$. The schedule also specifies the time interval during which the job j will be executed. This interval is denoted by the expected start time S_j and completion time C_j. We do not consider job preemption, therefore $C_j - S_j = p_j$

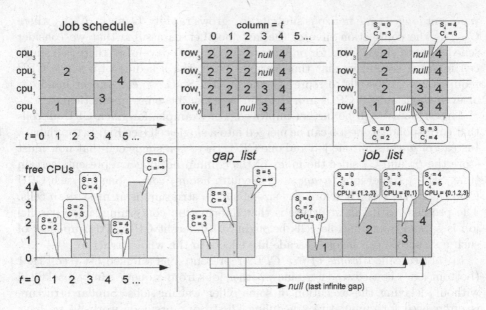

Fig. 1. Various data representations of job schedule

holds. Clearly, if the executions of two different jobs j_1 and j_2 overlap in time then $\mathcal{CPU}_{j_1} \cap \mathcal{CPU}_{j_2} = \emptyset$. We now proceed to the description of the applied data representation.

3   Data Representation of the Schedule

As we have already mentioned, queue-based scheduling systems use queue(s) to store jobs prior their execution. Here the scheduling decisions are often taken at the very last moment — when some machine(s) become available. Therefore, schedule-like structures are not necessary unless some planning ahead is required [8]. On the other hand, as soon as some advanced features such as predictability, evaluation of the quality of the generated solution, optimization routines or even advanced reservations are considered, the schedule becomes very useful structure as it depicts the future behavior of the system. It allows to predict the behavior of the system, to use evaluation when analyzing the quality of the solution, as well as to introduce optimization. Similarly, if advanced reservations are applied [14] some form of schedule must be used to establish and maintain them properly.

A trivial implementation of schedule is often used for static problems [12] where a matrix-like two dimensional array is used (see Fig. 1 (top middle)). Each cell of this array represents a plan for given CPU (y-axis (rows)) and given time (x-axis (columns)). More specifically, each cell contains either the identifier of a job being planned for that time period or no value (*null*) when there is no job currently planned. However, such structure is not suitable for schedules that represent longer time horizons since its size grows rapidly, being $m \cdot C_{max}$, where C_{max} is the completion time of the last job. Let us assume that we consider schedule for a single CPU for one month ($C_{max} = 30$ days). Let there is a single cell for each second in that time period. Then, the schedule of a single CPU requires 2,592,000 cells to represent one month. Since we can expect hundreds or even thousands of CPUs in a Grid this solution becomes impractical.

This structure can be further improved. For example, for given CPU all cells that correspond to one job can be merged into a single cell (see Fig. 1 (top right)). Instead of p_j cells for one job and one CPU, there is a single cell that now must store the S_j and C_j since the index of the column no longer represents certain time. Still, parallel jobs ($usage_j > 1$) require $usage_j$ cells — one for each CPU from the $\mathcal{CPU}_j$ set. Therefore, the size of such a structure is at most $m \cdot n$ cells. The problem with this structure is that information concerning single parallel job is spread over multiple cells belonging to different CPUs. Also updates of such a structure can invoke cascade-like effects in the whole structure.

In [11], so called *profile of free CPUs* represented as a linked list (see Fig. 1 (bottom left)) is used to determine whether jobs from a queue can be backfilled without delaying the execution of some older waiting jobs. Similar structure is often used for cumulative scheduling [2]. In our previous work [9] we have proposed a representation, where the schedule is represented as a linear list of jobs (*job_list*) and a list of so called *gaps* (*gap_list*) that represents the free CPUs. The *gap_list* is an analogy of the profile used in [11]. Both jobs and gaps in the lists are ordered according to their expected start times. Each job in this list stores its S_j, C_j and $\mathcal{CPU}_j$. Therefore, complete information as required by the definition in Section 2 is stored in a single cell of the list. All these parameters are computed using *UpdateSchedule* procedure once some job is added into the schedule. If two or more jobs in the schedule have the same start time, then the one being assigned to the CPU with the smallest *id* becomes the predecessor of the remaining jobs in the *job_list* and so on. *Gaps* represent unused periods of CPU time. They appears every time the number of available CPUs in the existing schedule is greater than the number of CPUs requested by the job(s) in the given time period. Just like jobs, gaps hold information about their start time, duration and usage. Here usage expresses the number of available (idle) CPUs in this gap. Moreover, each gap has a pointer to the nearest following job. If there is no following job (gap at the end of the *schedule*) this pointer is set to *null*. For given time t, there is always at most one gap in the *gap_list*. Two successive gaps in the *gap_list* have either different usage or the completion time of the earlier gap is smaller than the start time of the later gap. Otherwise, such gaps are merged into a single, longer gap. Fig. 1 (bottom right) shows an example of the applied data structure.

The use of this structure represents several benefits. First of all, it is very compact as each job is represented by a single cell. It can be shown that *job_list* and *gap_list* contain at most $2n + 1$ cells [8]. Moreover, as all gaps in the current schedule are stored in a separate list, these can be quickly used when necessary. For example, *gap_list* can be used when adding new job into the schedule [9].

This is a common operation used in several popular algorithms such as EASY or Conservative Backfilling [11]. Here, two or more adjacent gaps can be used for the new job. The pointer of the first selected gap is used to place the job into the *job_list*. This "gap-filling" approach is very useful as it significantly increases system utilization while respecting the start times of previously added jobs.

The most important and also demanding operation is the schedule update procedure called *UpdateSchedule*. It is a crucial part of the applied solution as it guarantees that schedule remains up-to-date subject to dynamically changing situation. As discussed in Section 1, various scenarios such as early job completions, machine failures or schedule modifications performed, e.g., by optimization algorithms can cause inconsistencies in the existing schedule. Typically, inconsistencies would appear in the internal values of jobs in the *job_list* or in the *gap_list*. In such situation, the *UpdateSchedule* procedure must recompute the internal values of all jobs in the *job_list* list and also construct a new *gap_list*. Otherwise, the schedule is not consistent with the new situation. As these updates can appear frequently, they must be handled efficiently. The rest of this paper describes *UpdateSchedule* implementation, its computational complexity and an experimental evaluation of the actual *UpdateSchedule* performance.

3.1 *UpdateSchedule* Procedure

The pseudo code of the *UpdateSchedule* procedure is shown in Algorithm 1. It uses two inputs — the *job_list* which represents the schedule that shall be updated and an auxiliary data structure called *first_free_slots* which stores information about the first free time slot on each working CPU. Using them, the *UpdateSchedule* procedure computes new and up-to-date "coordinates" for all n jobs, starting with the first job in *job_list* and continuing in the linear order of the list (lines 2–11). Formally, based on the *first_free_slots* structure and using known job's $usage_j$ and p_j parameters, new and up-to-date S_j, C_j and CPU_j values are computed for each job j in the *job_list*.

Algorithm 1. *UpdateSchedule(job_list, first_free_slots)*

1: *gap_list* := null;
2: **for** i := 1 to n **do**
3:      j := select i-th job in the *job_list*;
4:      S_j := find earliest start time S_j using the *first_free_slots*;
5:      C_j := $S_j + p_j$;
6:      CPU_j := compute the set of assigned CPUs;
7:      **if** gap(s) appeared "in front" of j **then**
8:          append gap(s) that appeared "in front" of j to *gap_list*;
9:      **end if**
10: *first_free_slots* := set entries corresponding to CPUs from CPU_j equal to C_j;
11: **end for**

The update works as follows. At first, the previous *gap_list* is deleted (line 1) as it will be newly constructed during the update. Next, new and up-to-date

S_j, C_j and $\mathcal{CPU}_j$ values are computed for each job (lines 4–6) and the newly constructed *gap_list* is extended with gap(s) that appeared "in front" of the job j (lines 7–9). Such gap(s) is identified as the earliest start time S_j is being found[1]. Finally, the auxiliary *first_free_slots* structure is updated such that entries that correspond to CPUs assigned to job j ($\mathcal{CPU}_j$) are set equal to the expected completion time C_j of the job (line 10) and a new iteration starts.

Once the *UpdateSchedule* procedure finishes, all schedule-related parameters of jobs in *job_list* as well as the *gap_list* are up-to-date. Now we can closely describe how the earliest start time of each job is found. Naturally, we can find the earliest start time by scanning the completion time of every job "in front" of the currently updated job. However, this solution is impractical, as its complexity was shown to be quadratic with respect to the number of jobs [4,11]. Instead of that, we continuously maintain the *first_free_slots* structure that stores information about the first free slot on each CPU. The design of this structure is the key to the good performance. The simplest solution would use an unordered array of size m. Here, the i-th cell would represent the earliest time when i-th CPU becomes available. However, such data structure is not very efficient when searching for minimal values. In general, $usage_j \leq m$ therefore the number of operations required to find the earliest start time of job can grow up to m^2 as the minimum must be found $usage_j$-times. Then, for all n jobs the time complexity would be in $\mathcal{O}\left(n \cdot m^2\right)$ which is inefficient. Instead of that, we use a *binary heap* which is much more time-efficient when searching for minimal values [3], allowing to keep the time complexity of *UpdateSchedule* procedure in $\mathcal{O}\left(n \cdot m\right)$ as we show in the following text.

For our purpose, the binary heap is applied in the following fashion. Each node of the heap stores a key representing the earliest available time (t_e) on some CPU(s). Moreover, each node contains a list of CPU IDs that all become free at the time t_e. In another words, if the time t_e is the same for two or more CPUs, their IDs are stored in this list, while t_e becomes the node's key in the heap. The heap is constructed according to the key values. The minimal key is the root of the heap. Let s (size) be the number of nodes in the heap. Let IDs_i be the list of CPU IDs at the i-th node of the heap. Clearly, as soon as the system contains at least one CPU then $s > 0$ as well as $s \leq m$. The latter guarantees that there are at most m nodes in the heap. Finally, $\sum_{i=1}^{s}|IDs_i| = m$ assures that the total number of CPU IDs stored in the heap is the same as the number of CPUs (m). Using a binary heap, the complexity when finding the minimal node is in $\mathcal{O}\left(1\right)$, the minimal node can be extracted in $\mathcal{O}\left(\log m\right)$ and a new node is inserted within $\mathcal{O}\left(\log m\right)$ [3].

3.2   Complexity of the *UpdateSchedule* Procedure

We now proceed to the complexity analysis of the *UpdateSchedule* procedure.

---

[1] For example, once the start time of the third job S_3 is established (see Fig. 1 top left), one gap located between the first and the third job is found. The gap is detected as S_3 is greater than the earliest free time on cpu_0 which is equal to C_1 in this case.

Theorem 1. *Let m be the number of CPUs in the system and let n be the number of jobs in the job_list. Then the time complexity of UpdateSchedule procedure is in $\mathcal{O}(n \cdot m)$.*

Proof. We first analyze the complexity of the steps performed in one loop of Algorithm 1, i.e., the complexity of lines 3–10.

line 3: $\mathcal{O}(1)$.

line 4: $\mathcal{O}(usage_j \cdot \log m)$. In the worst case $usage_j$ nodes must be extracted from the heap to find the earliest start time S_j for the job j.[2] Often the situation is much better. Let r be the root node of the heap. Let $size_r$ be the number of CPU IDs stored in the root r ($size_r = |IDs_r|$). In the best case $size_r > usage_j$ which means that no node has to be extracted from the heap and the complexity of finding the earliest start time is in $\mathcal{O}(usage_j)$ as only $usage_j$ steps are needed to remove the requested IDs from the list in node r.

lines 5–6: $\mathcal{O}(usage_j)$. $1 + usage_j$ steps are required to compute C_j and $\mathcal{CPU}_j$.

lines 7–9: $\mathcal{O}(usage_j)$. The gap_list is updated using at most $usage_j$ steps, since for a given job j at most $usage_j$ gaps can appear "in front" of it [8].

line 10: $\mathcal{O}(usage_j + m)$. When the update of the $first\_free\_slots$ structure (i.e., the heap) is performed, two situations can appear. If the C_j is the same as the key of some existing node in the heap, this existing node is extended. At most $usage_j + m$ steps are needed as there are at most m nodes in the heap, and $usage_j$ steps are needed to update the IDs_i list in the selected node i. Otherwise, one new node is inserted in the heap ($usage_j + \log m$ steps). Together, the update of the $first\_free\_slots$ structure is in $\mathcal{O}(usage_j + m + \log m) = \mathcal{O}(usage_j + m)$.

So far we have clarified the complexity of one iteration of Algorithm 1 that updates one job. We may now extend it to all n jobs, thus describing the complexity of the *UpdateSchedule* procedure. Without the loss of generality we assume that at the start of the procedure all CPUs are currently free and working, i.e., there are no failed machines. Therefore, at the beginning the heap contains only one node that stores all CPU IDs (m). This initial node is created in $\mathcal{O}(m)$ steps. The update is performed for all n jobs. Clearly, for each job the algorithm extracts at most $usage_j$ nodes from the heap (see **line 4**) and inserts at most one node in the heap (see **line 10**). Therefore, at most n nodes can be inserted into the heap during the execution of *UpdateSchedule* procedure. Since at the beginning the heap contains only one node and every job inserts at most one node into the heap then — for all jobs together — the algorithm cannot extract more than n nodes during its execution, therefore for all n jobs the time to compute **line 4** is bounded by $\mathcal{O}(n \cdot \log m)$. Then, for all n jobs the **lines 5–6** and **lines 7–9** are performed, requiring $2 \cdot \sum_{j=1}^{n} usage_j$ steps which is in $\mathcal{O}\left(\sum_{j=1}^{n} usage_j\right)$. Finally, the auxiliary $first\_free\_slots$ structure is updated (see **line 10**), which

---

[2] In the worst case all extracted nodes contain only one CPU ID.

for n jobs requires $\left(\sum_{j=1}^{n} usage_j\right) + n \cdot m$ steps. Together, the complexity of *UpdateSchedule* is shown in Eqn. 1.

$$\mathcal{O}\left(m\right) + \mathcal{O}\left(n \cdot \log m\right) + \mathcal{O}\left(\sum_{j=1}^{n} usage_j\right) + \mathcal{O}\left(\left(\sum_{j=1}^{n} usage_j\right) + n \cdot m\right) (1)$$

Since $usage_j \leq m$ holds, this equation can be further simplified as shown in Eqn. 2. Clearly, the complexity of *UpdateSchedule* is in $\mathcal{O}\left(n \cdot m\right)$ which concludes the proof of Theorem 1.

$$\begin{aligned} \mathcal{O}\left(m\right) + \mathcal{O}\left(n \cdot \log m\right) + \mathcal{O}\left(n \cdot m\right) + \mathcal{O}\left(n \cdot m + n \cdot m\right) \\ = \mathcal{O}\left(m + n \cdot \left(\log m + m\right)\right) \\ = \mathcal{O}\left(n \cdot m\right) \end{aligned} \quad (2)$$

□

4   Experimental Evaluation

In the previous section we have formally demonstrated that the application of binary heap can significantly decrease the time complexity of the *UpdateSchedule* procedure. In this section we present a synthetic experiment where the performance of the *UpdateSchedule* procedure is experimentally evaluated, measuring *memory* and *runtime* requirements subject to changing number of jobs and CPUs in the simulated system.

In the simulation, both m and n are varying, representing different size and different load of the system respectively. For m, we considered following values: $100, 200, 500, 1,000, 2,000, \ldots, 10,000$. For n, following values were applied: $100, 500, 1,000, 2,000, 5,000$ and $10,000$. Job parameters were generated synthetically using uniform distribution. Following ranges were used: job execution time (1–86,400) seconds, number of CPUs required by a job (1–128). In this experiment, all jobs were available at the same moment (at $t = 0$) as it was not necessary to simulate different job arrival times in this case. Once all n jobs were created the initial schedule was generated randomly and the experiment started, measuring the amount of used RAM and the actual runtime of the *UpdateSchedule* procedure. For each combination of m and n the experiment was repeated 20 times with different seed and the mean was calculated. All experiments were computed using an Intel QuadCore 2.6 GHz desktop machine with 2 GB of RAM.

The amount of used RAM is shown in the top part of Fig. 2. It grows proportionally to the number of jobs in the schedule which sounds with the expectations mentioned in Section 3, where we have shown that the size of the schedule structure is proportional to n [8]. Fig. 2 (bottom) shows the actual runtime of the *UpdateSchedule* procedure, which is very good as even the largest schedule is updated within only 40 ms. As we observed, the use of binary heap played a crucial role here. When we used an unordered array instead (see Section 3.1) the runtime increased up to 1,004 ms for the same problem instance. Clearly, the application of more powerful data structures makes good sense, keeping the runtime in a decent level even for large job schedules.

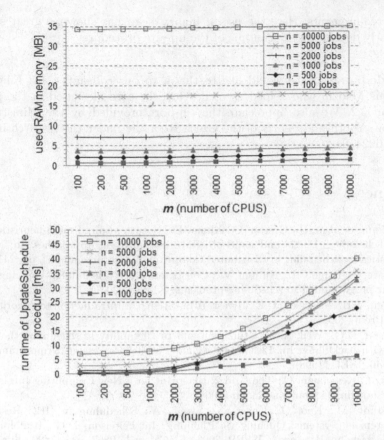

Fig. 2. Used RAM memory (top) and the runtime (bottom) of the *UpdateSchedule* procedure

Further experiments demonstrating applicability of described data structures on real-life data sets and standard benchmarks are available in [8].

5   Conclusion

This work has been motivated by the increasing popularity of advanced schedule-based techniques that represent promising direction when seeking for good performance in large scale computing systems such as Grids [15,7,6,11,14]. The dynamic character of the Grid system requires the use of efficient approaches when keeping the job schedule up-to-date. In this work we have described an efficient schedule update method designed to maintain large job schedules. All major features of the update procedure have been discussed, including the implementation details and the analysis of the computational complexity. Also an experimental evaluation has been presented showing the actual memory and runtime requirements. Here the use of binary heap has shown a great sense, significantly decreasing the runtime of the update procedure.

Acknowledgment. We would like to thank to our colleagues Jiří Filipovič and Matúš Madzin who helped us to develop the core idea used in the proof in Section 3.2. We also appreciate the support provided by the Ministry of Education, Youth and Sports of the Czech Republic under the research intent No. 0021622419.

References

1. Abraham, A., Liu, H., Grosan, C., Xhafa, F.: Nature inspired meta-heuristics for Grid scheduling: Single and multi-objective optimization approaches. In: Meta-heuristics for Scheduling in Distributed Computing Environments [17], pp. 247–272
2. Baptiste, P., Pape, C.L., Nuijten, W.: Constraint-based scheduling: Applying constraint programming to scheduling problems. Kluwer (2001)
3. Cormen, T.H., Leiserson, C.E., Rivest, R.L., Stein, C.: Introduction to Algorithms. MIT Press (2001)
4. Feitelson, D.G., Weil, A.M.: Utilization and predictability in scheduling the IBM SP2 with backfilling. In: 12th International Parallel Processing Symposium, pp. 542–546. IEEE (1998)
5. Foster, I., Kesselman, C.: The Grid 2: Blueprint for a New Computing Infrastructure, 2nd edn. Morgan Kaufmann (2004)
6. Hovestadt, M., Kao, O., Keller, A., Streit, A.: Scheduling in HPC Resource Management Systems: Queuing vs. Planning. In: Feitelson, D.G., Rudolph, L., Schwiegelshohn, U. (eds.) JSSPP 2003. LNCS, vol. 2862, pp. 1–20. Springer, Heidelberg (2003)
7. Keller, A., Reinefeld, A.: Anatomy of a resource management system for HPC clusters. Annual Review of Scalable Computing 3, 1–31 (2001)
8. Klusáček, D.: Event-based Optimization of Schedules for Grid Jobs. PhD thesis, Masaryk University (submitted, 2011)
9. Klusáček, D., Rudová, H.: Efficient Grid scheduling through the incremental schedule-based approach. Computational Intelligence: An International Journal 27(1), 4–22 (2011)
10. Klusáček, D., Rudová, H., Baraglia, R., Pasquali, M., Capannini, G.: Comparison of multi-criteria scheduling techniques. In: Grid Computing Achievements and Prospects, pp. 173–184. Springer, Heidelberg (2008)
11. Mu'alem, A.W., Feitelson, D.G.: Utilization, predictability, workloads, and user runtime estimates in scheduling the IBM SP2 with backfilling. IEEE Transactions on Parallel and Distributed Systems 12(6), 529–543 (2001)
12. Pinedo, M.: Scheduling: Theory, Algorithms, and Systems. Prentice-Hall (2002)
13. Sgall, J.: On-line scheduling – a survey. In: Fiat, A. (ed.) Dagstuhl Seminar 1996. LNCS, vol. 1442, pp. 196–231. Springer, Heidelberg (1998)
14. Smith, W., Foster, I., Taylor, V.: Scheduling with advanced reservations. In: International Parallel and Distributed Processing Symposium (IPDPS 2000), pp. 127–132 (2000)

15. Süß, W., Jakob, W., Quinte, A., Stucky, K.-U.: GORBA: A global optimising resource broker embedded in a Grid resource management system. In: International Conference on Parallel and Distributed Computing Systems, PDCS 2005, pp. 19–24. IASTED/ACTA Press (2005)
16. Xhafa, F., Abraham, A.: Meta-heuristics for Grid scheduling problems. In: Meta-heuristics for Scheduling in Distributed Computing Environments [17], pp. 1–37
17. Xhafa, F., Abraham, A.: Metaheuristics for Scheduling in Distributed Computing Environments. SCI, vol. 146. Springer, Heidelberg (2008)
18. Xhafa, F., Abraham, A.: Computational models and heuristic methods for Grid scheduling problems. Future Generation Computer Systems 26(4), 608–621 (2010)

Prefix-Free Regular Languages: Closure Properties, Difference, and Left Quotient*

Monika Krausová

Institute of Computer Science, P.J. Šafárik University,
Jesenná 5, 041 54 Košice, Slovakia
mon.krausova@gmail.com

Abstract. We show that the class of prefix-free languages is closed under intersection, difference, concatenation, square, and the k-th power and is not closed under complement, union, symmetric difference, Kleene star, reversal, cyclic shift, shuffle, and left quotient. Then, we study the state complexity of difference and left quotient of prefix-free regular languages. In both cases we get tight bounds. In the case of difference, the tight bound is $mn-m-2n+4$ and is met by binary languages. In the case of left quotient, the tight bound is 2^{n-1}. The bound is met by languages over $(n-1)$-letter alphabet and cannot be met using smaller alphabets.

1 Introduction

A language is prefix-free if it does not contain two strings one of which is a proper prefix of the other. Prefix-free languages are used in coding theory; for example, Huffman codes are prefix-free sets. Every minimal deterministic automaton recognizing a prefix-free regular language must have exactly one final state that goes to the dead state on every input symbol. Using this property, tight bounds on the state complexity of basic operations such as union, intersection, concatenation, star, and reversal have been obtained by Han *et al.* [1] and strengthen in [4,5], where also the tight bounds for symmetric difference and cyclic shift have been presented. The nondeterministic state complexity of basic operations has been studied in [2], and of cyclic shift and difference in [4], while [3] investigated the complexity of combined operations in the class of prefix-free languages.

Here we continue the research on properties of prefix-free languages. We start with closure properties. Then, we study the state complexity of difference and get the tight bound $mn-m-2n+4$. To prove tightness we use a binary alphabet. We next examine left quotient. The left quotient of regular languages has been investigated by Yu *at al.* in [7]. However, there is an error in the proof in [7], so we present a correct proof of the lower bound $2^n - 1$ on the state complexity of left quotient of regular languages. In the case of prefix-free languages, we get the tight bound 2^{n-1}. We show that the bound is tight for an alphabet consisting of at least $n - 1$ symbols. On the other hand, we prove that the bound cannot be met using any smaller alphabet.

* Research supported by VEGA grant 1/0035/09 "Combinatorial Structures and Complexity of Algorithms".

Z. Kotásek et al. (Eds.): MEMICS 2011, LNCS 7119, pp. 114–122, 2012.

2 Preliminaries

We assume that the reader is familiar with basic concepts of regular languages and finite automata and for unexplained notions we refer to [6].

For an alphabet Σ, let Σ^* be the set of all strings over Σ, including the empty string ε. A language is any subset of Σ^*. The difference of languages K and L over Σ is defined by $K - L = \{w \in \Sigma^* \mid w \in K \text{ and } w \notin L\}$, and left quotient of L by K is defined by $K \backslash L = \{x \in \Sigma^* \mid wx \in L \text{ for a string } w \text{ in } K\}$. We denote the power-set of a set X by 2^X.

A *deterministic finite automaton* (DFA) is a quintuple $M = (Q, \Sigma, \delta, s, F)$, where Q is a finite non-empty set of states, Σ is an input alphabet, $\delta : Q \times \Sigma \to Q$ is the transition function, $s \in Q$ is the initial state, and $F \subseteq Q$ is the set of final states. In this paper, all DFAs are assumed to be *complete*. The transition function δ is extended to the domain $Q \times \Sigma^*$ in a natural way. The *language accepted by DFA M* is the set of strings $L(M) = \{w \in \Sigma^* \mid \delta(s, w) \in F\}$.

A *nondeterministic finite automaton* (NFA) is a quintuple $M = (Q, \Sigma, \delta, S, F)$, where Q, Σ, and F are defined in the same way as for a DFA, S is the set of initial states, and δ is the nondeterministic transition function that maps $Q \times \Sigma$ to 2^Q. The transition function can be naturally extended to the domain $2^Q \times \Sigma^*$. The *language accepted by NFA M* is $L(M) = \{w \in \Sigma^* \mid \delta(S, w) \cap F \neq \emptyset\}$.

Two automata are *equivalent* if they recognize the same language. A DFA M is *minimal* if every DFA equivalent to M has at least as many states as M. It is well-known that a DFA is minimal if all of its states are reachable and pairwise distinguishable. The *state complexity* of a regular language L, sc(L), is the number of states in the minimal DFA recognizing language L.

Every NFA $(Q, \Sigma, \delta, S, F)$ can be converted to an equivalent deterministic automaton $(2^Q, \Sigma, \delta', S, F')$, where $\delta'(R, a) = \bigcup_{r \in R} \delta(r, a)$ for every set R in 2^Q and every symbol a in Σ, and $F' = \{R \in 2^Q \mid R \cap F \neq \emptyset\}$. We call the resulting DFA the *subset automaton* corresponding to NFA M. The subset automaton need not be minimal since some states may be unreachable or equivalent.

If u, v, w are strings in Σ^* and $w = uv$, then u is a *prefix* of w. If, moreover, $v \neq \varepsilon$, then u is a *proper prefix* of w. The empty string, ε, is a proper prefix of any string. A language is *prefix-free* if it does not contain two strings one of which is a proper prefix of the other.

3 Closure Properties

We start our investigation with the closure properties of the class of prefix-free regular languages. To prove the next result notice that every subset of a prefix-free language is a prefix-free language. Next, every language consisting of just one string is prefix-free.

Theorem 1. *The class of prefix-free regular languages is closed under intersection, difference, concatenation, square, and the k-th power and is not closed under complement, union, symmetric difference, Kleene star, reversal, cyclic shift, shuffle, and left quotient.*

Proof. Since every subset of a prefix-free language is a prefix-free language, the closeness under intersection and difference follows.

To show the closeness under concatenation, notice that having two DFAs such that both have just one final state going to the dead state on every input symbol, we can construct a DFA for concatenation as follows: First, remove the dead state of the first automaton and redirect all the transitions going to it to the dead state of the second DFA. Then, make the final state of the first automaton non-final and merge it with the initial state of the second automaton. The resulting DFA for concatenation has just one final state going to the dead state on every input symbol, therefore the concatenation is a prefix-free language.

The closeness under square and the k-th power follows from the closeness of the class of prefix-free regular languages under concatenation.

For all the other operations we present prefix-free languages such that the language resulting from the operation is not prefix-free:

Complement:	$\{a\}^c$	$\supseteq \{\varepsilon, aa, aaa\}$,
Union:	$\{a\} \cup \{ab\}$	$= \{a, ab\}$,
Symmetric difference:	$\{aa, ab\} \oplus \{ab, aab\}$	$= \{aa, aab\}$,
Kleene star:	$\{ab\}^*$	$\supseteq \{\varepsilon, ab, abab\}$,
Reversal:	$\{aa, abaa\}^R$	$= \{aa, aaba\}$,
Cyclic shift:	$Shift(\{aa, aba\})$	$= \{aa, aba, baa, aab\}$,
Shuffle:	$\{abb\} \sqcup \{a, ba\}$	$\supseteq \{abba, abbab\}$,
Left quotient:	$\{a, b\} \backslash \{aba, bbaba\}$	$= \{ba, baba\}$.

Hence, the non-closeness follows.   □

4   State Complexity of Difference

Now we turn our attention to the state complexity of difference of prefix-free regular languages. The operation of difference was not investigated in [1] at all. The upper bound and the ternary witness languages were claimed without any proof in [4]. Here we provide the proof of upper bound $mn - m - 2n + 4$, as well as binary worst-case examples.

Theorem 2. *Let $m \geq 4$, $n \geq 3$, and K and L be prefix-free regular languages with $sc(K) = m$ and $sc(L) = n$. Then, $sc(K - L) \leq mn - m - 2n + 4$ and the bound is tight in the binary case.*

Proof. First, we prove the upper bound. Let A and B be an m-state and an n-state DFAs over an alphabet Σ recognizing prefix-free languages and let their state sets be $P = \{0, 1, \ldots, m - 1\}$ and $Q = \{0, 1, \ldots, n - 1\}$, respectively, with the initial state 0 in both automata. Both automata must have exactly one final state that goes to the dead state on every input symbol. Without loss of generality, assume that states $m - 2$ and $n - 2$ are final, while states $m - 1$ and $n - 1$ are dead. Let the corresponding transition functions be δ_A and δ_B.

Construct the cross-product automaton for the difference $K - L$ as follows: $M = (P \times Q, \Sigma, \delta, [0, 0], F)$, where $\delta([p, q], a) = [\delta_A(p, a), \delta_B(q, a)]$ for all states $[p, q]$ in $P \times Q$ and all a in Σ, and $F = \{m - 2\} \times (Q - \{n - 2\})$, see Fig. 1.

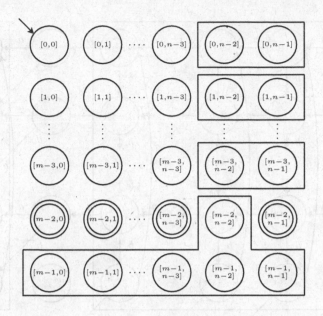

Fig. 1. The cross-product automaton for difference

Since states $m - 1$ and $n - 1$ are dead, all the states of the cross-product automaton M in row $m-1$, as well as state $[m-2, n-2]$, are dead. Next, all the states in row $m - 2$, except for state $[m - 2, n - 2]$, accept only the empty string, therefore are equivalent. Finally, the pairs of states $[i, n - 2]$ and $[i, n - 1]$, where $0 \le i \le m - 3$, are equivalent since they go to the same state on every symbol. Hence, the minimal DFA for the difference has at most $mn - m - 2n + 4$ states.

To prove tightness, consider prefix-free languages accepted by DFAs in Fig. 2. The cross-product automaton for their difference is shown in Fig. 3. Consider

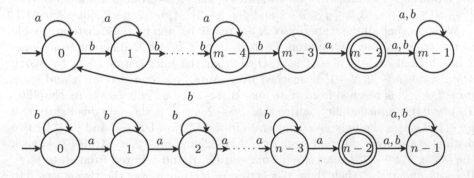

Fig. 2. Binary prefix-free languages meeting the bound $mn - m - 2n + 4$ for difference

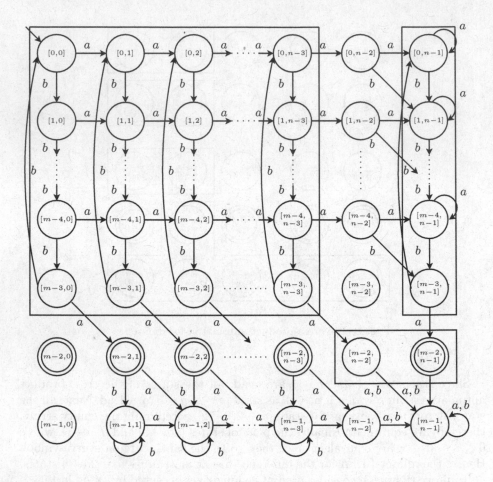

Fig. 3. The cross-product automaton for the difference of languages from Fig. 2

the following set of $mn - m - 2n + 4$ states of the cross-product automaton: $\mathcal{R} = \{[i,j]; 0 \le i \le m-3, 0 \le j \le n-1 \text{ and } j \ne n-2\} \cup \{[m-2, n-2], [m-2, n-1]\}$.

We show that all the states in set $\mathcal{R}$ are reachable and pairwise distinguishable in the cross-product automaton. Each state $[i,j]$ in set $\mathcal{R}$ different from $[m-2, n-2]$ and $[m-2, n-1]$ is reached from the initial state $[0,0]$ by string $a^j b^i$. State $[m-2, n-1]$ is reached from state $[m-3, n-1]$ by a and state $[m-2, n-2]$ is reached from state $[m-3, n-3]$ by a. This proves reachability. To prove distinguishability, notice that $[m-2, n-2]$ is the only dead state and $[m-2, n-1]$ is the only accepting state in set $\mathcal{R}$. Now let $[i,j]$ and $[k, \ell]$ be two distinct states in $\mathcal{R}$ different from $[m-2, n-2]$ and $[m-2, n-1]$. If $i < k$, then the string $a^n b^{m-3-i} a$ is accepted from state $[i,j]$ and rejected from state $[k, \ell]$. If $i = k$ and $j < \ell$, then there is a string in b^* that moves the two states into states $[0, j]$ and $[0, \ell]$ in row 0. Then, the string $a^{n-3-j} b^{m-3} a$ is rejected from state $[0, j]$ and accepted from state $[0, \ell]$. This concludes our proof.   □

5   State Complexity of Left Quotient

Yu *et al.* in [7] investigated the state complexity of left quotient of regular languages. They proved the upper bound $2^n - 1$ and presented binary language L, shown in Fig. 4, that meets the bound for $\Sigma^* \backslash L$. However, as shown below, their proof does not work, therefore we provide a correct proof. Then, we consider the case of prefix-free regular languages.

Theorem 3 ([7]). *Let K and L be regular languages with $\mathrm{sc}(K) = m$ and $\mathrm{sc}(L) = n$. Then, $\mathrm{sc}(K \backslash L) \leq 2^n - 1$ and the bound is tight in the binary case.*

Let us first show that the proof in [7] does not work. For tightness, let L be the language recognized by the DFA in Fig. 4. The paper [7] claims that in the subset automaton corresponding to the NFA for $\Sigma^* \backslash L$, every non-empty subset X of the state set $\{0, 1, \ldots, n-1\}$ is reached from the initial state $\{0, 1, \ldots, n-1\}$ by the string $x_0 x_{n-1} \cdots x_1$, where for every j with $0 \leq j \leq n-1$, $x_j = a$, if $j \in X$, and $x_j = b$ otherwise. Assume $n = 6$ and let $X = \{2, 3, 5\}$. State X should be reached from the initial state $\{0, 1, 2, 3, 4, 5\}$ by string $babaab$. However, we have $\{0, 1, 2, 3, 4, 5\} \xrightarrow{b} \{0, 2, 3, 4, 5\} \xrightarrow{a} \{0, 1, 3, 4, 5\} \xrightarrow{b} \{0, 2, 4, 5\} \xrightarrow{a} \{0, 1, 3, 5\} \xrightarrow{a} \{0, 1, 2, 4\} \xrightarrow{b} \{0, 2, 3, 5\}$.

Proof. To get an n-state NFA for language $K \backslash L$ from an n-state DFA A for L, it is enough to make initial all the states of DFA A that can be reached from the initial state of A by a string in language K. In the corresponding subset automaton, the empty set cannot be reached since DFA A for L is assumed to be complete. This gives the upper bound $2^n - 1$.

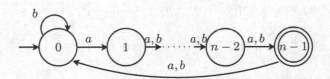

Fig. 4. Binary witness language for left quotient by Σ^*

For tightness, let $K = a^* \cup a^* b^{m-2}$. Language K contains all strings in a^* and has state complexity m. Let L be the language recognized by the DFA shown in Fig. 4. Then, in the NFA for language $K \backslash L$, obtained from the DFA for L, all the states are initial. The string a^{n-1-i} is accepted by the NFA for $K \backslash L$ only from state i. It follows that all the states in the corresponding subset automaton are pairwise distinguishable since two distinct subsets must differ in a state i, therefore the string a^{n-1-i} distinguishes them.

We prove the reachability of all the non-empty subsets by induction on the size of subsets. The set $\{0, 1, \ldots, n-1\}$ is the initial state of the subset automaton, therefore is reachable. Assume that every subset of size $k+1$, where $1 \leq k \leq n-1$

is reachable and let $X = \{i_1, i_2, \ldots, i_k\}$, where $0 \leq i_1 < i_2 < \cdots < i_k \leq n - 1$, be a subset of size k.

First, let $i_1 = 0$ and $i_2 \geq 2$, thus X contains 0 and does not contain 1. Take $Y = \{0, i_2 - 1, \ldots, i_k - 1, n - 1\}$. Then, $|Y| = k + 1$, therefore Y is reachable by the induction hypothesis. State X is reached from state Y by b.

Now let $i_1 = 0$, $i_2 = 1$, and ℓ be the minimal state in $\{0, 1, \ldots, n-1\}$, that is not in X; such a state must exist since $|X| < n$. Take $Y = \{(x - (l - 1)) \bmod n \mid x \in X\}$. Then, $|Y| = k$ and Y contains 0 and does not contain 1. Thus state Y is reachable as shown in the first case. State X is reached from Y by a^{l-1}.

Finally, let $i_1 > 0$. Take $Y = \{x - i_1 \mid x \in X\}$. Then, $|Y| = k$ and Y contains 0, thus state Y is reachable as shown in the two cases above. State X is reached from Y by a^{i_1}. This proves reachability and concludes the proof.   □

Theorem 4. *Let K and L be prefix-free regular languages over an alphabet Σ with $\mathrm{sc}(K) = m$ and $\mathrm{sc}(L) = n$, where $m, n \geq 3$. Then, $\mathrm{sc}(K \backslash L) \leq 2^{n-1}$. The bound is tight if $|\Sigma| \geq n - 1$, but cannot be met using any smaller alphabet.*

Proof. Since L is prefix-free, the DFA for L has the dead state. Before constructing an NFA for $K \backslash L$, we omit the dead state. This gives the upper bound.

To prove tightness, let $\Sigma = \{a_1, a_2, \ldots, a_{n-1}\}$. Let L be the language accepted by the DFA with states $1, 2, \ldots, n$, of which 1 is the initial state, $n - 1$ is the sole accepting state, n is the dead state, and in which for $i = 1, 2, \ldots, n - 1$, by a_i, states $1, 2, \ldots, i - 1$ go to itself, each state j with $i \leq j \leq n - 1$ goes to state $j + 1$, and state $n - 1$ goes to state n, see Fig. 5 for every instance of i.

We define language K so that in the NFA for language $K \backslash L$, all the states in $\{1, 2, \ldots, n-1\}$ would be initial. To this aim we consider two cases: If $m \geq n$, then let

$$K = a_2 + a_1 a_3 + a_1^2 a_4 + \cdots + a_1^{n-3} a_{n-1} + a_1^{n-3} a_{n-2} + a_1^{m-2}$$

$$= a_2 + \sum_{i=1}^{n-3} a_1^i a_{i+2} + a_1^{n-3} a_{n-2} + a_1^{m-2},$$

and if $m < n$, then let

$$K = a_2 + a_1 a_3 + a_1^2 a_4 + \cdots + a_1^{m-4} a_{m-2} + a_1^{m-3} a_1^* (a_{m-1} + a_m + \cdots + a_{n-1})$$

$$= a_2 + \sum_{i=1}^{m-4} a_1^i a_{i+2} + a_1^{m-3} a_1^* (a_{m-1} + a_m + \cdots + a_{n-1}),$$

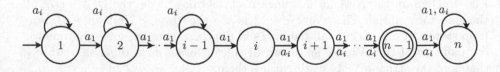

Fig. 5. Transitions on symbol a_1 and a_i

see Fig. 6 for $n = 6$, in which all omitted transitions go to the dead states 6 and 4, respectively. In both cases, the strings $a_1^{i-2}a_i$ with $2 \le i \le n - 1$ as well as the string $a_1^{n-3}a_{n-2}$ are in K, therefore all the states in the NFA for $K \backslash L$ are initial.

Since the string a_1^{n-1-i} is accepted by this NFA only from state i, all the states in the corresponding subset automaton are pairwise distinguishable. Now we prove that all the non-empty subsets of $\{1, 2, \dots, n - 1\}$ are reachable in the subset automaton. The set $\{1, 2, \dots, n - 1\}$ is the initial state of the subset automaton. Let $X = \{1, 2, \dots, n - 1\} - \{i_1, i_2, \dots, i_k\}$, where $1 \le k \le n - 1$ and $1 \le i_1 < i_2 < \cdots < i_k$, be a subset. Then, X is reached from the initial subset $\{1, 2, \dots, n - 1\}$ by string $a_{i_1} a_{i_2} \cdots a_{i_k}$.

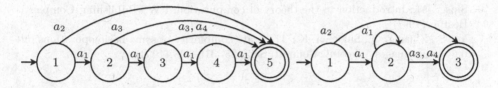

Fig. 6. Automaton for language K; $n = 5, m = 6$ (left) and $n = 5, m = 4$ (right)

To see that the bound cannot be met for a smaller alphabet, denote by Q the initial state $\{1, 2, \dots, n-1\}$. Then, every set $Q - \{i\}$ must be reached either from Q or from a set $Q - \{j\}$. Since we omitted the dead state, no transitions go from state $n - 1$. Therefore, the second case is possible only if $j = n - 1$. However, if $Q - \{n-1\}$ goes to $Q - \{i\}$, then Q goes to $Q - \{i\}$ as well. It follows that every set $Q - \{i\}$ must be reached from the initial state Q, therefore $|\Sigma| \ge n - 1$. $\square$

6   Conclusions

We investigated closure properties and the state complexity of difference and left quotient of prefix-free regular languages. We showed that the class of prefix-free regular languages is closed under intersection, difference, concatenation, square, and the k-th power and is not closed under complement, union, symmetric difference, Kleene star, reversal, cyclic shift, shuffle, and left quotient. We proved that the state complexity of difference of prefix-free regular languages is $mn - m - 2n + 4$ and we provided binary worst-case example. In the case of left quotient, we presented a correct proof of a lower bound $2^n - 1$ in the case of regular languages. Then, we dealt with the left quotient of prefix-free regular languages and showed that its state complexity is 2^{n-1} by providing witness languages over an alphabet of size $n - 1$. We also proved that the upper bound cannot be met using smaller alphabets.

References

1. Han, Y.-S., Salomaa, K., Wood, D.: Operational state complexity of prefix-free regular languages. Automata, Formal Languages, and Related Topics, 99–115 (2009)
2. Han, Y.-S., Salomaa, K., Wood, D.: Nondeterministic state complexity of basic operations for prefix-free regular languages. Fund. Inform. 90, 93–106 (2009)
3. Han, Y.-S., Salomaa, K., Yu, S.: State Complexity of Combined Operations For Prefix-Free Regular Languages. In: Dediu, A.H., Ionescu, A.M., Martín-Vide, C. (eds.) LATA 2009. LNCS, vol. 5457, pp. 398–409. Springer, Heidelberg (2009)
4. Jirásková, G., Krausová, M.: Complexity in prefix-free regular languages. In: McQuillan, I., Pighizzini, G., Trost, B. (eds.) Proc. 12th DCFS, pp. 236–244. University of Saskatchewan, Saskatoon (2010)
5. Krausová, M.: Prefix-free languages and descriptional complexity. Bachelor thesis. P. J. Šafárik University, Košice, Slovakia (2010) (in Slovak)
6. Sipser, M.: Introduction to the theory of computation. PWS Publishing Company, Boston (1997)
7. Yu, S., Zhuang, Q., Salomaa, K.: The state complexity of some basic operations on regular languages. Theoret. Comput. Sci. 125, 315–328 (1994)

Noise Injection Heuristics
for Concurrency Testing

Bohuslav Křena, Zdeněk Letko, and Tomáš Vojnar

FIT, Brno University of Technology, Czech Republic

Abstract. Testing of concurrent software is difficult due to the non-determinism present in scheduling of concurrent threads. Existing testing approaches tackle this problem either using a modified scheduler which allows to systematically explore possible scheduling alternatives or using random or heuristic noise injection which allows to observe different scheduling scenarios. In this paper, we experimentally compare several existing noise injection heuristics both from the point of view of coverage of possible behaviours as well as from the point of view of error discovery probability. Moreover, we also propose a new noise injection heuristics which uses concurrency coverage information to decide where to put noise and show that it can outperform the existing approaches in certain cases.

1 Introduction

Concurrency software testing and analysis is hard due to the non-deterministic nature of scheduling of concurrent threads. Static analysis and model checking do not scale well when analysing such programs due to the large interleaving space they need to explore. Testing and dynamic analysis scale well but usually do not analyse all possible interleavings. The number of different interleavings spot during repeated executions of the same test can be increased either by using a *deterministic scheduler* or by injecting of so-called *noise* into test executions.

Deterministic schedulers [12] control thread scheduling decisions during a program execution and so can systematically explore the interleaving space up to a certain extent. Such tools can be seen as light-weight model checkers. Noise injection tools [3,11] inject calls to a noise maker routine into the program code. Threads executing the modified code then enter the noise maker routine that decides—either randomly or based on some heuristics—whether to cause a noise. The noise causes a delay in the current thread, giving other threads opportunity to make a progress.

Coverage metrics are used to measure how many *coverage tasks* (i.e., monitored events such as reachability of a certain line) defined by a *coverage model* have been covered during test execution(s) so far. Concurrency coverage metrics [14,2,7] can be used to track how many different concurrency-related tasks have been covered, and hence how many different interleavings have been witnessed.

This paper presents two contributions to the research on noise injection techniques. First, we propose a *new heuristics* which uses coverage information to

Z. Kotásek et al. (Eds.): MEMICS 2011, LNCS 7119, pp. 123–135, 2012.

select places in an execution of a given code where to put a noise. We also propose
a way to determine the strength of the noise needed to suitably affect the behaviour of tested programs. Second, we address the current lack of experimental
evaluations of the various noise injection heuristics by *systematic comparison* of
several noise injection techniques available in the well-known IBM Concurrency
Testing Tool (ConTest) [3] as well as our new heuristics on a set of test cases
of different size. The comparison is based on the coverage obtained under one
selected concurrency coverage metric, the needed execution time, and the rate
of manifestation of concurrency errors in the testing runs.

We in particular focus on concurrent programs written in Java. We use our
infrastructure for search-based testing called SearchBestie [8] to run multiple
tests with different parameters and to collect their results and IBM ConTest [3]
for noise injection and concurrency coverage measurement. Although our comparison could certainly be further extended, we believe that the comparison
provides results missing in the existing literature on noise injection. Moreover,
the comparison shows that our new heuristics may in certain cases provide an
improvement in the testing process.

2   Existing Noise Injection Heuristics

Existing works discuss three main aspects of heuristic noise injection: (1) how
to make noise, i.e., which type of noise generating mechanism should be used,
(2) where to inject noise during a test execution, i.e., at which program location
and at which of its executions, and (3) how to minimise the amount of noise
needed for manifestation of an already detected error when debugging. This
work mainly targets the first two aspects. More information on debugging can
be found, e.g., in [5].

There exist several ways how a scheduler decision can be affected in Java.
In [3], three different noise seeding techniques are introduced and evaluated on
a single-core processor. The *priority* technique changes priorities of threads. This
technique did not provide good results. The *yield* technique injects one or more
calls of `yield()` which causes a context switch. The *sleep* technique injects
one call of `sleep()`. Experiments showed that the sleep technique provided
best results in all cases. However, when many threads were running, the yield
technique was also effective.

The current version of the IBM ConTest tool comes with several more noise
seeding techniques [9]. The *wait* technique injects a call of `wait()`. The concerned threads must first obtain a special shared monitor, then call `wait()`,
and finally release the monitor. The *synchYield* technique combines the yield
technique with obtaining the monitor as in the wait technique. The *busyWait*
technique does not obtain a monitor but instead loops for some time. The *haltOneThread* technique [13] occasionally stops one thread until any other thread
cannot run. Finally, the *timeoutTamper* heuristics randomly reduces the time-
out used when calling `sleep()` in the tested program (to test that it is not used
for synchronisation). All the above mentioned seeding techniques except the priority technique are parameterised by the so-called *strength of noise*. In the case

of techniques based on `sleep` and `wait`, the strength gives the time to wait. In the case of `yield`, the strength says how many times the yield should be called.

Next, we discuss techniques for determining where to put a noise. IBM Con-Test allows to inject a noise before and after any concurrency-related event (namely, access to class member variables, static variables, and arrays, calls of `wait`, `interrupt`, `notify`, `monitorenter`, and `monitorexit` routines). The *rstest* [11] tool considers as possibly interesting places before concurrency-related events only. Moreover, rstest uses a simple escape analysis and a lockset-based algorithm to identify so-called *unprotected accesses* to shared variables. The unprotected access reads or writes a variable which is visible to multiple threads without holding an appropriate lock. This optimisation reduces the number of places where the noise can be put but suppresses ability to detect some concurrency errors, e.g., high-level data races or deadlocks where all accesses to problematic variables are correctly guarded by a lock.

It is discussed in [3,11,5] that putting noise on every possible place is inefficient and only a few relevant context switches are critical for the concurrency error. Also, putting noise in a certain place (*ploc*—program location [3]) in the execution can either help to spot the concurrency error or mask it completely. Therefore, several heuristics for choosing places where to put a noise were proposed, e.g., in [3,11,1,6,4,13].

The simplest heuristics is based on a *random noise* [3,11]. This heuristics puts a noise before/after an executed *ploc* with a given probability. The probability is the same for all *ploc*s in the execution. It was shown in [1] that focusing random noise only on a single variable over which a data race exists increases the probability of spotting the error. The authors also propose a heuristics which helps to choose a suitable variable without additional information from a data race detector. In [4], the noise injection problem is reformulated as a *search problem*, and a genetic algorithm is used to determine *ploc*s suitable for noise injection. The fitness function used prefers solutions with a low number of *ploc*s where a noise is put (size), a high amount of noise in less *ploc*s (entropy), and a high probability of spotting the error (efficiency). In [6], several *concurrency antipatterns* are discussed, and for each of them, a suitable scheduling scenario that leads to manifestation of the corresponding concurrency error is presented, but the paper contains no practical evaluation of the proposed heuristics.

A few heuristics based on concurrency coverage models have been published. Coverage-directed generation of interleavings presented in [3] considers two coverage models. The first model determines whether the execution of each method was interrupted by a context switch. The second model determines whether a method execution was interrupted by any other method. The level of methods used here is, according to our opinion, too coarse. In [13], a coverage model considers, for each synchronisation primitive, various distinctive situations that can occur when the primitive is executed (e.g., in the case of a synchronised block defined using the Java keyword `synchronised`, the tasks are: *synchronisation visited, synchronisation blocking* some other thread, and *synchronisation blocked* by some other thread). A forcing algorithm then injects noise at corresponding synchronisation primitive *ploc*s to increase the coverage. None of these two heuristics focuses on accesses to shared variables which can limit their ability to discover some concurrency errors, e.g., data races.

3   A New Coverage-Based Noise Injection Heuristics

Our new heuristics is motivated by our recent experiences with concurrency coverage metrics [7]. The heuristics primarily answers the question where to inject noise during a test run (the noise can be caused by any of the `wait`, `sleep`, or `yield` seeding techniques). In the heuristics, we consider only *ploc*s that appear before concurrency-related events as suitable for noise injection. Our heuristics targets both accesses to shared variables as well as the use of synchronisation primitives. Our goal is to be able to discover all kinds of concurrency errors. Our heuristics monitors the frequency of a *ploc* execution during a test and puts a noise at the given *ploc* with a probability biased wrt. this frequency—the more often a *ploc* is executed the lower probability is used. Furthermore, our heuristics also derives the strength of a noise to be used from the timing of events observed in previous executions of the test (although for determining the strength of noise, alternative approaches can be used too).

The testing process with our noise injection heuristics works in the following four steps. (1) No noise is produced, and a set of covered tasks of our coverage metric together with information on relative timing of appearance of monitored concurrency-related events are generated during the first execution of the test. (2) A set of the so-called *noise tuples* is generated from the gathered information. (3) Random noise at the *ploc*s included in the noise tuples is generated, and the average frequency of execution of these *ploc*s within particular threads is gathered during the next test execution. (4) Biased random noise of strength computed wrt. the collected statistics is (repeatedly) produced at the collected *ploc*s. Coverage information is updated during each execution, and new noise tuples are constantly learnt. Likewise, all other collected statistics are updated during each test run. Due to performance reasons, only one thread is influenced by noise at a time. We now explain the above introduced steps in more detail.

Our coverage model considers coverage tasks of the form $(t_1, ploc_1, t_2, ploc_2)$. There are two situations when a task is covered. First, a task is covered if a thread t_1 accesses a shared variable v at $ploc_1$, and subsequently a thread t_2 accesses v at $ploc_2$, which is a typical scenario critical for occurrence of concurrency-related errors. If t_1 owns a monitor when accessing v at $ploc_1$, another task $(t_1, ploc_3, t_2, ploc_2)$ where $ploc_3$ refers to the location where t_1 obtained the last monitor is also covered. This is motivated by considering the relative position of locking a critical section in one thread and using it in another thread as important. Second, a new task is covered if a thread t_1 releases a monitor obtained at $ploc_1$, and subsequently a thread t_2 obtains the monitor at $ploc_2$. Each covered task is annotated by the number of milliseconds that elapsed between the events on which the task is based. The threads are identified in an abstract way based on the history of their creation in the same way as in [7].

Our heuristics injects noise before a location $ploc_1$ executed by a thread t_1 if a task $(t_1, ploc_1, t_2, ploc_2)$ has been covered within some previous execution. This way, our heuristics tries to reverse the order in which the locations are executed. The coverage information collected during previous runs is transformed into *noise tuples* of the form $(t_1, ploc_1, min, max, orig, exec)$. Here, t_1 identifies a thread and $ploc_1$ the program location where to put a noise. The two next values give the minimal and maximal number of milliseconds that elapsed between the events defining the given coverage task. These values can be used for determining the strength of noise to be used as a delay of length randomly chosen from between the values. If there are multiple coverage tasks with the same couple $(t_1, ploc_1)$, min and max are computed from all such tasks. The $orig$ value contains an identification of the run where the couple $(t_1, ploc_1)$ was spot for the first time. In order to limit values of min and max, their update is possible only within a limited number of test executions after the $orig$ run. Finally, the $exec$ value contains the average number of times the couple $(t_1, ploc_1)$ is executed during a test execution. It is used to bias the probability of noise injection at $ploc_1$.

In repeated executions of a test, the so far computed noise tuples are loaded, and the noise is generated at program locations given by them with the probability computed from the number of times the locations have been executed (the $exec$ value). The computation is shown in Alg. 1. The base probability is obtained as $1/exec$ to be higher for $plocs$ that are executed rarely. The minimal noise probability accepted by ConTest is 0.001, and so

```
1 if exec > 0 then
2     prob = 1 / exec;
3     if prob < 0.004 then
4         prob = 0.001;
5     else prob = prob/4;
6 else prob = 0.01;
```

Alg. 1. Computing probability of noise generation

all lower computed probabilities are set to this value. Higher probabilities are divided by 4 to keep the noise injection frequency reasonably low (25 % for a $ploc$ which is executed once during each test). This is motivated by our observation that higher probability than 25 % degrades test performance and usually does not provide considerably better results. The limit can be changed if necessary. If the $exec$ value is not yet available, the probability of 0.01 is used.

4   A Comparison of Noise Injection Techniques

This section presents an experimental evaluation of selected noise injection techniques available in ConTest as well as of the above newly proposed heuristics. We evaluate these techniques on a set of 5 test cases shown in Table 1 which gives the number of classes the test cases consist of and the concurrency error present in them (if there is one). The *sunbank* test case runs 4 threads representing bank clients each performing a set of transfers. There is a data race on a variable containing the total amount of money in the bank. The *airlines* [7] test case represents an artificial air ticket reservation system. During each test, 4 threads representing ticket resellers serve requests of 8 client threads. The test case contains a high-level atomicity violation.

The three other programs in Table 1 are real-life case studies. The *crawler* case study [1] is a skeleton of an older version of a major IBM software. In this test case, 16 threads simulate serving of remote requests. A data race can manifest here if a certain very rare timing condition is met during a shutdown sequence. The *ftpserver* case study [7] is an early development

Table 1. Test cases

Test	Classes	Concur. error
sunbank	2	data race
airlines	8	atom. viol.
crawler	19	data race
ftpserver	120	data race
tidorbj	1399	none

version of an open-source FTP server. The server creates a new thread for each connection. The code contains several data races, out of which we focus only on those producing a `NullPointerException`. Finally, the *tidorbj* test case is an open source CORBA-compliant object resource broker [10]. We used the *echo_concurrent* test case available in the distribution. The test starts 10 clients, each sending a set of requests to the server. This test case does not contain any known concurrency error.

During each test run, we measure coverage wrt. a chosen metric—namely, *Avio** [7]. This metric has been chosen due to its very good ratio of providing good results from the point of view of suitability for saturation-based or search-based testing and a low overhead of measuring the achieved coverage (and hence its suitability for performing many tests with minimal interference with tested programs—still, in the future, more experiments with other metrics could be done). Note that the Avio* metric that we use for evaluation of the testing is different than the specialised metric that we have proposed above as a means for driving the noise injection. In particular, the *Avio** coverage metric focuses on accesses to shared variables and collects triplets consisting of two subsequent accesses $a1, a3$ to a shared variable v from a thread and the last access $a2$ to v from another thread that interleaved accesses $a1$ and $a3$. Besides coverage information, we monitor execution times and occurrences of the known errors. Collection of this information of course affects thread scheduling of the monitored test cases, but the influence is the same for all performed executions. All tests were executed on multi-core machines running Linux and Java version 1.6.

To recall from Section 2, IBM ConTest provides 5 basic techniques for noise seeding: *yield, sleep, wait, busyWait,* and *synchYield*. In addition, the so-called *mixed* technique simply randomly chooses one technique from the others. The probability of causing a noise at a *ploc* is driven by the *noise frequency* (*nFreq*) parameter ranging from 0 (no noise) to 1000 (always). We limit this parameter to values 0, 50, 100, 150, and 200. Higher values cause significant performance degradation and are therefore not considered. The mentioned basic noise seeding techniques can be combined in ConTest with two further techniques—*haltOneThread* and *timeoutTamper*. The approach of setting a certain noise frequency to control when some noise is generated can then be combined with restricting the noise generation to events related to (certain) shared variables (the *sharedVar* heuristics). Finally, ConTest provides a so-called *random* setting under which it randomly selects and combines its parameters.

Table 2. Relative improvement of error detection when using different types of noise

test case	nFreq	sleep	busyWait	wait	sYield	yield	mixed	average
sunbank	50	1.63	1.32	2.28	0.45	1.60	0.85	1.36
	100	3.05	2.48	4.22	0.00	0.38	3.62	2.29
	150	4.18	1.68	2.52	0.00	4.85	2.03	2.54
	200	3.85	3.12	6.13	0.00	4.47	2.50	3.34
airlines	50	1.13	1.13	0.65	0.67	3.06	0.91	1.26
	100	2.44	1.45	1.34	1.88	5.48	1.35	2.32
	150	0.21	1.89	1.42	1.83	5.21	0.47	1.84
	200	1.90	0.23	0.58	1.93	5.54	1.15	1.89
ftpserver	50	0.36	0.34	0.56	0.94	0.91	0.49	0.60
	100	0.21	0.48	0.28	0.90	0.96	0.35	0.53
	150	0.36	0.22	0.30	0.98	0.95	0.31	0.52
	200	0.20	0.60	0.29	0.99	0.90	0.31	0.55
average		1.63	1.24	1.71	0.88	2.86	1.19	1.59

Each of our 5 test cases was tested with 496 different noise injection configurations. We collected data from 60 executions for each configuration. This way, we obtained a database of 148,800 results. Then, we computed average cumulated values for sequences of 1, 10, 20, 30, 40, and 50 randomly chosen results of each configuration (the length of the sequence is denoted as $SeqLen$ below). These average results represent average values that one obtains when executing the given configuration $SeqLen$ times.

Due to limited space, only two analyses of the results are presented here: (1) A comparison of the efficiency of the different noise seeding techniques available in ConTest together with the influence of the noise frequency on them. (2) A comparison of the efficiency of the ConTest's heuristics restricting noise generation to events related to (certain) shared variables and our newly proposed heuristics for deciding where to generate noise in a testing run. Hence, the first comparison is mainly about the types of noise seeding and partially about where the noise is generated in a test execution whereas the second comparison is mainly about the latter issue.

4.1   A Comparison of ConTest's Noise Seeding Settings

In this subsection, we focus on the influence of the different noise seeding techniques and the noise frequency on how the testing results are improved in comparison to testing without noise injection (but with the collection of data about the testing enabled, which also influences the scheduling). Since ConTest does not allow one to use its *timeoutTamper* and *haltOneThread* noise seeding techniques without one of its basic noise seeding techniques, we first study the effect of the basic noise seeding techniques, which are activated via the `noiseType` parameter of ConTest. Then we focus on the effect of the *timeoutTamper* and *haltOneThread* seeding techniques.

Table 2 shows the relative improvement of error detection that we observed when using different basic noise seeding techniques available in ConTest. Both the *haltOneThread* and *timeoutTamper* seeding techniques were disabled, the random noise injection heuristics was enabled, and *SeqLen=50*. Additionally, we also consider the ConTest setting which randomly chooses among basic noise seeding techniques before each test execution (referred as *mixed* in the table). The entries of the table give the ratio of the number of error manifestations observed when using noise injection of the respective type against the number of error manifestations without any noise setting enabled. Moreover, average values are provided for a better comparison. Values lower than 1.00 mean that the appropriate configuration provided a worse result than without noise. Higher values mean that noise of the appropriate type provides better results. For instance, 1.25 means that the given type of noise on average detected an error by 25 % more often. Results for the *crawler* and *tidorbj* test cases are omitted because there were no errors detected by the considered test configurations in those test cases.

The table illustrates that noise injection affects each test case differently— sometimes it helps, sometimes not. The use of noise almost always very significantly helps in the cases of *sunbank* and *airlines*, but it does not help in the case of *ftpserver*. Also, the different seeding techniques perform differently in the different test cases, and one cannot claim a clear winner among them (although *yield* seems to be often winning). The *wait* technique helps the most in the *sunbank* test case while *yield* provides the best improvement in the *airlines* test case. In the case of *ftpserver*, no technique provides improvement. Significant influence of *nFreq* is visible in the *sunbank* test case, but in the *ftpserver* case, it seems that *nFreq* has no influence. The effect of *nFreq* in *airlines* has no clear tendency. Nevertheless, overall, the table demonstrates that choosing a suitable noise seeding technique can rapidly improve the probability of detecting an error at least in some cases.

Further, we have also performed experiments on how using the different basic noise seeding techniques available in ConTest impacts upon coverage obtained under the Avio* metric. The obtained results can be summarised by saying that the obtained improvement due to the use of noise injection was smaller in this case, and the differences among the noise seeding techniques were smaller too. The best improvement was achieved using the *busyWait* technique (about 45 %) in the *crawler* and *ftpserver* test cases.

Table 3 shows influence of the *timeoutTamper* and *haltOneThread* noise seeding techniques as well as their combination on error detection (in the table, t_0/t_1 indicates whether *timeoutTamper* is disabled or enabled, and h_0/h_1 indicates whether *haltOneThread* is disabled or enabled, respectively). As said above, these techniques cannot be used without any basic noise seeding techniques in ConTest, and therefore average values computed from results obtained with

Table 3. Influence of the *haltOneThread* and *timeoutTamper* techniques on error detection

test case	t_0		t_1	
	h_0	h_1	h_0	h_1
sunbank	2.54	0.95	1.93	1.72
airlines	1.84	2.55	1.61	2.29
ftpserver	0.52	0.61	0.34	0.45

different basic noise seeding techniques are reported. Results for *nFreq=150* and *seqLen=50* are used. Like in Table 2, the ratio of the number of manifested errors against the number of manifested errors when no noise is used is presented. The table shows that *timeoutTamper* and *haltOneThread* also affect each test case differently. The *haltOneThread* technique significantly helps in the *airlines* test case, slightly helps in the *ftpserver*, but it is harmful in the *sunbank* test case. The *timeoutTamper* technique provides worse results in all shown test cases. On the other hand, in the *crawler* test case (not shown in the table since no error is detected in it without noise injection), testing with *timeoutTamper* enabled and *haltOneThread* disabled was the only configuration of ConTest that allowed an error to manifest (in 7 % of the executions).

Table 4 illustrates the influence of the *time-outTamper* and *haltOneThread* noise seeding techniques on the coverage obtained under the Avio* coverage metric. The table clearly shows that the effect of *timeoutTamper* is very important for the *crawler* test case. As we have already said, this test case is a skeleton of one IBM software product. When developers extracted the skeleton, they modeled its environment using timed routines. The *timeoutTamper* heuristics influences these timeouts in a way leading to significantly better results. The effects of the considered techniques in the other examples are then none or very small.

Table 4. Influence of the *haltOneThread* and *timeoutTamper* techniques on Avio* coverage

	t_0		t_1	
test case	h_0	h_1	h_0	h_1
sunbank	1.04	1.03	1.04	1.06
airlines	0.85	0.81	0.77	0.86
crawler	1.15	1.30	3.91	3.78
ftpserver	1.04	1.04	1.09	1.07
tidorbj	0.95	0.95	0.95	0.96

The same trends as described above can also be seen from results of experiments that we have performed with different values of *nFreq*. Our results indicate that there is no optimal configuration, and for each test case and each testing goal, one needs to choose a different testing configuration. For instance, the best configuration for the *crawler* test case is a combination of the *busyWait* and *timeoutTamper* noise seeding techniques with *nFreq* set to 200 if the goal is to increase the error detection probability. On the other hand, the testing configuration with *yield*, *timeoutTamper*, and *nFreq* set to 150 provides the best improvement of the Avio* coverage in this test case. In some cases, using a random injection of noise does not provide any improvement as can be seen from the *tidorbj* test case. A significant improvement in this case is achieved only when the noise heuristics discussed in the following section are used.

4.2 A Comparison of Heuristics for Determining Where to Generate Noise

This subsection concentrates on the influence of the ConTest's heuristics restricting noise generation to events related to shared variables and on the influence of our new heuristics proposed in Section 3. In addition, the scenario in which ConTest randomly chooses its own parameters is also considered. In particular, Table 5 compares the mentioned heuristics according to the number of Avio* covered tasks divided by the time needed to execute the tests. Intuitively, this relativised comparison favours techniques that provide a high coverage with a low

Table 5. A relativised comparison of heuristics restricting places where to put noise

position	configuration	airlines	crawler	ftpserver	sunbank	tidorbj	average
1	0_1_1_1-0-one_0-0	7.0	2.7	9.2	4.8	7.7	6.3
2	0_1_0_1-0-one_0-0	5.0	2.7	11.5	4.5	8.8	6.5
3	0_0_0_0-0-all_1-0	2.6	17.7	2.5	7.6	2.3	6.6
4	1_0_0_0-0-all_0-0	10.3	3.2	10.3	5.3	5.0	6.8
5	0_1_0_1-1-one_0-0	11.8	5.0	11.8	4.0	8.7	8.3
6	0_1_1_1-1-one_0-0	9.5	7.5	15.7	3.5	7.2	8.7
7	0_0_1_1-0-one_0-0	5.2	18.0	3.0	9.7	9.3	9.0
8	0_0_0_1-0-one_0-0	6.3	17.8	2.8	10.0	8.7	9.1
9	0_0_0_1-1-one_0-0	8.7	15.8	10.8	7.8	7.0	10.0
10	0_0_1_1-1-one_0-0	10.8	14.5	9.5	10.5	7.5	10.6
11	0_0_0_0-0-all_0-0	5.0	19.2	11.0	12.0	10.5	11.5
12	0_0_0_0-0-all_1-1	3.7	23.0	19.0	6.7	13.0	13.1
13	0_1_0_1-0-all_0-0	14.7	5.5	19.0	15.3	14.7	13.8
14	0_1_0_0-0-all_0-0	17.2	7.5	17.0	12.3	16.0	14.0
15	0_1_0_1-1-all_0-0	17.3	6.8	18.2	11.0	17.2	14.1
16	0_1_1_1-0-all_0-0	17.8	6.5	13.7	17.3	15.5	14.2
17	0_1_1_1-1-all_0-0	14.3	9.3	16.0	16.8	14.7	14.2
18	0_0_1_1-0-all_0-0	13.0	14.3	9.5	19.8	16.7	14.7
19	0_0_0_1-1-all_0-0	14.0	16.8	14.3	16.0	13.7	15.0
20	0_1_1_0-0-all_0-0	16.2	10.3	17.8	14.8	16.5	15.1
21	0_0_1_1-1-all_0-0	15.3	16.0	9.7	19.8	15.2	15.2
22	0_0_0_1-0-all_0-0	18.2	17.3	11.8	16.3	17.3	16.2
23	0_0_1_0-0-all_0-0	19.2	18.5	9.8	19.3	18.0	17.0

overhead, and therefore punishes techniques that either put too much noise into test executions or provide a poor coverage only. Based on our experiments, we have also compared the heuristics according to the number of Avio* covered coverage tasks only (thus providing a non-relativised comparison) as well as according to how often an error is manifested (either taking into account the needed testing time or not). Due to space restrictions, we do not present these latter comparisons in detailed tables here, but we summarize them in the text.

The *configuration* column of Table 5 describes the considered noise injection configuration. A configuration consists of five parts delimited by the "_" character. The meaning of these parts is as follows: (Part 1) The ConTest *random* parameter: if set to 1, ConTest parameters considered in Parts 2–4 are set randomly before each execution. (Part 2) If set to 1, the *timeoutTamper* heuristics is enabled. (Part 3) If set to 1, the *haltOneThread* heuristics is enabled. (Part 4) This part is divided into three sub-parts delimited by "-". The first sub-part indicates whether the ConTest's heuristics limiting noise generation to events related to shared variables is enabled. The second sub-part says whether the noise is also put to other *ploc*s than accesses to shared variables. Finally, the third sub-part says whether the noise is put to *all* shared variables or *one* randomly chosen before each execution. (Part 5) This last part encodes the setting of our noise injection heuristics. It consists of two sub-parts delimited by "-". The first sub-part says whether our noise injection heuristics is enabled and the second one whether our noise strength computation is enabled too. For further information concerning ConTest configuration, we refer the reader to Section 2 or ConTest documentation [9].

For each considered test case (i.e., airlines, crawler, etc.), we rank the test configurations according to the obtained results—rank 1 is the best, rank 23 is the worst. More precisely, the entries of the table under the particular test cases contain average ranks obtained across the different basic noise types of ConTest. The average rank over all the test cases is provided in the last column. The test configurations are then sorted according to their average rank, giving us their final position in the evaluation of the 23 configurations. We use the final position to identify the configurations in the following text.

As before, the table shows that the efficiency of the different heuristics vary for different test cases. Our heuristics (at position 3) achieved the best results in three out of five test cases (*airlines*, *ftpserver*, and *tidorbj*). The heuristics was not evaluated as the overall winner due to the poor results that it achieved in the *crawler* test case. On the other hand, our heuristics was evaluated as the best for *crawler* when considering the probability of error detection. In fact, there were only three configurations (3, 16, and 18) which were able to detect the very rarely manifesting error in the *crawler* test case. Our heuristics increased the probability of spotting the error the most and achieved the best result in both relativised and non-relativised comparisons. In the other considered test cases, our heuristics was always in the first third of the average results when considering the relativised probability of error detection. As for results of our heuristics in the non-relativised cases of both the Avio* coverage and the probability of error detection, our heuristics achieved worse results (still mostly being in the first half of all the configurations). Hence, based on the results, we can claim that our new heuristics seems to be a good choice when one needs to test bigger programs, especially when having a limited time for testing.

The use of our noise injection heuristics combined with the newly proposed noise strength computation ended at position 12 in Table 5. The results achieved in the various test cases differ more significantly for this configuration than when using the new noise injection heuristics only. Relatively good results were obtained for the *sunbank* and *airlines* test cases, bad results for the other test cases. Similar results were obtained for the relativised Avio* coverage. This is caused by the newly proposed noise strength computation that sometimes puts a considerable amount of noise to places where it might be interesting. This leads to poor results in relativised comparisons where the time plays an important role. On the other hand, the use of our noise injection heuristics combined with the newly proposed noise strength computation provided better results than using our noise injection heuristics only in the non-relativised comparisons because it was able to examine more different interleavings. It was even evaluated as the best for the *tidorbj* test case in the non-relativised comparison using the Avio* coverage. To sum up, we may advice to use the combination of both of the newly proposed heuristics to test bigger programs when performance degradation is not a problem.

Table 5 also clearly shows effectiveness of the ConTest's shared variable heuristics focused on a single randomly chosen shared variable. Configurations based on this heuristics occupy eight from the ten first positions in the table and provide good results also in other considered comparisons. The overall best results were obtained by the combination of this heuristics with the *timeoutTamper* and *haltOneThread* noise heuristics (position 1), which is again mainly due to the effect of the *timeoutTamper* heuristics in the *crawler* test case. Hence, our results prove conclusions presented in [1] that focusing noise on a single variable randomly chosen for each test execution improves the overall test coverage.

Our results then also show that some heuristics trying to restrict the position where to put noise in an intelligent way provide worse results than the configuration with generating noise at random places in test executions (position 11). Finally, we have to admit that surprisingly good results were often provided by the random setting of ConTest too (position 4). This approach provided good results especially in the relativised comparisons and the best result for the *airlines* test case and the criterion of maximizing the probability of error manifestation. Results of this configuration were of course considerably worse for the non-relativised comparison where the execution time is not considered. We suggest to use this configuration when the execution time is important, and one has no idea how the test case is affected by different noise injection techniques.

Results presented in Table 5 were computed for *seqLen=20* and *nFreq=150*. We also examined the influence of changing these paramaters. Our results show that *seqLen* has a minimal impact on the results. Configurations that were evaluated as good after 10 executions of the test were very similarly rated after 50 executions. The *nFreq* parameter which controls how often the noise is caused influenced our results more. Differences were usually up to two positions with three exceptions. Those exceptions represent the ConTest random setting and both versions of our heuristics which in fact do not use the *nFreq* parameter. All three configurations obtain a better ranking when *noiseFreq=50* and non-relativised results are considered. As for relativised results, the ConTest random setting obtained the best overall ranking in both considered evaluation schemes. Our noise injection heuristics used without the newly proposed noise strength computation remained among the best three configurations, still beating the ConTest random configuration in some test results. The combined use of both newly proposed heuristics lost when considering the Avio* coverage, but remained well-ranked when considering the error detection probability. Therefore, we suggest to use the ConTest random setting or our noise injection heuristics without the newly proposed noise strength computation in cases when the amount of noise needs to be very low.

5   Conclusions

We have provided a comparison of multiple noise injection heuristics that was missing in the current literature. We have also proposed a new, original noise injection heuristics, winning over the existing ones in some cases. We show that there is no silver bullet among the existing noise injection heuristics although some of them are on average winning in certain testing scenarios. Based on our experiences, we have given several suggestions on how to test concurrent programs using the noise injection approach. Our future work includes further improvements of our heuristics, a further investigation of the influence of noise on different programs, and an evaluation of some heuristics [4,6] not yet implemented and tested in our framework. The obtained results are also important for our current work which applies search techniques for automatic identification of a suitable configuration (or configurations) for specific test cases [7,8].

Acknowledgement. This work was supported by the Czech Science Foundation (projects no. P103/10/0306 and 102/09/H042), the Czech Ministry of Education (projects COST OC10009 and MSM 0021630528), the EU/Czech IT4Innovations Centre of Excellence project CZ.1.05/1.1.00/02.0070, and the internal BUT project FIT-11-1.

References

1. Ben-Asher, Y., Farchi, E., Eytani, Y.: Heuristics for Finding Concurrent Bugs. In: Proc. of IPDPS 2003. IEEE CS (2003)
2. Bron, A., Farchi, E., Magid, Y., Nir, Y., Ur, S.: Applications of Synchronization Coverage. In: Proc. of PPoPP 2005. ACM (2005)
3. Edelstein, O., Farchi, E., Nir, Y., Ratsaby, G., Ur, S.: Multithreaded Java Program Test Generation. IBM Systems Journal 41, 111–125 (2002)
4. Eytani, Y.: Concurrent Java Test Generation as a Search Problem. ENTCS 144 (2006)
5. Eytani, Y., Latvala, T.: Explaining Intermittent Concurrent Bugs by Minimizing Scheduling Noise. In: Bin, E., Ziv, A., Ur, S. (eds.) HVC 2006. LNCS, vol. 4383, pp. 183–197. Springer, Heidelberg (2007)
6. Farchi, E., Nir, Y., Ur, S.: Concurrent Bug Patterns and How To Test Them. In: Proc. of IPDPS 2003. IEEE CS (2003)
7. Křena, B., Letko, Z., Vojnar, T.: Coverage Metrics for Saturation-based and Search-based Testing of Concurrent Software. To appear in Proc. of RV (2011), http://www.fit.vutbr.cz/~iletko/pub/rv11paper.pdf
8. Křena, B., Letko, Z., Vojnar, T., Ur, S.: A Platform for Search-based Testing of Concurrent Software. In: Proc. of PADTAD 2010. ACM (2010)
9. Nir-Buchbinder, Y., Farchi, E., Tzoref-Brill, R., Ur, S.: IBM Contest Documentation (May 2005), http://www.alphaworks.ibm.com/tech/contest
10. Soriano, J., Jimenez, M., Cantera, J.M., Hierro, J.J.: Delivering Mobile Enterprise Services on Morfeo's MC Open Source Platform. In: Proc. of MDM 2006. IEEE CS (2006)
11. Stoller, S.D.: Testing Concurrent Java Programs Using Randomized Scheduling. In: Proc. of RV 2002. ENTCS, vol. 70(4). Elsevier (2002)
12. Šimša, J., Bryant, R., Gibson, G.: DBug: Systematic Testing of Unmodified Distributed and Multi-threaded Systems. In: Groce, A., Musuvathi, M. (eds.) SPIN Workshops 2011. LNCS, vol. 6823, pp. 188–193. Springer, Heidelberg (2011)
13. Trainin, E., Nir-Buchbinder, Y., Tzoref-Brill, R., Zlotnick, A., Ur, S., Farchi, E.: Forcing Small Models of Conditions on Program Interleaving for Detection of Concurrent Bugs. In: Proc. of PADTAD 2009. ACM (2009)
14. Yang, C.-S.D., Souter, A.L., Pollock, L.L.: All-DU-Path Coverage for Parallel Programs. In: Proc. of ISSTA 1998. ACM (1998)

Low GPU Occupancy Approach
to Fast Arithmetic Coding in JPEG2000

Jiří Matela[1,3], Martin Šrom[3], and Petr Holub[2,3]

[1] Faculty of Informatics
[2] Institute of Computer Science,
Masaryk University, Botanická 68a, 602 00 Brno, Czech Republic
[3] CESNET z.s.p.o., Zikova 4, 162 00 Prague, Czech Republic
{matela,hopet}@ics.muni.cz, 208213@mail.muni.cz

Abstract. Arithmetic coding, and especially adaptive MQ-Coding of JPEG2000, is a serial process, which does not match specifics of GPUs as massively parallel processors well. In this paper we study and evaluate several approaches to acceleration of the MQ-Coding using commodity GPU hardware, including our proposal of a new enhanced renormalization procedure. We conclude with a "low occupancy approach" and 5.6–16× average speedup when compared to the state of the art multi-threaded CPU implementations.

1 Introduction

Besides the compression performance superior to the JPEG standard, the JPEG2000 [1,2] provides a number advanced features (e.g. multiple resolution support, progressive format, optional lossless compression, or region of interests coding) at cost of much higher computational demands. Figure 1 presents a simplified block diagram of the JPEG2000 compression system. Input image data consists of one or more color components, which can be optionally transformed into a different target color space. Prior to actual compression, the image data is transformed using the discrete wavelet transform (DWT) [3] and optionally quantized [4] to reduce volume of the data to be compressed. The actual compression is performed by the Embedded Block Coding with Optimal Truncation (EBCOT) [5] consisting of two tiers: Tier-1 of the algorithm is context-based adaptive binary arithmetic coder, while Tier-2 serves for the purposes of data formation and rate allocation of the resulting stream.

The input to the EBCOT is partitioned into so called *code-blocks*. Each code-block is independently processed by context-modeling and arithmetic MQ-Coder modules in Tier-1 [6]. The context modeller analyzes bit structure of a code-block and collects contextual information (CX) that is passed together with bit values (D) to the arithmetic coding module for binary compression. The EBCOT Tier-1 is known to be computationally very intensive—most of JPEG2000 processing time is spent in Tier-1 [7,8].

Attracted by their raw computing power and affordability, a number of general-purpose computing approaches on commodity GPUs has been implemented.

Z. Kotásek et al. (Eds.): MEMICS 2011, LNCS 7119, pp. 136–145, 2012.

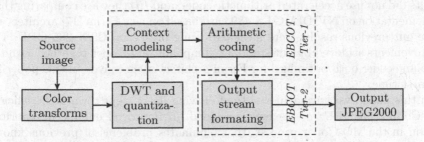

Fig. 1. JPEG2000 compression chain diagram

We have opted for CUDA [9] because of its flexibility and ability to utilize maximum performance of GPUs in real applications. GPU architectures are designed to run thousands of threads in parallel. In CUDA, the threads are grouped into so called thread blocks and warps, where the threads can cooperate using synchronization primitives, shared memory (fast, visible within a thread block only), and global memory (slower, visible to all threads). Fastest memory for each thread is registers, but their number is limited—if compound amount of registers requested on a multiprocessor is exceeded, the data is spilled to a slow local memory by the CUDA compiler. Threads within the same warp should follow the same execution path; otherwise thread divergence is introduced and divergent execution paths are serialized (SIMT). These architecture specifics of GPUs call for algorithms that allow for fine-grained parallelization with minimum instruction divergence and good use of the memory hierarchy. High-enough ratio of arithmetic operations to memory accesses is needed in order to mask memory latency.

Related Work. Acceleration of the compression steps up to the context modeling for GPU has been studied by several groups [10,11,12], but an efficient implementation of the MQ-Coding is still an open question. When accelerating the EBCOT Tier-1 as whole using GPUs, it should be noted that co-design of the context modeling on a GPU and the MQ-Coding on a CPU is not appropriate since the amount of data between these two steps increases multiple times and data transfer over buses would become a bottleneck.

A natural approach to the parallel MQ-Coder is on code-block level, utilized by CUJ2K [12]. Limited work has been done on general parallelization of the coder [13], while most of the work focuses on VLSI architectures [14,15,16].

A recent study by Le et al. [10] also focused on the GPU acceleration of the JPEG2000 EBCOT processing. Their context modeller uses parallelization principles published by us previously [11]. Authors state their novel contribution is a fully parallel design of the arithmetic coder, which is, however, incompatible with the JPEG2000 MQ-Coder. Discussion of their results also shows that the introduced parallelism of the arithmetic coder doesn't bring any significant improvement for GPUs. Le et al. claim their approach is about 2× faster than our previous results, which is incorrect for two reasons: *(i)* our previously published results did not use accelerated arithmetic coder, and *(ii)* they are comparing their implementation on NVIDIA GTX 480 card based on new Fermi [17] architecture, while our previous results were measured using pre-Fermi GTX 285 GPU. The improvements achieved by our standard-compliant MQ-Coder together with the bit plane coder both optimized for Fermi architecture are given in this paper for the first time.

In this paper, we have achieved the following novel steps toward the efficient MQ-Coding on GPU: *a)* we have provided an improved enhanced renormalization in the MQ-Coder process, that eliminates problems of previous known designs, *b)* surveyed and analyzed state of the art parallelization techniques from the perspective of GPU architectures; *c)* studied optimum occupancy from performance perspective; *d)* evaluated performance of accelerated EBCOT Tier-1 compression on real-world systems.

2   Arithmetic Coding in JPEG2000

JPEG2000 standard uses MQ-Coding [18,19], which is a variant of an arithmetic Q-Coder. The Q-Coder works with a notion of a *more probable symbol* (MPS) and a *less probable symbol* (LPS)—the prevailing value (0 or 1) is mapped to the MPS while the other value becomes the LPS. The coding process results in a number C and uses an interval A which is split into two sub-intervals $[0, AQ)$ and $[AQ, A]$, where Q is the probability of MPS occurrence. For each bit on input, the coding will proceed as follows:

MPS	$A = A(1 - Q)$	$C = C + AQ$
LPS	$A = AQ$	$C = C$

In order to minimize the number of multiplications, which are more complex than summations, the A interval is kept close to $A \approx 1$ and the multiplications may be replaced by $A(1 - Q) \approx A - Q$ and $AQ \approx Q$. More precisely A is kept in interval $[0.75, 1.5]$ using so called *renormalization* process: both A and C are multiplied by 2 until $A \geq 0.75$ (see Figure 3).

MQ-Coder is an adaptive variant of Q-Coder, where the meaning of the MPS and the LPS adapts during the coding process to obtain better results. Each input symbol $D \in \{0, 1\}$ is assigned a context value CX, which determines mapping of the MPS and the LPS, an estimate of LPS probability, and other coder state information. Thus all the D symbols with the same CX share some coder state.

Implementation of the MQ-Coder requires two 32-bit registers for A and C and a lookup table. Structure of C register is as follows:

$$\texttt{0000 cbbb bbbb bsss xxxx xxxx xxxx xxxx}$$

where b represents output bits for ByteOut procedure (for meaning of the other bits, see [18, p. 187]). During the computation, an index $I(CX)$ into the lookup table is maintained for each context; starting with initial values according to

```
A = A - Qe;
if A < 0x8000
    if A < Qe
        A = Qe;
    else
        C = C + Qe;
    I(CX) = NMPS;
    RENORMALIZE;
else
    C = C + Qe;
```

```
A = A - Qe;
if A < Qe
    C = C + Qe;
else
    A = Qe;
I(CX) = NLPS;
RENORMALIZE;
```

Fig. 2. MQ-Coder MPS coding (a–left) and LPS coding (b–right) procedures

JPEG2000 specification, it evolves according to the symbols read and records in the lookup table. The lookup table contains 46 rows with the following columns: $I(CX)$ – index value, Qe – LPS probability estimate; $NMPS/NLPS$ – next index under MPS/LPS; $SWITCH$ – MPS/LPS swap indicator. The renormalization occurs when $A < 0x8000$. The MQ-Coder MPS and LPS coding procedures are depicted in Figure 2.

The MQ-coder is highly sequential: modifications of the A and C registers depend on previously coded symbols due to the evolving state guided by the lookup table. Parallelism is only allowed on the level of code blocks, which is too coarse for GPUs—smaller latency-sensitive images (e.g., real-time 720p video encoding) do not have enough code blocks; even for larger images, there is still a problem with large amount of resources required by a single parallel process. Beyond the default mode, there are optional modes in the JPEG2000 standard [1, Chapter 12]: combination of RESET, RESTART and CAUSAL enables parallel coding passes at cost of slightly lower coding efficiency. But these modes are optional and forbidden by some important standards based on the JPEG2000, e.g., Digital Cinema Initiative (DCI) [20] which is widely used for video distribution in digital cinematography.

3   Accelerating MQ-Coder Using GPU

Basic binary arithmetic coding algorithms can be parallelized using parallel prefix sum suitable for GPU platforms [21]. Context-based nature of MQ-Coder, however, inhibits application of this method to a great extent.

When accelerating MQ-Coder using modern GPUs we have to deal with *coarse data granularity* and *data-dependant conditional branches* which are the properties of the algorithm restricting utilisation of GPU processing power.

Coarse Data Granularity. The smallest independent data block is a code-block (possibly slightly refined by RESET+RESTART+CAUSAL). Such a data block cannot be normally processed internally in parallel, thus each thread has to process its own data block. Small number of data blocks may produce not enough working warps to mask global memory or instruction pipeline latency. There are also consequences for large amount of local data and global memory access pattern compared to a whole thread block processing a common shared data block.

Data-Dependant Conditional Branches. Because the MQ-Coder algorithm contains conditional branches, threads in a warp are taking divergent execution paths. In the SIMT model, width of an issued instruction is then dynamically narrowed and performance is wasted.

3.1   MQ-Coder Concurrency and Speedup Techniques

As a basis for our GPU MQ-Coder we have chosen an open source CPU implementation of MQ-Coder from OpenJPEG library. Except for several minor changes the code was copied as is, so that we could compare performance of the same code on CPUs and GPUs. Because of the coarse data granularity, the GPU code was executed with each of 64 threads in a thread block processing a single code-block. This basic GPU MQ-Coder was 7× faster than OpenJPEG on the CPU and 1.9× faster than highly optimized proprietary Kakadu CPU implementation. Results discussed throughout this section are also summarized in Figure 4.

Transition to Registers. Local data structures and arrays are likely to be placed not in the registers but in slower local memory [9, Chap. 5.3.2.2]. Despite the local memory is cached in an L1 cache, the registers are still much faster. The basic MQ-Coder implementation stores A, C, and CT symbols in a structure placed into local memory. We have modified the code to use registers where possible. Results were 2.4× and almost 17× faster than basic GPU and CPU codes respectively.

Enhanced Renormalization. The original MQ-Coder algorithm checks A and starts renormalization (Figure 3a) whenever its value drops under $0x8000$ threshold. The renormalization process then NS-times cyclically doubles value of A and C registers till $A > 0x8000$. Enhanced renormalization described by Min et al. [13] omits the cyclical doubling by precomputing the NS using static lookup table with registers A and C being shifted by this number in single pass. There are, however, two issues with that algorithm: *(a)* it introduces overhead of the lookup table and *(b)* it does not handle overflows correctly in all cases.

Instead of the lookup table, we propose using Count Leading Zeros (CLZ) instruction, which is common on CPUs as well as GPUs and returns the number of consecutive zero bits starting at the most significant bit. Based on our experiments, this is as fast as the lookup table approach both on GPUs and CPUs and avoids the storage overhead of the lookup table.

Regarding the second problem, compressed data is sent to output every time the value of counter CT drops to zero during the renormalization process. The CT counts how many ByteOut bit positions are left in the C register. The algorithm proposed in [13] compares number of shift steps NS and number of ByteOut positions left CT and splits the renormalization procedure into two steps whenever $NS > CT$ [13, Fig. 6]. The algorithm is correct except for occasions

```
while ( A < 0x8000 ) {
    A = A << 1;
    C = C << 1;
    CT = CT - 1;
    if ( CT == 0 )
        ByteOut();
}
```

```
A = A << NS;
if ( CT > NS ) {
    C = C << NS; CT = CT - NS;
} else {
    C = C << CT; NS = NS - CT;
    ByteOut();
    if ( CT > NS ) {
        C = C << NS; CT = CT - NS;
    } else {
        C = C << CT; NS = NS - CT;
        ByteOut();
        CT = CT - NS; C = C << NS;
    }
}
```

Fig. 3. Original (a–left) and revised enhanced (b–right) renormalization

when $NS - CT > 8$. We have therefore proposed revised enhanced renormalization (Figure 3b) which is as fast as [13], functionally equivalent to JPEG2000 original and about 39% faster than original when implemented on a GPU.

Loop Unrolling. Loop unrolling was proposed in [14,22], suggesting to process several consecutive MPS symbols at once, iff renormalization does not take its place during the coding and all the consecutive MPS symbols have been assigned same context CX. Under this condition new values of the registers A and C can be computed according to equations $A = A - n \times Qe$ and $C = C + n \times Qe$, where n is number of consecutive symbols having the same CX. Such equations are enumerated using a single MAD instruction on a GPU. We evaluated that for our image data set, 17%–25% of all CX,D pairs was grouped into sequences of MPS with same CX value. We considered sequences of length from 2 to 32.

To detect the sequences and find out their length during the coding, we have implemented a parallel lookup algorithm, checking for potential sequence when a MPS is detected on the input. The CUDA kernel was launched in such a configuration that each group of 4 threads was concurrently processing a single code-block. We have chosen 4 threads because vast majority of the sequences was not longer than 4. Our measurements demonstrate average 31% slowdown due to overhead of the parallel lookup routine and mainly due to fact that majority of CX,D pairs is coded sequentially, which means that the majority of the threads intended to process particular code-block is idling most of the time.

Prefix Sum. The prefix sum technique enhances previously described loop unrolling by considering all sequences of MPS regardless value of their contexts CX. In this case the portion of MPS sequences rises to 35%–50%. Because different contexts have different probability estimate Qe, values of A and C registers cannot be updated by the single MAD instruction. Qe values have to be summed up to form $Qe_{total} = \sum_{i=0}^{n-1} Qe_i$ which is in turn used to update the registers $A = A - Qe_{total}$ and $C = C + Qe_{total}$. Similarly to [21], the value of the aggregated probability estimate can be concurrently computed using parallel prefix sum algorithm. Similarly to the loop unrolling, this technique resulted in 24%

slowdown on average due to its complexity, overhead of sequence lookup routine and the fact, that most of the threads were idling on solitary symbols.

Chunk Data Loading. Because of coarse data granularity, every thread processes different data locations which also means that threads do not follow coalesced global memory access pattern. Data loading could be sped up if a single thread issues more data fetches or if it uses bit-level parallelism through wider fetches [23]. We have opted for 64-bit fetches through data type double and every thread performed 16 such loads in each step of a computation. This resulted in 33% speedup on average.

3.2   Low GPU Occupancy Approach

In order to find optimum configuration of the computation, we have analyzed its performance dependence on occupancy of the GPU. CUDA occupancy is defined as a ratio of a number of resident warps to the maximum number of resident warps supported by a multiprocessor [9]. A common optimization is to increase occupancy in order to hide latency of global memory access (GMA) and instruction pipeline latency (IP). Since occupancy is determined by amount of shared memory and registers used, a typical endeavour is to reduce resources consumption just to increase occupancy which could yield speed up. Higher occupancy, nevertheless, helps to hide GMA latency only for memory-bound kernels—i.e., when throughput of global memory causes performance bottleneck—and IP latency is typically hidden at occupancy counting about 22 or 6 warps per multiprocessor on Fermi and pre-Fermi platforms respectively [9]. On the other hand, lower occupancy allows for more registers and more cache per a single thread. Availability of more registers may be advantageous for computations with many variables of simple local data types. Larger amount of data cache may be helpful when more complex local data structures are placed to the local memory. Occupancy could be further reduced through instruction level parallelism when a batch of independent arithmetic or data loading instructions is issued [23].

For our GPU accelerated MQ-Coder implementation, the best results have been achieved at 33% occupancy (Figure 4). When compared to 100% occupancy, a 1080p image was processed 1 ms/13% faster and a 4K image 9 ms/45% faster. Because our code does not feature sufficient portion of instruction level parallelism, the performance drops significantly at lower occupancies.

3.3   Experimental Results and Discussion

All results throughout this paper have been measured on a personal computer sporting Core i7 @3GHz, 6GB RAM, NVIDIA GTX 580, Linux operating system, GCC 4.4.3 and CUDA 4.0. As input data we have used the The New Test Images set[1] of 8 bit RGB images in 1920×1080 (1080p, full HD) resolution. To measure performance with respect to the resolution of an input image, we have used an image of nature[2] in 720p (1280×720), 1080p (1920×1080), 4K (4096×2160)

---

[1] http://www.imagecompression.info/test_images/
[2] http://adventuretykes.com/wp-content/uploads/2010/11/MG_0079.jpg

Table 1. *(a)* Performance of CPU and GPU implementations of the MQ-Coder and *(b)* overall JPEG2000 and EBCOT Tier-1 performance. n t describes number of threads used by the multi-threaded CPU implementation. CUJ2K performance in *(a)* is only estimated based on average ratio 0.34 of MQ-Coder in Tier-1 in other implementations.

(a)	720p	1080p	4K	(b) 1080p	Total	Tier-1
OpenJPEG 1.4	157 ms	316 ms	1081 ms	OpenJPEG 1.4	1204 ms	958 ms
Jasper 1.900.1	89 ms	178 ms	594 ms	Jasper 1.900.1	1179 ms	883 ms
Kakadu 6.4 (4 t)	41 ms	84 ms	284 ms	Kakadu 6.4 (4 t)	218 ms	182 ms
CUJ2K 1.1	≈25 ms	≈49 ms	≈166 ms	CUJ2K 1.1 (GPU)	280 ms	143 ms
CUDA GPU	**7.3 ms**	**8.1 ms**	**17.6 ms**	**CUDA GPU**	**N/A**	**14.1 ms**

resolutions. All the measured JPEG2000 implementations have been set to lossless mode with code-block 32×32 px, and 5 level DWT. CUDA kernels have been executed at 33% occupancy with 64 threads per a thread-block, without any shared memory used, and with preference for L1 caching.

Part *(a)* of Table 1 compares MQ-Coder performance of several CPU and GPU implementations, both open-source and commercial. Data is provided for images of 720p, 1080p, and 4K resolutions. Data for the MQ-Coder in CUJ2K implementations are only estimates based on average ratio 0.34 of MQ-Coder in Tier-1 in other implementations. The results show that the performance of our MQ-Coder implementation scales with amount of data processed. The 720p image is coded only 0.8 ms faster than image in 1080p which has about twice as much resolution and the 4K image is coded about 2× faster but it has 4× more pixels than the 1080p image. When compared to the CUJ2K our implementation is 3.4× to 9.4× faster and it is 5.6× to 61× faster than the CPU implementations.

Part *(b)* presents total and Tier-1 compression times of the individual codes on 1080p image data. The total time is provided to give an idea of what fraction of the total time Tier-1 consumes. It also shows that our entire GPU EBCOT Tier-1 implementation is 68× faster than OpenJPEG, 63× faster than reference JasPer, 13× faster than commercial multi-threaded Kakadu, and about 10× faster than another GPU implementation CUJ2K on 1080p image. The result of 14.1 ms also allows real-time compression requirements of full HD (1080p) video data. We did not include results presented in [10] because of its incompatibility with JPEG2000 standard. To give approximate comparison, noting [10] used 3.3× more data (5 MP, CMYK) and ≈15% slower GPU using the same Fermi architecture, their results are equivalent to 71 ms for Tier-1, which is 5× slower compared to our results.

Figure 4 summarizes performance impact of the algorithm and GPU-related optimizations described in the Sections 3.1 and 3.2. The table contains execution times in milliseconds for each optimization and resolution in the left column and speedups relative to the basic GPU implementation in the right column. All the optimizations are implemented in registers, since the register optimization improved performance of all the optimizations. As noted in Section 3.1, loop unrolling and prefix sum techniques slowed down the basic register

	720p		1080p		4K	
GPU Basic	38.0 ms	–	45.0 ms	–	92.9 ms	–
GPU R	16.2 ms	2.3×	18.9 ms	2.4×	48.5 ms	1.9×
GPU R+ERN	11.9 ms	3.2×	14.9 ms	3.0×	44.9 ms	2.1×
GPU R+LU	18.1 ms	2.1×	31.2 ms	1.4×	87.1 ms	1.1×
GPU R+PS	20.9 ms	1.8×	25.7 ms	1.8×	64.6 ms	1.4×
GPU R+CL	12.1 ms	3.1×	13.2 ms	3.4×	27.7 ms	3.4×
GPU R+ERN+CL	7.3 ms	5.2×	8.1 ms	5.6×	17.6 ms	5.3×

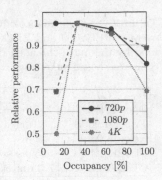

Fig. 4. Performance impact of individual optimizations (left) and occupancy–performance relation (right). R – implementation in registers; ERN – revised enhanced renormalization; LU – loop unrolling; PS – prefix sum; CL – chunk loading.

implementation. The resulting implementation therefore combines the use of registers, revised enhanced renormalization, and chunk loading optimizations.

4   Conclusion and Future Work

In this paper, we have studied various approaches to implementing and optimizing the arithmetic MQ-Coder for GPU platforms. We have proposed a novel enhanced normalization process compliant with the JPEG2000 standard. Together with implementing the computations in the registers and with the specific chunk loading strategy, these turned out to be effective optimizations, while the loop unrolling and the prefix sums lead to deterioration of the performance. We have also investigated dependency of the GPU occupancy on the performance and figured out that the optimum performance is achieved with as low occupancy as 33% because of the amount of resources required by each parallel process. The experimental results show 5.6–16× and 3–9× performance increase over the current multi-threaded CPU implementations and GPU implementations of MQ-coder respectively, and 13–68× and 10× increase for entire EBCOT Tier-1 over existing CPU and GPU implementations respectively. The results indicate that the presented GPU design will allow for the real-time JPEG2000 compression of 1080p video and in a multi GPU configurations it will allow even real-time 4K video compression. The process of resource utilization optimization stressed the importance of further research into automation of performance tuning.

Acknowledgments. This project has been supported by the grants LM2010005 and GD102/09/H042 and MSM0021622419 research intent.

References

1. Taubman, D.S., Marcellin, M.W.: JPEG2000: Image Compression Fundamentals, Standards, and Practice. Springer, Heidelberg (2002)
2. ISO/IEC 15444-1: JPEG2000 image coding system—part 1: Core coding system (2004)

3. Daubechies, I., Sweldens, W.: Factoring wavelet transforms into lifting steps. J. Fourier Anal. Appl. 4, 247–269 (1998)
4. Marcellin, M.W., Lepley, M.A., Bilgin, A., Flohr, T.J., Chinen, T.T., Kasner, J.H.: An overview of quantization in JPEG2000. Signal Processing: Image Communication 17(1), 73–84 (2002)
5. Taubman, D.: High performance scalable image compression with EBCOT. IEEE Trans. Image Process. 9(7), 1158–1170 (2000)
6. Rabbani, M., Joshi, R.: An overview of the JPEG2000 still image compression standard. Signal Processing: Image Communication 17(1), 3–48 (2002)
7. Lian, C.J., Chen, K.F., Chen, H.H., Chen, L.G.: Analysis and architecture design of block-coding engine for EBCOT in JPEG2000. IEEE Trans. Circuits Syst. Video Technol. 13(3), 219–230 (2003)
8. Matela, J., Rusňák, V., Holub, P.: GPU-based sample-parallel context modeling for EBCOT in JPEG2000. In: MEMICS 2010 – Selected Papers. OpenAccess Series in Informatics (OASIcs), vol. 16, pp. 77–84. Schloss Dagstuhl–Leibniz-Zentrum fuer Informatik, Dagstuhl (2011)
9. NVIDIA: NVIDIA CUDA C Programming Guide 4.0. NVIDIA (2011)
10. Le, R., Bahar, I.R., Mundy, J.L.: A novel parallel Tier-1 coder for JPEG2000 using GPUs. In: IEEE SASP 2011, pp. 129–136 (2011)
11. Matela, J., Rusňák, V., Holub, P.: Efficient JPEG2000 EBCOT Context Modeling for Massively Parallel Architectures. In: Data Compression Conference (DCC 2011), Snowbird, USA, pp. 423–432 (2011)
12. Weiß, A., Heide, M., Papandreou, S., Fürst, N., Balevic, A.: CUJ2K: a JPEG2000 encoder in CUDA. Technical report, IPVS, Universität Stuttgart (2009)
13. Min, B., Yoon, S., Ra, J., Park, D.S.: Enhanced renormalization algorithm in MQ-coder of JPEG2000. In: IEEE ISITC 2007, pp. 213–216 (2007)
14. Dyer, M., Taubman, D., Nooshabadi, S., Gupta, A.: Concurrency techniques for arithmetic coding in JPEG2000. IEEE Trans. Circuits Syst. I 53(6), 1203–1213 (2006)
15. Liu, K., Zhou, Y., Song Li, Y., Ma, J.F.: A high performance MQ encoder architecture in JPEG2000. Integration, the VLSI Journal 43(3), 305–317 (2010)
16. Rhu, M., Member, S., Park, I.C., Member, S.: Optimization of Arithmetic Coding for JPEG2000. IEEE Transactions on Circuits and Systems 20(3), 446–451 (2010)
17. NVIDIA: NVIDIA's Next Generation CUDA Compute Architecture: Fermi. NVIDIA (2009)
18. Acharya, T., Tsai, P.S.: JPEG2000 Standard for Image Compression: Concepts, algorithms and VLSI architectures. Wiley Interscience, New York (2004)
19. Christopoulos, C., Skodras, A., Ebrahimi, T.: The JPEG2000 still image coding system: An overview. IEEE Trans. Consum. Electron. 46(4), 1103–1127 (2000)
20. DCI: Digital Cinema System Specification v. 1.2, http://www.dcimovies.com/DCIDigitalCinemaSystemSpecv1_2.pdf (2008)
21. Balevic, A.: Parallel Variable-Length Encoding on GPGPUs. In: Lin, H.-X., Alexander, M., Forsell, M., Knüpfer, A., Prodan, R., Sousa, L., Streit, A. (eds.) Euro-Par 2009. LNCS, vol. 6043, pp. 26–35. Springer, Heidelberg (2010)
22. Feygin, G., Gulak, P., Chow, P.: Architectural advances in the VLSI implementation of arithmetic coding for binary image compression. In: DCC 1994, pp. 254–263 (1994)
23. Volkov, V.: Better Performance at Lower Occupancy. In: GPU Technology Conference (2010)

Using Dimensionality Reduction Method for Binary Data to Questionnaire Analysis

Jakub Mažgut[1], Martina Paulinyová[2], and Peter Tiňo[3]

[1] Faculty of Informatics and Information Technologies,
Slovak University of Technology, Slovakia
mazgut@fiit.stuba.sk
[2] Department of Child Psychiatry, Child University Hospital,
Faculty of Medicine, Comenius University, Slovakia
mpaulinyova@gmail.com
[3] School of Computer Science,
University of Birmingham, United Kingdom
P.Tino@cs.bham.ac.uk

Abstract. In this paper we introduce a modified version of existing dimensionality reduction method for binary data, weighted logistic principal component analysis (WLPCA). We propose to fit the basis vectors of the latent natural parameter subspace in a successive procedure instead of fitting them at ones, so the vectors will be sorted by an explanation power of the data in term of model likelihood. Based on our modified WLPCA model, we present a methodology for analyzing binary (true/false) questionnaires. The purpose of the methodology is to bring the authors of questionnaires a global overview of relationships between questions based on the correlations of binary answers. In the experiment we employ our proposed model to analyze psychiatric questionnaire, namely the Junior Temperament and Character Inventory (JTCI). The results suggest that our methodology can yield interesting relationships between questions and that our modified model is better suited for such an analysis as the existing versions of the logistic principal component analysis model.

Keywords: dimensionality reduction, binary data, principal component analysis.

1 Introduction

Most of us have filled in a questionnaire of one kind or other for various purposes. In the basic form, the questionnaire is a research instrument consisting of a series of questions for the purpose of gathering information from respondents. Designing any questionnaire to be really effective is a complicated process. Even translation of the questionnaire requires several confirmatory steps, especially in psychiatric domain [5].

In this work, we focus on an analysis of questionnaire from psychiatric domain, but the model and the methodology can be used to analyze any binary

Z. Kotásek et al. (Eds.): MEMICS 2011, LNCS 7119, pp. 146–154, 2012.
© Springer-Verlag Berlin Heidelberg 2012

questionnaire. To introduce the process of evaluation of validity and reliability and to point out existing problems we describe the process of translating a Junior Temperament and Character Inventory (JTCI) from English to another language.

Firstly, the text of JTCI must be translated from the original English version to the desired language and then independently translated back by bilingual professionals. Usually, the reverse translation must be approved by authors of the original questionnaire [5]. Then the questionnaire is administered to the respondents and acquired data are collected. When the data are collected, statistical methods are used to evaluate the validity and reliability of the questionnaire. In questionnaires, the questions are usually divided into theoretical groups based on the general construct that each question tracks. One of the confirmatory tests is a test that compares the theoretical structure (groups of questions) with the structure (factors) obtained from data by dimensionality reduction methods, principal component analysis (PCA) or factor analysis (FA) [4]. If PCA or FA reveals similar structure to the theoretical groups of questions, it is considered as a sign of properly designed questionnaire. However, the PCA and FA are often used in their basic forms that are suitable for modeling real-valued data assuming Gaussian noise model and not suitable for modeling the binary data. Note that, using such models to analyze binary data is a common practice in psychiatric domain (e.g.: [4,7]) and can lead to misleading results.

To further validate the design of questionnaire, an internal consistency of each group of questions is measured by Cronbach alpha. The higher the Cronbach alpha, the higher level of internal consistency for analyzed group of questions. Often the first version of questionnaire does not pass the evaluation process (e.g. [7,4]) and the authors must inspect which questions to change or completely remove. To address such problems, we propose a methodology based on an appropriate model for binary data to visualize an overview of relationships between questions based on the correlations of their binary answers.

2   Dimensionality Reduction Methods for Binary Data

Principal component analysis (PCA) [3] is a widely used method for applications such as dimensionality reduction, lossy data compression, feature extraction and visualization of multivariate data. The method discovers a orthogonal projection of the data onto a lower dimensional linear space, known as the *principal subspace*, such that the mean squared distance between the data points and their projections is minimized.

While the mean-centering operations and mean squared distance criteria of PCA are naturally suited to real-value data, they are not generally appropriate for binary data [6]. The first attempt to expand the PCA for binary and other data types was made by Collins et al. in [2]. They derived generalized criteria for dimensionally reduction of data types that can be modeled by exponential family of distributions and presented an iterative algorithm. A drawback of the algorithm is that the optimizations required at each iteration do not have a simple closed form for the Bernoulli distribution used for binary data.

Schein et al. eliminated the drawback of Collins's approach and proposed in [6] an iterative algorithm for generalized PCA embedding the Bernoulli distribution for binary data, logistic principal component analysis (LPCA). An alternating least squares method is used to fit the model parameters, where update rules have a simple closed form and are guaranteed at each iteration to improve the model likelihood. Furthermore, Zivkovic extended the LPCA model with weights [8], so the model considers individual data sample and dimension selectively, depending on the corresponding weights.

In our opinion, the name logistic principal component analysis is misleading. There are significant fundamental differences between PCA and LPCA: (1) PCA finds linear projections that maximize the variance of projected data while LPCA finds projections that maximize the model likelihood based on Bernoulli distributions; (2) PCA diagonalizes the correlation matrix producing uncorrelated factors while LPCA produces only linearly independent factors; (3) PCA assumes an unit variance across variables while LPCA does not.

3   The Model

In this chapter we propose a modified version of the WLPCA model. According to the previously mentioned differences between PCA and LPCA we decided to not use the name PCA and denote our model as weighted dimensionality reduction for binary data (WDRBD).

Consider binary N-dimensional vector $\mathbf{a} \in \{0,1\}^N$. Assume we are given a set of M such vectors organized into a data matrix $\mathbf{A}$ as row vectors, $\mathbf{A} = \{\mathbf{a}_1, \mathbf{a}_2, ..., \mathbf{a}_M\}^T$ and each element $a_{m,n}$ of the vector $\mathbf{a}_m$, $m = 1, 2, ..., M$, $n = 1, 2, ..., N$, is independently Bernoulli distributed with parameter (mean) $p_{m,n}$: $P(a_{m,n}|p_{m,n}) = p_{m,n}^{a_{m,n}} \cdot (1 - p_{m,n})^{1-a_{m,n}}$. The distribution can be equivalently parametrized through log-odds (natural parameter) $\theta_{m,n} = \log(p_{m,n}/(1-p_{m,n}))$, so the canonical link function linking the natural parameter with the mean is the logistic function $p_{m,n} = \sigma(\theta_{m,n}) = (1 + e^{-\theta_{m,n}})^{-1}$. For each data vector $\mathbf{a}_m$, $m = 1, 2, ..., M$, the LPCA has $P(\mathbf{a}_m|\boldsymbol{\theta}_m) = \prod_{n=1}^N P(a_{m,n}|\theta_{m,n})$, where $P(a_{m,n}|\theta_{m,n}) = \sigma(\theta_{m,n})^{a_{m,n}} \cdot \sigma(-\theta_{m,n})^{1-a_{m,n}}$.

Zivkovic [8] extended the model by introducing the weights $w_{m,n} \in \mathbb{R}^+$ for each data sample m and dimension n. The higher the value of $w_{m,n}$, the higher the importance of data element $a_{m,n}$. If we collect all the parameters $\theta_{m,n}$ in a matrix $\Theta \in \mathbb{R}^{M \times I}$ and assume the data vectors are independently generated, the model likelihood reads

$$L(\Theta) = \prod_{m=1}^{M} \prod_{n=1}^{N} P(a_{m,n}|\theta_{m,n})^{w_{m,n}}. \tag{1}$$

So far the values in the parameter vectors $\boldsymbol{\theta}_m$ were unconstrained. Schein et al. constrained all the N-dimensional parameter vectors $\boldsymbol{\theta}_m \in \mathbb{R}^N$ (one for each data vector $\mathbf{a}_m$) to lie in a subspace spanned by the reduced set of basis vectors $\mathbf{U} = \{\mathbf{u}_1, ..., \mathbf{u}_R\}$ where $R \leq N$ and bias (offset) vector Δ [6]:

$$\boldsymbol{\theta}_m = \sum_{r=1}^{R} q_{m,r} \cdot \mathbf{u}_r + \Delta, \tag{2}$$

where $\mathbf{q}_m = (q_{m,1}, q_{m,2}, ..., q_{m,r})$, $q_{m,r} \in \mathbb{R}$ are the mixing coefficients for the data vector $a_{m,n}$.

To get parameter updates, authors of [6] take advantage of the fact that while the logarithm of likelihood (1) is not convex in the parameters, it is convex in any parameter, if the others are kept fixed. This leads to an iterative estimation scheme described in a great detail in [6,8]. From the model likelihood definition and updates formulas can be seen that there is no pressure for the basis vectors $\mathbf{U}$ to be orthogonal or ordered by the degree of explaining the variation in data. Furthermore, the direction of correlations can be captured (hidden) as linear combinations of basis vectors and not represented straight-forward by the direction of vectors as it is in the real-valued PCA model. So to use the WLPCA model in a similar manner to the PCA for visualizing the data in 2- or 3- dimensional space spanned by basis vectors with largest explanatory power in order to identify uniform or atypical groups of data samples can be misleading.

In order to address such problems, we propose to update the parameters for each basis vector in successive procedure. Firstly, we fit the bias vector Δ, then the first basis vector $\mathbf{u}_1$ with corresponding mixing coefficients $q_{m,1}, m = 1, \ldots, M$, then the second vector with mixing coefficients and so on. According to this scheme, the model log-likelihood for ℓ-th basis vector and mixing coefficients as a form

$$\mathcal{L}(\Theta^{(\ell)}) = \sum_{m=1}^{M} \sum_{n=1}^{N} w_{m,n} \left[a_{m,n} \log \sigma(\theta_{m,n}^{(\ell)}) + (1 - a_{m,n}) \log \sigma(-\theta_{m,n}^{(\ell)}) \right], \tag{3}$$

where

$$\theta_{m,n}^{(\ell)} = q_{m,\ell} \cdot u_{\ell,n} + \delta_{m,n}^{(\ell)}, \tag{4}$$

$$\delta_{m,n}^{(\ell)} = \begin{cases} \Delta_i & \text{if } \ell = 1 \\ \sum_{r=1}^{(\ell-1)} q_{m,r} \cdot u_{r,n} + \Delta_i & \text{if } \ell > 1. \end{cases} \tag{5}$$

To get analytical parameter updates, we use the trick of [6] and derive the updating formulas from log-likelihood lower bound. Derivation of the parameter updates is rather involved and (due to space limitations) we only present the update formulas. Maximizing the lower bound of the model likelihood (3) with respect to bias vector Δ leads to

$$\Delta_n = \frac{\sum_{m=1}^{M} w_{m,n} (2 a_{m,n} - 1)}{\sum_{m=1}^{M} w_{m,n} t_{m,n}},$$

where $t_{m,n} = (\tanh(\theta_{m,n}/2)/\theta_{m,n}$. The bias vector Δ can be though as a centering of the data in case of real-valued numbers and classical PCA method.

Maximizing the lower bound of the model likelihood with respect to basis vectors $u_{\ell,n}$ and mixing coefficients $q_{m,\ell}$ leads to the following update formulas:

$$u_{\ell,n} = \frac{\sum_{m=1}^{M} w_{m,n}(2a_{m,n} - 1 - t_{m,n}\,\delta_{m,n}^{(\ell)})\,q_{m,\ell}}{\sum_{m=1}^{M} w_{m,n}\,t_{m,n}\,q_{m,\ell}^2}, \tag{6}$$

$$q_{m,\ell} = \frac{\sum_{n=1}^{N} w_{m,n}(2a_{m,n} - 1 - t_{m,n}\delta_{m,n}^{(\ell)})\,u_{\ell,n}}{\sum_{n=1}^{N} w_{m,n}\,t_{m,n}\,u_{\ell,n}^2}, \tag{7}$$

where $\ell = 1, 2, \ldots, R$ is the basis index.

4   Data

In this work, we focus on analysis of a Junior Temperament and Character Inventory (JTCI) but the model and methodology can be used to analysis any binary questionnaire. The JTCI questionnaire was developed to assess a Cloninger's biosocial model of personality in children and adolescent [5]. Assessing the biosocial model is important to distinguishing a psychopathology of the respondent. The importance of the JTCI in psychiatry supports the fact that it was translated and validated in more than 15 countries around the world [5,7].

In the experiments, we used the data gathered from Slovak version of JTCI [5]. The authors provided 773 fully filled questionnaires. Each filled questionnaire represents 108 yes/no (binary) answers. We collected the data to a binary matrix with 773 rows (data samples) and 108 columns (data attributes/questions). The questions are divided into two main groups, temperament and character questions. Furthermore, the temperament group is divided into four temperamental subgroups (traits): novelty seeking, harm avoidance, reward dependence and persistence. The character group is divided into three subgroups (traits): self-directedness, cooperativeness and self-transcendence.

5   Questionnaire Analysis

The goal of a methodology presented in this chapter is to bring a global overview over the structure of questions based on the correlations of binary answers and helps to suggest questions that need to be further analyzed in order to increase the reliability of a given questionnaire. The existing evaluation methods that employ PCA and FA are based on separating high and low values (extremes) of basis vectors coefficients (e.g. [4]). The basis vector coefficients can be thought as correlation coefficients between the question and particular factor represented by the basis vector. In other words, high correlated (positive or negative) questions with one factor creates a group.

Instead of analyzing each basis vector independently, we proposed to visualize the questions in two-dimensional plot based on their coefficients of 2 selected basis vectors. This allow us to inspect also the inter-factor correlations of questions. We employ LPCA, WLPCA and WDRBP models to find 2-dimensional subspaces (2 factors) of the binary questionnaire data, plot the questions (attributes) based on their correlations with factors and not the projections of filled questionnaires (data samples) to the subspace determinated by mixing coefficients as it is a common practice. For our dataset, larger number of factors (3 and more) did not reveal more useful information.

Several works (e.g. [4]) use the PCA or FA to analyze the JTCI temperament and character questions separately while other works (e.g. [1]) analyze the whole dataset at once. The reason is that the dependency between temperament and character traits is not straightforward. The temperament traits are assumed to be biologically rooted and stable across time while character traits are based on social, cognitive and personality development and are expected to mature throughout the life span [4]. However, analyzing the questions separately can cause a loss of information while on the other side analyzing the whole set of questions can cause mixing of the factors. In our methodology based on WDRBD, we are able through the weights to set a trade-off between the scenarios of analyzing the questions separately and analyzing the whole set.

The Fig. 1 shows the analyses of correlations of temperament questions with 2 factors obtained by different models and setups. The upper-left plot shows results for LPCA model analysis of the whole set of questions and plotted are only the temperament questions. Upper-right plot visualizes the results for LPCA analyzing only the temperament questions. Lower-left plot shows the results of our proposed WDRBD model where we set the weights for temperament questions to 1 and for character questions to 0.2. We got similar results for weights from interval 0.1 to 0.4. At last, the lower-right plot visualizes the analysis by WLPCA model with the same weights as we used in the setup with WDRBD model. As could be seen from the plots, our WDRBD model separates the questions of different types more clearly than the rest of the models. In the similar manner we also analyzed the character questions and yield similar results that are shown in Fig. 2.

Furthermore, to confirm the robustness of the results from WDRBD model, we tested the threshold of minimum data samples that are necessary to achieve the same separation of groups of questions. The sampling test has shown that only 150 random samples out of 773 questionnaires are enough to get the same results.

To further analyze the visualization by WDRBD, we use the same setup as in the previous case and instead of plotting the questions as marks we use the question identification numbers. The plot is depicted in Fig. 3. At first, we inspected the questions that are separated from their groups. The question 18 from persistence group is clearly separated. According to authors of the Slovak version of JTCI a lot of children had problem understanding this question. Besides that, if we remove the question, the internal consistency of the persistence group measured by Cronbach alpha raise significantly from 0,44 (low level) to 0,58 (moderate level). Note that, improving the internal consistency of the questions is a crucial step in tweaking the questionnaire. Another clearly separated questions from their group are questions 3, 26, 42, and 92 from novelty seeking.

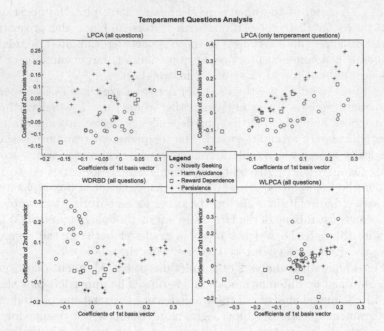

Fig. 1. 2D plots of temperament questions based on the coefficients along 1st and 2nd basis vectors

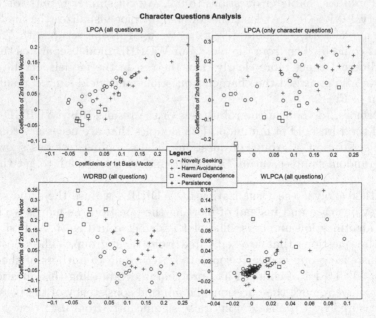

Fig. 2. 2D plots of character questions based on the coefficients along 1st and 2nd basis vectors

Again, if we remove these questions, the Cronbach alpha of the group raise from 0,71 to 0,75. For a more involved analysis, we inspected the meaning of questions that are 'close' to each other and marked the groups of questions with similar meaning by ellipses in Fig 3. Group C-1 includes questions about illness and tiredness that are related [5], group C-4 questions about sad movies and sad stories, group C-2 about filings when she or he is trying new things or meets strange people, group C-5 groups questions about loneliness, C-6 about secrecy, C-2 about endeavor and C-3 about decisiveness. As could be seen from the detailed analysis, WDRBD model is capable to visualize the questions with some level of general topographic organization, where 'close' questions have similar character.

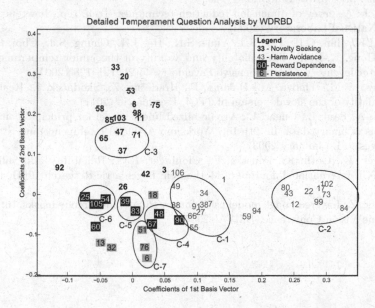

Fig. 3. A detailed analysis of temperament questions based on the WDRBD model. Groups of questions with similar meaning and close position in the plot are marked by ellipses.

6   Conclusion

In our work, we investigated the possibility of using dimensionality reduction methods for analyzing a binary questionnaire to bring a different view of the intrinsic relationships between questions. For that purpose we proposed an weighted dimensionality reduction method for binary data (WDRBD) based on the existing weighted logistic principal component analysis (WLPCA).

The experiments with real dataset of binary answers to Slovak version of Junior Temperament and Character Inventory (JTCI) [5] have shown that our proposed methodology based on WDRBD model can reveal an interesting relationships between questions that can be useful for further analysis of the questions by authors of the questionnaires.

Acknowledgements. This work was partially supported by the Scientific Grant Agency of Slovak Republic, grant No. VG1/0508/09 and by the Slovak Research and Development Agency under the contract No. APVV-0208-10.

References

1. Asch, M.: Psychometric properties of a french version of the junior temperament and character inventory. European Child Adolescent Psychiatry 18(3), 144–153 (2009)
2. Collins, M., Dasgupta, S., Schapire, R.E.: A generalization of principal component analysis to the exponential family. In: Advances in Neural Information Processing Systems. MIT Press, Cambridge (2002)
3. Fodor, I.: A survey of dimension reduction techniques. Tech. rep., Lawrence Livermore National Laboratory (2002)
4. Lyoo, I.K., Han, C.H., Lee, S.J., Yune, S.K., Ha, J.H., Chung, S.J., Choi, H., Seo, C.S., Hong, K.-E.M.: The reliability and validity of the junior temperament and character inventory. Comprehensive Psychiatry 45(2), 121–128 (2004)
5. Paulinyová, M., Tiňová, M., Halama, P., Hradečná, Z., Škodáček, I.: Realiability and validity of the slovak version of JTCI. Psychiatrie (2011)
6. Schein, A., Saul, L., Ungar, L.: A generalized linear model for principal component analysis of binary data. In: 9th Int. Workshop Artificial Intelligence and Statistics, Key West, FL (January 2003)
7. Schmeck, K., Goth, K., Poustka, F., Cloninger, R.C.: Reliability and validity of the JTCI. International Journal of Methods in Psychiatric Research 10(4), 172–182 (2001)
8. Zivkovic, Z.: Layered image model using binary PCA transparency masks. In: British Machine Vision Conference, BMVA (2007)

Generalized Maneuvers in Route Planning

Petr Hliněný and Ondrej Moriš

Faculty of Informatics, Masaryk University
Botanická 68a, 602 00 Brno, Czech Republic
{hlineny,xmoris}@fi.muni.cz

Abstract. We study an important practical aspect of the route planning problem in real-world road networks – *maneuvers*. Informally, maneuvers represent various irregularities of the road network graph such as turn-prohibitions, traffic light delays, round-abouts, forbidden passages and so on. We propose a generalized model which can handle arbitrarily complex (and even negative) maneuvers, and outline how to enhance Dijkstra's algorithm in order to solve route planning queries in this model without prior adjustments of the underlying road network graph.

1 Introduction

Since mass introduction of GPS navigation devices, the *route planning problem*, has received considerable attention. This problem is in fact an instance of the well-known single pair shortest path (SPSP) problem in graphs representing real-world road networks. However, it involves many challenging difficulties compared to ordinary SPSP. Firstly, classical algorithms such as Dijkstra's [4], A* [6] or their bidirectional variants [11] are not well suited for the route planning despite their optimality in wide theoretical sense. It is mainly because graphs representing real-world road networks are so huge that even an algorithm with linear time and space complexity cannot be feasibly run on typical mobile devices.

Secondly, these classical approaches disregard certain important aspects of real-world road networks, namely route restrictions, traffic regulations, or actual traffic info. Hence a route found by such algorithms might not be optimal or not even feasible. Additional attributes are needed in this regard.

The first difficulty has been intensively studied in the past decade, and complexity overheads of classical algorithms have been largely improved by using various preprocessing approaches. For a brief overview, we refer the readers to [2,3,12] or our [7]. In this paper we focus on the second mentioned difficulty as it is still receiving significantly less attention.

Related Work. The common way to model required additional attributes of road networks is with so called *maneuvers*; Definition 2.1. Maneuvers do not seem to be in the center of interest of route-planning research papers: They are either assumed to be encoded into the underlying graph of a road network, or they are addressed only partially with rather simple types of restriction attributes such as turn-penalties and path prohibitions.

Z. Kotásek et al. (Eds.): MEMICS 2011, LNCS 7119, pp. 155–166, 2012.

Basically, the research directions are represented either by modifications of the underlying graph during preprocessing [8,10,15], or by adjusting a query algorithm [9,13] in order to resolve simple types of restrictions during queries.

The first, and seemingly the simplest, solution is commonly used as it makes a road network graph maneuver-free and so there is no need to adjust the queries in any way. Unfortunately, it can significantly increase the size of the graph [14]; for instance, replacing a single turn-prohibition can add up to eight new vertices in place of one original [5]. A solution like this one thus conflicts with the aforementioned (graph-size) objectives. Another approach [1] uses so-called dual graph representation instead of the original one, where allowed turns are modeled by dual edges.

To summarize, a sufficiently general approach for arbitrarily complex maneuvers seems to be missing in the literature despite the fact that such a solution could be really important. We would like to emphasize that all the cited works suffer from the fact that they consider only "simple" types of maneuvers.

Our Contribution. Firstly, we introduce a formal model of a generic maneuver – from a single vertex to a long self-intersecting walk – with either positive or negative effects (penalties); being enforced, recommended, not recommended or even prohibited. Our model can capture virtually any route restriction, most traffic regulations and even some dynamic properties of real-world road networks.

Secondly, we integrate this model into Dijkstra's algorithm, rising its worst-case time complexity only slightly (depending on a structure of maneuvers). The underlying graph is not modified at all and no preprocessing is needed. Even though our idea is fairly simple and relative easy to understand, it is novel in the respect that no comparable solution has been published to date. Furthermore, some important added benefits of our algorithm are as follows:

- It can be directly used bidirectionally with any alternation strategy using an appropriate termination condition; it can be extended also to the A* algorithm by applying a "potential function to maneuver effects".
- Many route planning approaches use Dijkstra or A* in the core of their query algorithms, and hence our solution can be incorporated into many of them (for example, those based on a reach, landmarks or various types of separators) quite naturally under additional assumptions.
- Our algorithm tackles maneuvers "on-line" – that is no maneuver is processed before it is reached. And since the underlying graph of a road network is not changed (no vertices or edges are removed or added), it is possible to add or remove maneuvers dynamically even during queries to some extent.

2   Maneuvers: Basic Terms

A *(directed) graph* $G = (V, E)$ is a pair of a finite set V of vertices and a finite multiset $E \subseteq V \times V$ of edges (self-loops and parallel edges are allowed). The vertex set of G is referred to as $V(G)$, its edge multiset as $E(G)$. A *subgraph H* of a graph G is denoted by $H \subseteq G$.

A walk $P \in G$ is an alternating sequence of vertices and edges $(u_0, e_1, u_1, \ldots, e_k, u_k) \subseteq G$ such that $e_i = (u_{i-1}, u_i)$ for $i = 1, \ldots, k$, the multiset of all edges of a walk P is denoted by $E(P)$. *A concatenation* $P_1 . P_2$ of walks $P_1 = (u_0, e_1, u_1, \ldots, e_k, u_k)$ and $P_2 = (u_k, e_{k+1}, u_{k+1}, \ldots, e_l, u_l)$ is the walk $(u_0, e_1, u_1, \ldots, e_k, u_k, e_{k+1}, \ldots, e_l, u_l)$. If $P_2 = (u, f, v)$ represents a single edge, we write $P_1 . f$. If edges are clear from the graph, then we write a walk simply as $(u_0, u_1, \ldots, u_k)$.

A walk Q is a *prefix* of another walk P if Q is a subwalk of P starting with the same index, and analogically with *suffix*. The *prefix set* of a walk $P = (u_0, e_1, \ldots, e_k, u_k)$ is $Prefix(P) = \{(u_0, e_1, \ldots, e_i, u_i) | \ 0 \le i \le k\}$, and analogically $Suffix(P) = \{(u_i, e_{i+1}, \ldots, e_k, u_k) | \ 0 \le i \le k\}$. A prefix (suffix) of a walk P thus is a member of $Prefix(P)$ $(Suffix(P))$, and it is *nontrivial* if $i \ge 1$.

The weight of a walk $P \subseteq G$ with respect to a weighting $w : E(G) \mapsto \mathbb{R}$ of G is defined as $\sum_{e \in E(P)} w(e)$ and denoted by $|P|_w$. *A distance* from u to v in G, $\delta_w(u, v)$, is the minimum weight of a walk $P = (u, \ldots, v) \subseteq G$ over all such walks and P is then called *optimal* (with respect to weighting w). If there no such walk then $\delta_w(u, v) = \infty$. *A path* is a walk without repeating vertices and edges.

Virtually any route restriction or traffic regulation in a road network, such as turn-prohibitions, traffic lights delays, forbidden passages, turn-out lanes, suggested directions or car accidents by contrast, can be modeled by *maneuvers* – walks having extra (either positive or negative) "cost effects". Formally:

Definition 2.1 (Maneuver). A maneuver M *of* G *is a walk in* G *that is assigned a penalty* $\Delta(M) \in \mathbb{R} \cup \infty$. *A set of all maneuvers of* G *is denoted by* $\mathcal{M}$.

Remark 2.2. A maneuver with a negative or positive penalty is called *negative* or *positive*, respectively. Furthermore, there are two special kinds of maneuvers the *restricted* ones of penalty 0 and the *prohibited* ones of penalty ∞.

The cost effect of a maneuver is formalized next:

Definition 2.3 (Penalized Weight). *Let* G *be a graph with a weighting* w *and a set of maneuvers* $\mathcal{M}$. *The* penalized weight *of a walk* $P \subseteq G$ *containing the maneuvers* $M_1, \ldots, M_r \in \mathcal{M}$ *as subwalks is defined as* $|P|_w^{\mathcal{M}} = |P|_w + \sum_{i=1}^{r} \Delta(M_i)$.

Then, the intended meaning of maneuvers in route planning is as follows.

- If a driver enters a restricted maneuver, she must pass it completely (cf. Definition 2.4); she must obey the given direction(s) regardless of the cost effect. Examples are headings to be followed or specific round-abouts.

- By contrast, if a driver enters a prohibited maneuver, she must not pass it completely. She must get off it before reaching its end, otherwise it makes her route infinitely bad. Examples are forbidden passages or temporal closures.

- Finally, if a driver enters a positive or negative maneuver, she is not required to pass it completely; but if she does, then this will increase or decrease the cost of her route accordingly. Negative maneuvers make her route better (more desirable) and positive ones make it worse. Examples of positive maneuvers are, for instance, traffic lights delays, lane changes, or left-turns. Examples of negative ones are turn-out lanes, shortcuts, or implicit routes.

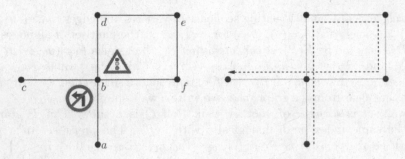

Fig. 1. A road network containing maneuvers $M_1 = (a, ab, b, bc, c)$ with $\Delta(M_1) = \infty$ (prohibited left turn) and $M_2 = (a, ab, b, bf, f)$ with $\Delta(M_2) = 1$ (right turn traffic lights delay). All edges have weight 1. The penalized weight of the walk (a, ab, b, bc, c) is $2 + \infty$, the penalized weight of the walk $(a, ab, b, bf, f, fe, e, ed, d, db, b, bd, c)$ is $6 + 1$. Therefore the optimal walk (with respect to the penalized weight) from a to c is $(a, ab, b, bd, d, de, e, ef, f, fb, b, bc, c)$ with the penalized weight $6 + 0$.

Definition 2.4 (Valid Walk). *Let $G, w, \mathcal{M}$ be as in Definition 2.3. A walk P in G is valid if and only if $|P|_w^{\mathcal{M}} < \infty$ and, for any restricted maneuver $M \in \mathcal{M}$, it holds that if a nontrivial prefix of M is a subwalk of P, then whole M is a subwalk of P or a suffix of P is contained in M (that is P ends there).*

We finally get to the summarizing definition. A structure of a road network is naturally represented by a graph G such that the junctions are represented by $V(G)$ and the roads by $E(G)$. The chosen cost function (for example travel time, distance, expenses) is represented by a *non-negative* weighting $w : E(G) \mapsto \mathbb{R}_0^+$ assigned to G, and the additional attributes such as traffic regulations are represented by maneuvers as above. We say that two walks Q_1, Q_2 are *divergent* if, up to symmetry between Q_1, Q_2, a nontrivial prefix of Q_1 is contained in Q_2 but the whole Q_1 is not a subwalk of Q_2. Moreover, we say that Q_2 *overhangs* Q_1 if a nontrivial prefix of Q_2 is a suffix of Q_1 (particularly, $E(Q_1) \cap E(Q_2) \neq \emptyset$).

Definition 2.5 (Road Network). *Let G be a graph with a non-negative weighting w and a set of maneuvers $\mathcal{M}$. A road network is the triple $(G, w, \mathcal{M})$. Furthermore, it is called* proper *if:*

  i. no two restricted maneuvers in $\mathcal{M}$ are divergent,

  ii. no two negative maneuvers in $\mathcal{M}$ overhang one another, and

  iii. for all $N \in \mathcal{M}$, $\Delta(N) \geq -|N|_w^{\mathcal{M} \setminus \{N\}}$ (that is, the penalized weight of every walk in G is non-negative).

Within a road network, only valid walks (Definition 2.4) are allowed further, and the distance from u to v, $\delta_w^{\mathcal{M}}(u, v)$, is the minimum penalized weight (Definition 2.3) of a valid walk $P = (u, \ldots, v) \subseteq G$; such a walk P is then called *optimal with respect to the penalized weight*. If there is no such walk, then $\delta_w^{\mathcal{M}}(u, v) = \infty$. See Fig. 1.

Motivation for the required properties i.–iii. in Definition 2.5 is of both natural and practical character: As for i., it simply says that no two restricted maneuvers are in a conflict (that is no route planning deadlocks). Point ii. concerning only negative maneuvers is needed for a fast query algorithm, and it is indeed a natural requirement (to certain extent, overhanging maneuvers can be modeled without overhangs). We remark that other studies usually allow no negative maneuvers at all. Finally, iii. states that no negative maneuvers can result in a negative overall cost of any walk – another very natural property. In informal words, a negative penalty of a maneuver somehow "cannot influence" suitability of a route before entering and after exiting the maneuver.

2.1 Strongly Connected Road Network

The traditional graph theoretical notion of strong connectivity also needs to be refined, it must suit our road networks to dismiss possible route planning traps now imposed by maneuvers.

First, we need to define a notion of a *"context"* of a vertex v in G – a maximal walk in G ending at v such that it is a proper prefix of a maneuver in $\mathcal{M}$, or $\emptyset$ otherwise. A set of all such walks for v is denoted by $\mathcal{X}_\mathcal{M}$. For example, on the road network depicted on Fig. 1, $\mathcal{X}_\mathcal{M}(b) = \{(a, b), \emptyset\}$. More formally:

Definition 2.6. *Let $\mathcal{M}$ be a set of maneuvers. We define*

$$\mathcal{X}_\mathcal{M}(v) \overset{def}{=} \big\{ X \in Prefix^<(\mathcal{M}) \,|(v) \in Suffix(X)\big\} \cup \{\emptyset\}$$

$$Prefix^<(M) \overset{def}{=} Prefix(M) \setminus \{M\}, \quad Prefix^<(\mathcal{M}) \overset{def}{=} \bigcup_{M \in \mathcal{M}} Prefix^<(M).$$

This $\mathcal{X}_\mathcal{M}(v)$ is the maneuver-prefix set at v, that is the set of all proper prefixes of walks from $\mathcal{M}$ that end right at v, including the mandatory empty walk. An element of $\mathcal{X}_\mathcal{M}(v)$ is called a context *of the position v within the road network.*

The reverse graph G^R of G is a graph on the same set of vertices with all of the edges reversed. Let $(G, w, \mathcal{M})$ be a road network, a reverse road network *is defined as $(G^R, w^R, \mathcal{M}^R)$, where $w^R : E(G^R) \mapsto \mathbb{R}_0^+$, $\forall (u, v) \in E(G^R) : w^R(u, v) = w(v, u)$ and $\mathcal{M}^R = \{M^R | M \in \mathcal{M}\}$, $\forall M^R \in \mathcal{M}^R : \Delta(M^R) = \Delta(M)$.*

Definition 2.7. *A road network $(G, w, \mathcal{M})$ is* strongly connected *if, for every pair of edges $e = (u', u)$, $f = (v, v') \in E(G)$ and for each possible context $X = X_1 \cdot e \in \mathcal{X}_\mathcal{M}(u)$ of u in G and each one of v in G^R, that is $Y^R = Y_1^R \cdot f^R \in \mathcal{X}_{\mathcal{M}^R}(v)$, there exists a valid walk starting with X and ending with Y.*

We remark that Definition 2.7 naturally corresponds to strong connectivity in an amplified road network modeling the maneuvers within underlying graph.

3   Route Planning Queries

At first, let us recall classical Dijkstra's algorithm [4]. It solves SPSP[1] problem a graph G with a non-negative weighting w for a pair $s, t \in V(G)$ of vertices.

---

[1] Given a graph and two vertices find a shortest path from one to another.

- The algorithm maintains, for all $v \in V(G)$, a *(temporary) distance estimate* of the shortest path from s to v found so far in $d[v]$, and a predecessor of v on that path in $\pi[v]$.

- The scanned vertices, that is those with $d[v] = \delta_w(s, v)$, are stored in the set T; and the reached but not yet scanned vertices, that is those with $\infty > d[v] \geq \delta_w(s, v)$, are stored in the set Q.

- The algorithm work as follows: it iteratively picks a vertex $u \in Q$ with minimum value $d[u]$ and relaxes all the edges (u, v) leaving u. Then u is removed from Q and added to T. *Relaxing* an edge (u, v) means to check if a shortest path estimate from s to v may be improved via u; if so, then $d[v]$ and $\pi[v]$ are updated. Finally, v is added into Q if is not there already.

- The algorithm terminates when t is scanned or when Q is empty.

Time complexity depends on the implementation of Q; such as it is $\mathcal{O}(|E(G)| + |V(G)| \log |V(G)|)$ with the Fibonacci heap.

3.1 $\mathcal{M}$-Dijkstra's Algorithm

In this section we will briefly sketch the core ideas of our natural extension of Dijkstra's algorithm. We refer a reader to Algorithm 1 for a full-scale pseudocode of this $\mathcal{M}$-Dijkstra's algorithm.

1. Every vertex $v \in V(G)$ scanned during the algorithm is considered together with its context $X \in \mathcal{X}_\mathcal{M}(v)$ (Definition 2.6); that is as a pair (v, X). The intention is for X to record how v has been reached in the algorithm, and same v can obviously be reached and scanned more than once, with different contexts. For instance, b can be reached with the empty or (a, b) contexts on the road network depicted on Fig. 1.

2. Temporary distance estimates are stored in the algorithm as $d[v, X]$ for such vertex-context pairs (v, X). At each step the algorithm selects a next pair (u, Y) such that it is minimal with respect to the following partial order $\leq_\mathcal{M}$.

   Remark 3.1. Partial order $\leq_\mathcal{M}$:

   $$(v_1, X_1) \leq_\mathcal{M} (v_2, X_2) \overset{\text{def}}{\Longleftrightarrow} \begin{array}{l} (d[v_1, X_1] < d[v_2, X_2] \vee \\ (d[v_1, X_1] = d[v_2, X_2] \wedge X_1 \in \mathit{Suffix}(X_2))). \end{array}$$

3. Edge relaxation from a selected vertex-context pair (u, Y) respects all maneuvers related to the context Y (there can be more such maneuvers). If one of them is restricted, then only its unique (cf. Definition 2.5, i.) subsequent edge is taken, cf. Algorithm 1, RESTRICTEDDIRECTION.

   Otherwise, every edge $f = (u, v)$ is relaxed such that the distance estimate at v – together with its context as derived from the concatenation $(Y.f)$ – is (possibly) updated with the weight $w(f)$ plus the sum of penalties of all the maneuvers in $(Y.f)$ ending at v, cf. Algorithm 1, RELAX.

4. If an edge relaxed is the first one of a negative maneuver, a specific process is executed before scanning the next vertex-context pair. See below.

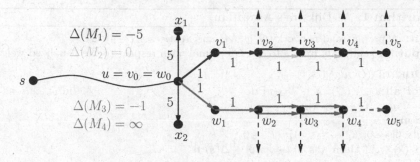

Fig. 2. A road network containing two negative maneuvers, $M_1 = (v_0, \ldots, v_5)$ and $M_3 = (w_0, \ldots, w_5)$, a restricted maneuver $M_2 = (v_2, v_3, v_4)$, and a prohibited maneuver $M_4 = (w_2, w_3, w_4)$. When u is being processed (with its implicit context), x_1, x_2 and v_1, w_1 are relaxed normally. Furthermore, negative maneuver processing is executed for both M_1 and M_3. As a result, v_5 will be immediately reached and inserted to Q with distance estimate equal to that of u which is less than those of x_1, x_2 (5 from u) and of v_1, w_1 (1 from u). On the other hand, w_5 will not be reached in the process because the distance estimate of w_4 bounces to ∞ while handling M_4.

3.2   Processing Negative Maneuvers

Note that the presence of a maneuver of negative penalty *may violate* the basic assumption of ordinary Dijkstra's algorithm; that relaxing an edge never decreases the nearest temporary distance estimate in the graph. An example of such a violation can be seen in Fig. 2, for instance, at vertex v_5 which would not be processed in its correct place by ordinary Dijkstra's algorithm. That is why a negative maneuver M must be processed by $\mathcal{M}$-Dijkstra's algorithm at once – whenever its starting edge is relaxed, cf. Algorithm 1, PROCESSNEGATIVE.

Suppose that an edge $f = (u, v)$ is relaxed from a selected vertex-context pair (u, X) and there is a negative maneuver $M = (v_0, f_1, v_1, \ldots, v_{n-1}, f_n, v_n)$, $u = v_0$, $v = v_1$ starting with f (that is $f = f_1$), processing negative maneuver M works as follow:

1. Vertex-context pairs $(v_i, X_i), 0 \leq i \leq n$ along M are scanned one by one towards the end of M. The other vertices leaving these v_i are ignored.

2. Scanned vertex-context pairs are added to Q and their distance estimates are updated, but none of them is added into T. They must be properly scanned during the main loop of the algorithm.

3. This process terminates when the end (v_n, X_n) is reached or the distance estimate of some (v_i, X_i) bounces to ∞ (that is there is a prohibited maneuver ending at v_i) or when some restricted maneuver forces us to get off M (and thus M cannot be completed).

Algorithm 1. $\mathcal{M}$-Dijkstra's Algorithm

Input: A proper road network $(G, w, \mathcal{M})$ and vertices $s, t \in V(G)$.
Output: A valid walk from s to t in G optimal with respect to the penalized weight.

$\mathcal{M}$-DIJKSTRA$(G, w, \mathcal{M}, s, t)$
1: **for all** $v \in V(G)$, $X \in \mathcal{X}_{\mathcal{M}}(v)$ **do**   /* Initialization. */
2:      $d[v, X] \leftarrow \infty$; $\pi[v, X] \leftarrow \bot$
3: **done**
4: $d[s, \emptyset] \leftarrow 0$; $Q \leftarrow \{(s, \emptyset)\}$; $T \leftarrow \emptyset$
5: **if** $(s) \in \mathcal{M}$ **then** $d[s, \emptyset] \leftarrow d[s, \emptyset] + \Delta(s)$ **fi**

   /* The main loop starts at $(s, \emptyset)$ and terminates when either all reachable vertex-
   context pairs have been scanned or when t is reached with some of its contexts. */

6: **while** $Q \neq \emptyset \wedge [\nexists X \in \mathcal{X}_{\mathcal{M}}(t) \text{ s.t. } (t, X) \in T]$ **do**
7:      $(u, X) \leftarrow \min_{\leq_{\mathcal{M}}}(Q)$; $Q \leftarrow Q \setminus \{(u, X)\}$ /* Recall $\leq_{\mathcal{M}}$ (Remark 3.1) */
8:      $F \leftarrow$ RESTRICTEDDIRECTION(u, X) /* Possible restricted dir. from u. */
9:      **if** $F = \emptyset$ **then** $F \leftarrow \{(u, v) \in E(G) \mid v \in V(G)\}$ **fi**
10:      **for all** $f = (u, v) \in F$ **do**
11:          RELAX(u, X, f, v)
12:          **for all** $M = (u, f, v, \ldots) \in \mathcal{M}$ s.t. $\Delta(M) < 0 \wedge |E(M)| > 1$ **do**
13:              PROCESSNEGATIVE(X, M)
14:          **done**   /* Negative man. starting with f are processed separately. */
15:      **done**
16:      $T \leftarrow T \cup \{(u, X)\}$
17: **done**
18: CONSTRUCTWALK(G, d, π) /* Use "access" information stored in $\pi[v, X]$. */

LONGESTPREFIX(P) : a walk $P' \subseteq G$
        /* The longest (proper) prefix of some maneuver contained as a suffix of P */
1: $P' \leftarrow \max_{\subseteq} \left[(Suffix(P) \cap Prefix^{<}(\mathcal{M})) \cup \{\emptyset\} \right]$
          where $Prefix^{<}(\mathcal{M}) \stackrel{\text{def}}{=} \bigcup_{M \in \mathcal{M}} Prefix(M) \setminus \{M\}$
2: **return** P'

RESTRICTEDDIRECTION(u, X) : $F \subseteq E(G)$
        /* Looking for edge f leaving u that follows in a restricted man. in context X.*/
1: $F \leftarrow \{f = (u, v) \in E(G) \mid \exists \text{ restricted } R \in \mathcal{M} :$
          $E(X) \cap E(R) \neq \emptyset \wedge Suffix(X.f) \cap Prefix(R) \neq \emptyset\}$
2: **return** F

RELAX(u, X, f, v) /* Relaxing an edge f from vertex u with context X. */
1: $\delta \leftarrow w(f) + \sum_{N \in \mathcal{N}} \Delta(N)$ where $\mathcal{N} = \mathcal{M} \cap Suffix(X.f)$
2: $X' \leftarrow$ LONGESTPREFIX$(X.f)$
3: **if** $d[u, X] + \delta < d[v, X']$ **then**
4:      $Q \leftarrow Q \cup \{(v, X')\}$; $d[v, X'] \leftarrow d[u, X] + \delta$; $\pi[v, X'] \leftarrow (u, X)$
5: **fi**

PROCESSNEGATIVE$(X, M = (v_0, e_1, \ldots, e_n, v_n))$
1: $i \leftarrow 1$; $X_0 \leftarrow X$; $F \leftarrow \emptyset$ /* Relaxing sequentially all the edges of M. */
2: **while** $i \leq n \wedge d[v_{i-1}, X_i] < \infty \wedge F = \emptyset$ **do**

```
3:      RELAX(v_{i-1}, X_{i-1}, e_i, v_i)
4:      X_i ← LONGESTPREFIX(X_{i-1}.e_i); F ← RESTRICTEDDIRECTION(v_i, X_i)\{e_{i+1}}
5:      i ← i + 1
6: done
```

3.3   Correctness and Complexity Analysis

Assuming validity of Definition 2.5 ii. in a proper road network, correctness of above $\mathcal{M}$-Dijkstra's algorithm can be argued analogously to a traditional proof of Dijkstra's algorithm. Hereafter, the time complexity growth of the algorithm depends solely on the number of vertex-context pairs.

Theorem 3.2. *Let a proper road network* $(G, w, \mathcal{M})$ *and vertices* $s, t \in V(G)$ *be given.* $\mathcal{M}$-*Dijkstra's algorithm (Algorithm 1) computes a valid walk from* s *to* t *in* G *optimal with respect to the penalized weight, in time* $\mathcal{O}\big(c_{\mathcal{M}}^2 |E(G)| + c_{\mathcal{M}} |V(G)| \log(c_{\mathcal{M}} |V(G)|)\big)$ *where* $c_{\mathcal{M}} = \max_{v \in V(G)} |\{M \in \mathcal{M} \,|\, v \in V(M)\}|$ *is the maximum number of maneuvers per vertex.*

Proof. We follow a traditional proof of ordinary Dijkstra's algorithm with a simple modification – instead of vertices we consider vertex-context pairs as in Definition 2.7 and in Algorithm 1.

For a walk P let $\chi(P) = \max_{\subseteq} \big[(\mathit{Suffix}(P) \cap \mathit{Prefix}^{<}(\mathcal{M})) \cup \{\emptyset\} \big]$ denote the context of the endvertex of P with respect to maneuvers $\mathcal{M}$. Let P_x stand for the prefix of P up to a vertex $x \in V(P)$. The following invariant holds at every iteration of the algorithm:

i. For every $(u, X) \in T$, the final distance estimate $d[u, X]$ equals the smallest penalized weight of a valid walk P from s to u such that $X = \chi(P)$. Every vertex-context pair directly accessible from a member of T belongs to Q.

ii. For every $(v, X') \in Q$, the temporary distance estimate $d[v, X']$ equals the smallest penalized weight of a walk R from s to v such that $X' = \chi(R)$ and, moreover, $(x, \chi(R_x)) \in T$ for each internal vertex $x \in V(R)$ (except vertices reached during PROCESSNEGATIVE, if any).

This invariant is trivially true after the initialization. By induction we assume it is true at the beginning of the while loop on line 6, and line 7 is now being executed – selecting the pair $(u, X) \in Q$. Then, by minimality of this selection, (u, X) is such that the distance estimate $d[u, X]$ gives the optimal penalized weight of a walk P from s to u such that $X = \chi(P)$. Hence the first part of the invariant (concerning T, line 16) will be true also after finishing this iteration.

Concerning the second claim of the invariant, we have to examine the effect of lines 8–15 of the algorithm. Consider an edge $f = (u, v) \in E(G)$ starting in u, and any walk R from s to v such that $\chi(R_u) = X$. Since $\chi(R)$ must be contained in $X.f$ by definition; it is, RELAX, line 2, $\chi(R) = X'$. Furthermore, every maneuver contained in R and not in R_u must be a suffix of $X.f$ by definition. So the penalized weight increase δ is correctly computed in RELAX, line 1. Therefore, RELAX correctly updates the temporary distance estimate $d[v, X']$ for every such f. Finally, any negative maneuver starting from u along f is correctly reached towards its end w on line 13, its distance estimate is updated by successive relaxation of its edges and, by Definition 2.5, ii. and iii., this distance estimate of w and its context is not smaller than $d[u, X]$; thus the second part of claimed invariant remains true.

Validity of a walk is given by line 8 – RESTRICTEDDIRECTION, that is enforcing entered restricted maneuvers; and line 1 in RELAX – δ grows to infinity when completing prohibited maneuvers, "if" condition on line 3 in RELAX is then false and therefore prohibited maneuver cannot be contained in an optimal walk.

Lastly, we examine the worst-case time complexity of this algorithm. We assume G is efficiently implemented using neighborhood lists, the maneuvers in $\mathcal{M}$ are directly indexed from all their vertices and their number is polynomial in the graph size, and that Q is implemented as Fibonacci heap.

– The maximal number of vertex-context pairs that may enter Q is

$$m = |V(G)| + \sum_{M \in \mathcal{M}} (|M| - 1) \le c_{\mathcal{M}} \cdot |V(G)|,$$

and time complexity of the Fibonacci heap operations is $O(m \log m)$.

– Every edge of G starting in u is relaxed at most those many times as there are contexts in $\mathcal{X}_{\mathcal{M}}(u)$ and edges of negative maneuvers are relaxed one more time during PROCESSNEGATIVE. Hence the maximal overall number of relaxations is

$$r = \sum_{u \in V(G)} |\mathcal{X}_{\mathcal{M}}(u)| \cdot out\text{-}deg(u) + q \le (c_{\mathcal{M}} + 1) \cdot |E(G)|$$

where q is the number of edges belonging to negative maneuvers.

– The operations in RELAX on line 1, LONGESTPREFIX as well as RESTRICTED-DIRECTION can be implemented in time $O(c_{\mathcal{M}})$.

The claimed runtime bound follows.   □

Notice that, in real-world road networks, the number $c_{\mathcal{M}}$ of maneuvers per vertex is usually quite small and independent of the road network size, and thus it can be bounded by a reasonable minor constant. Although road networks in practice may have huge maneuver sets, particular maneuvers do not cross or interlap too much there. for example, $c_{\mathcal{M}} = 5$ in the current OpenStreetMaps of Prague.

4   Conclusion

We have introduced a novel generic model of maneuvers that is able to capture almost arbitrarily complex route restrictions, traffic regulations and even some dynamic aspects of the route planning problem. It can model anything from single vertices to long self-intersecting walks as restricted, negative, positive or prohibited maneuvers. We have shown how to incorporate this model into Dijkstra's algorithm so that no adjustment of the underlying road network graph is needed. The running time of the proposed Algorithm 1 is only marginally larger than that of ordinary Dijkstra's algorithm (Theorem 3.2) in practical networks.

Our algorithm can be relatively straightforwardly extended to a bidirectional algorithm by running it simultaneously from the start vertex in the original network and from the target vertex in the reversed network. A termination condition must reflect the fact that chained contexts of vertex-context pairs scanned in both directions might contain maneuvers as subwalks. Furthermore, since the A* algorithm is just an ordinary Dijkstra's algorithm with edge weights adjusted by a potential function, our extension remains correct for A* if the road network is proper (Definition 2.5, namely iii.) even with respect to this potential function.

Finally, we would like to highlight that, under reasonable assumptions, our model can be incorporated into many established route planning approaches.

Acknowledgements. We would like to thank the reviewers, who took the time to carefully read our paper and suggested many small, but helpful corrections, additions, and improvements to our original submission.

References

1. Anez, J., De La Barra, T., Perez, B.: Dual graph representation of transport networks. Transportation Research Part B: Methodological 30(3), 209–216 (1996)
2. Cherkassky, B., Goldberg, A.V., Radzik, T.: Shortest paths algorithms: Theory and experimental evaluation. Mathematical Programming 73(2), 129–174 (1996)
3. Delling, D., Sanders, P., Schultes, D., Wagner, D.: Engineering Route Planning Algorithms. In: Lerner, J., Wagner, D., Zweig, K.A. (eds.) Algorithmics of Large and Complex Networks. LNCS, vol. 5515, pp. 117–139. Springer, Heidelberg (2009)
4. Dijkstra, E.: A note on two problems in connexion with graphs. Numerische Mathematik 1, 269–271 (1959)
5. Gutierrez, E., Medaglia, A.: Labeling algorithm for the shortest path problem withturn prohibitions with application to large-scale road networks. Annals of Operations Research 157, 169–182 (2008), doi:10.1007/s10479-007-0198-9
6. Hart, P.E., Nilsson, N.J., Raphael, B.: Correction to "A formal basis for the heuristic determination of minimum cost paths". SIGART Bull. 1(37), 28–29 (1972)
7. Hliněný, P., Moriš, O.: Scope-Based Route Planning. In: Demetrescu, C., Halldórsson, M.M. (eds.) ESA 2011. LNCS, vol. 6942, pp. 445–456. Springer, Heidelberg (2011)
8. Jiang, J., Han, G., Chen, J.: Modeling turning restrictions in traffic network for vehicle navigation system. In: Proceedings of the Symposium on Geospatial Theory, Processing, and Applications (2002)
9. Kirby, R.F., Potts, R.B.: The minimum route problem for networks with turn penalties and prohibitions. Transportation Research 3, 397–408 (1969)
10. Pallottino, S., Scutella, M.G.: Shortest path algorithms in transportation models: classical and innovative aspects. Technical report, Univ. of Pisa (1997)

11. Pohl, I.S.: Bi-directional and heuristic search in path problems. PhD thesis, Stanford University, Stanford, CA, USA (1969)
12. Schultes, D.: Route Planning in Road Networks. PhD thesis, Karlsruhe University, Karlsruhe, Germany (2008)
13. Villeneuve, D., Desaulniers, G.: The shortest path problem with forbidden paths. European Journal of Operational Research 165(1), 97–107 (2005)
14. Winter, S.: Modeling costs of turns in route planning. GeoInformatica 6, 345–361 (2002), doi:10.1023/A:1020853410145
15. Ziliaskopoulos, A.K., Mahmassani, H.S.: A note on least time path computation considering delays and prohibitions for intersection movements. Transportation Research Part B: Methodological 30(5), 359–367 (1996)

STANSE: Bug-Finding Framework for C Programs

Jan Obdržálek, Jiří Slabý, and Marek Trtík

Masaryk University, Brno, Czech Republic
{obdrzalek,slaby,trtik}@fi.muni.cz

Abstract. STANSE is a free (available under the GPLv2 license) modular framework for finding bugs in C programs using static analysis. Its two main design goals are 1) ability to process large software projects like the Linux kernel and 2) extensibility with new bug-finding techniques with a minimal effort. Currently there are four bug-finding algorithms implemented within STANSE: AUTOMATONCHECKER checks properties described in an automata-based formalism, THREADCHECKER detects deadlocks among multiple threads, LOCKCHECKER finds locking errors based on statistics, and REACHABILITYCHECKER looks for unreachable code. STANSE has been tested on the Linux kernel, where it has found dozens of previously undiscovered bugs.

1 Introduction

During the last decade, bug-finding techniques based on static analysis have finally come of age. One of the papers to really stir interest was [2], showing that static analysis can efficiently find many interesting bugs in real-world code. This work eventually led to a successful commercial tool called COVERITY [10]. Over the years, several other successful tools, like CODESONAR [9] or KLOCWORK [12], appeared. However, such fully-featured tools are neither free to obtain, nor is their code available (e.g. for developing new algorithms or tailoring the existing tools to specific tasks). The existing free tools are usually severely limited in what they can do (e.g. UNO [15], SPARSE [14], SMATCH [13]). One notable exception is FINDBUGS [5,11], a successful tool working on Java code. STANSE is intended to fill this gap for the C language. It can be seen in two ways:

1. STANSE is a robust framework (written predominantly in Java) for implementing diverse static analysis algorithms. An implemented algorithm can be immediately evaluated on large real-world software projects written in C as the framework is capable to process such projects (for example, it can process the whole Linux kernel). An implementation of such an algorithm within the framework is called a *checker*.
2. As STANSE already contains four checkers, it can be also seen as a working static analysis tool.

The paper is structured as follows. Section 2 describes the functionality provided by the framework, while Section 3 is devoted to the four existing checkers.

Z. Kotásek et al. (Eds.): MEMICS 2011, LNCS 7119, pp. 167–178, 2012.

In Section 4 we present some results of running STANSE on the Linux kernel. The last section summarises the basic strengths of STANSE and mentions some directions of future development.

2   Framework Functionality

The STANSE framework is modular and fully open. It is designed to allow static analysis of large software projects like Linux kernel. Furthermore it is aimed to reduce effort when implementing a new static analysis technique. Architecture of the framework is depicted in Fig. 1, and is more or less standard. The bug-finding algorithms are implemented as *checkers*, and will be described in more detail in Section 3. In this section we focus on the functionality of the framework itself, describing only the non-standard or for some other reason interesting features.

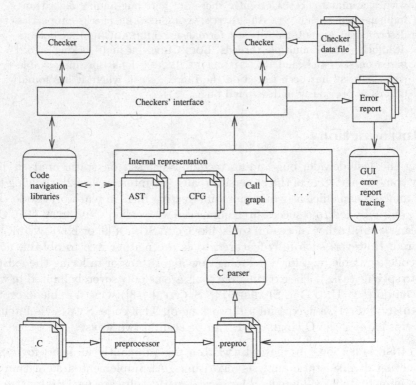

Fig. 1. STANSE framework architecture

2.1   Configuration

The STANSE framework contains data structures capturing a configuration of an analysis to be performed. We always need to know what source files to analyse and by what checkers. That information we call *configuration*.

There are several ways how to tell STANSE which source files to analyse. Besides the standard possibilities (a given file, all files from a given directory, all files listed in a list), STANSE can also derive all the necessary information from a project Makefile. In this case, STANSE also remembers compiler flags for preprocessing purposes. This functionality is inspired by the SPARSE [14] tool.

The user must also specify the checkers which should be run on the configured source files. There can be many checkers running simultaneously in STANSE. However they cannot share any data and proceed independently. Checkers themselves can also be configured through their own configuration files. The configuration can be passed to the STANSE framework either via command line arguments, or using the graphical interface.

2.2 Parsing Source Files

The STANSE framework can process source files written in C, more specifically in the ISO/ANSI C99 standard together with most of the GNU C extensions. This allows STANSE to process software projects like the Linux kernel. We are currently working on support of other languages, in particular C++, a prototype implementation for which is included in the distribution. The parsing pipeline, including a preprocessing the source files by the standard GNU C preprocessor, is depicted at the bottom in Fig. 1. It is important to note that we do not parse the source files in a sequence one by one as they appear in a configuration. Since we use streaming (which we discuss later), the pipeline is applied as needed for each individual source file.

The parser used in STANSE is generated using the ANTLR tool from our own annotated C grammar. The reason for us to write our own parser was that at the time we started to develop STANSE we could not find free parser which, while being suitable for our purposes, would be able to parse most of the GNU C. (Linux Kernel makes heavy use of GNU C language extensions.) There is one notable exception: CLANG, which is slowly improving and will be able to handle the Linux kernel in the near future. However, in its current form it still contains bugs and cannot be used reliably. Our plan is to switch from our parser to CLANG once it becomes stable and feature complete.

Also, one may object that we could use the parser from the GNU compiler (GCC). Unfortunately this parser, and most importantly its internal structures, is not suitable for our purposes. For example the CFG is built on the top of RTL or tree representation (we encourage the reader to look into the GCC manual where these are described).

2.3 Program Internal Representation

Once the code is parsed, it is represented using STANSE's *internal structures*: a call graph among functions, a control flow graph (CFG) for each function, and an abstract syntax tree (AST) for the whole file. Subtrees in the AST are referenced from appropriate CFG nodes. We show these structures in the middle of Fig. 1. All these structures can be dumped in a textual or graphical form.

Since we aim at large software projects consisting of hundreds or thousands of modules (compilation units), it is often impossible in practice to store the corresponding internal structures in the memory all at the same time. The STANSE framework therefore applies automatic *streaming* of the internal structures. This is currently performed on a module basis. Instead of parsing all source modules in the beginning, a module is streamed in only when STANSE needs to access some internal structure belonging to the module. In other words, the internal structures are constructed on demand, in a lazy manner.

If the memory occupied by internal structures exceeds a given limit, some internal structures have to be freed before another module is streamed in. The structures to be freed are selected using the LRU (least recently used) approach: STANSE discards all internal structures of the module whose structures are not accessed for the longest time. If the discarded structure is accessed again later, the corresponding module is streamed back in. Both laziness of internal structures and streaming are completely invisible to checkers.

In the current implementation of streaming, each source file streamed out from the memory is completely discarded. STANSE does not back up already parsed internal structures into auxiliary files before discarding. As a consequence, when internal structures of the discarded file are needed again, STANSE starts the parsing pipeline of the file from scratch to recreate requested internal structures. Although loading of previously parsed internal structures from auxiliary files would speed up the streaming process, profiling of STANSE's performance on the Linux kernel has not shown streaming to be a performance bottleneck. However this could be easily changed if streaming performance becomes a problem in the future.

2.4   Pointer Analysis in Stanse

Since C programs tend to heavily use pointers, it almost always becomes a necessity to use some form of pointer analysis. There are many different known approaches to pointer analysis, differing in speed and accuracy. As each bug-finding/program analysis technique may have different requirements regarding pointer analysis, a framework like STANSE should ideally implement several different pointer analysis techniques and provide them to its checkers.

Nevertheless, the STANSE framework currently provides just two pointer analyses: *Steensgaard*'s [7] and *Shapiro-Horowitz*'s [6]. Both analyses are *may* analyses – they compute an over-approximation of an accurate solution. The *Steensgard*'s analysis is very fast and it is widely used in practice. On the other hand it is not very accurate. The *Shapiro-Horowitz*'s analysis allows parametrisation between *Steensgard*'s and *Andersen*'s analyses. One can therefore balance between speed of *Steensgard*'s analysis and accuracy of *Andersen*'s one.

2.5   Matching Language Constructs

Many static analyses change their internal state only on some subset of program expressions. For example, when finding race conditions in a parallel program, one may only focus on expressions involving synchronisation, while ignoring all others. The STANSE framework therefore provides a specification language for determining a set of program expressions.

The language defines a collection of *patterns*. Each pattern is supposed to identify a single specific kind of sub-trees in AST of analysed program. A pattern itself is therefore also a sub-tree of AST, where some of its vertices are "special". They allow to define a set of possible sub-trees at that vertex.

This is, however, not the only possible approach. For example, in the METAL [1] specification language, a C expression can be directly parametrised to define a set. The solution we implemented exploits the fact that checkers in STANSE work with AST intensively, and therefore identifying expressions in terms of AST is very practical.

2.6   Traversing Internal Representation

Although a checker may need to work with the internal structures in an arbitrary way, most checkers walk through CFGs using some standard strategy. To prevent unnecessary reimplementations, the most important and heavily used traversal methods are implemented directly inside the framework. With this functionality, one can implement a new checker (or its part) by specifying

- whether it should go through CFGs forwards or backwards, breadth-first or depth-first,
- whether the interprocedural walk-through should be performed or not (if not, the function calls are ignored), and
- a method (callback) to be called for each visited node in a CFG.

This makes implementation of new algorithms extremely simple.

For example, when a checker needs to implement a forward flow-sensitive analysis, it may ask the STANSE framework to traverse paths in CFGs in forward depth-first manner. This can be implemented by a single call to a function `traverseCFGToDepthForward`, which takes as an argument a CFG and a subclass of STANSE class `CFGPathVisitor`. In this class the checker defines the action which should be taken whenever a CFG node is visited (already in the requested order). The checker implements the action in a method `visit` of the subclass.

In addition, for those interprocedural analyses which do not construct summaries STANSE provides an automated traversal among different CFGs according to function calls (involving automated parameters passing and value returning). Again, this can be done using a single call to the STANSE framework.

The functionality described in this section is shown in Fig. 1 as "Code navigating libraries".

2.7   Support for Function Summaries

Interprocedural analyses typically build function summaries. Unfortunately, these summaries may differ from one analysis to another. Nevertheless, quite common part in building many summaries is passing formal and actual parameters to call sites and mapping return values to appropriate variables. Therefore, the STANSE framework provides classes simplifying the parameter passing and values returning for checkers. These classes also provide a conversion of a given expression in the caller into an equal expression in the called function. The conversion can also be required in the opposite direction, i.e. for returned values.

2.8   The Concept of Checkers

In the STANSE framework a checker is an implementation of some concrete static analysis technique. Each checker has an access to a shared internal structure of analysed source files. They are also provided with an access to the algorithms providing navigation in those structures. This is done by an interface between checkers and internal structure and libraries of the framework. The interface is depicted in Fig. 1 right bellow the checkers.

The checkers are integrated in the framework of STANSE using concrete factory design pattern. Therefore, to insert a new checker to the framework one needs to implement generic checker interface and register it to the checkers' factory of the framework. Then it gains a full access to the features of the framework accessible through the discussed interface.

It is very easy to integrate a new checker into STANSE. The process requires only three simple steps to be fully functional. The first step is to create a subclass of STANSE abstract class `Checker`, say `MyChecker`. The most important method to implement is `check`. There the analysis algorithm should be implemented.

The second step is to integrate the newly created class into the framework. This means implementation of `MyCheckerCreator`, a subclass of `CheckerCreator` abstract class. And the final step is to register the class `MyCheckerCreator`. It comprises adding a line `registerCheckerCreator(new MyCheckerCreator())` at the end of `CheckerFactory.java`.

2.9   Processing Errors

Once a checker finds an error, it reports the error back to the framework in the form of an annotated *error trace* - a path in the analysed code demonstrating this error. A datatype is provided in the STANSE framework to describe an error. In the framework there are then several possibilities how to present the error traces back to the user of STANSE: they can be printed to the console, displayed using a built-in error trace browser in the GUI (see Fig. 2), or saved to an external file in XML format. This XML file has a wide variety of possible applications. For example, we supply a tool transforming the XML file into an SQLITE database. The database is supplemented with a web interface allowing to browse errors in the database via a web browser. Using the web browser or the built-in graphical error browser, one can mark errors as real bugs or false positives. STANSE also provides various statistics of errors like number of errors per checker, frequency of errors of the same kind, percentage of false positives (based on user feedback).

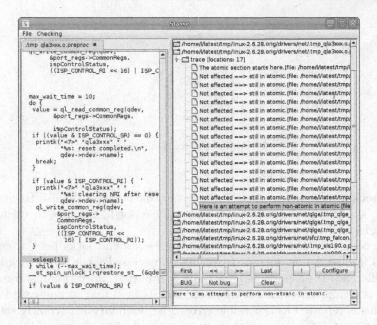

Fig. 2. Error trace browser in the STANSE GUI

Error reporting and tracing pipeline is depicted to the right of interface and internal representation of Fig. 1.

3   Checkers

In this section we briefly describe the four currently available checkers. All four checkers are provided with sample configuration so that they can be used instantly, however they can be configured differently when necessary.

AutomatonChecker is heavily influenced by [2]. It takes, as an input, a set of finite-state automata that describe the properties we want to check, patterns which match against the code to be checked, and finally transitions, i.e. pairing of patterns and automaton state changes. Properties like locking discipline, interrupt management, null pointer dereference, dangling pointers and many others can be described this way.

An example of the locking checker is presented in Fig. 3. The automaton starts in the unlocked state (U) and a transition is made when there is an outgoing edge from the current state with a pattern matching the action currently performed by the analysed program. E.g. if there is an unlock action while the automaton is in an unlocked state, an error is reported.

Compared to the implementation described in [2] and [4], our technique differs in several aspects. In particular, we do not use metacompilation, automata are not input-language specific (a pattern matching is used instead), and the interprocedural analysis is done in the context of a single input file.

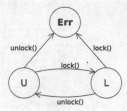

Fig. 3. Automaton for locks checking

LockChecker accounts statistics about variable accesses. It also tracks which locks are locked while each of the variable is accessed. Again both variable accesses and locks are specified by patterns.

Then, combining the information about accesses and locks held, it counts a statistics in how many cases each variable is accessed while some lock is held. If the difference is proportional, an error is reported. So if, for instance, some variable is changed 99 times while some lock is held and in one case the lock is not, this is reported as a possible error. The boundary is currently set to 70, so that at least 70% of accesses must be under locks. The rest (30%) is then reported. This work is based upon [3].

ThreadChecker aims to check for possible deadlocks in concurrent programs. The technique is based on the notions of locksets of [8] and deadlock detection by looking for cycles in *resource allocation graphs (RAGs)*. THREADCHECKER first tries to identify the parts of the code which can run in parallel, as different threads. This is performed by searching of functions instantiating threads (such as pthread_create). Or, for the Linux kernel, we also specify manually which hooks may be run parallel.

Then the checker builds a set of *dependency graphs* for each such thread. A dependency graph statically represents possible locksets during one execution of a thread. Dependency graphs are then combined and transformed into RAGs. If there is a circular lock dependency, RAG contains a cycle. In such case an error is reported to the user.

ReachabilityChecker searches CFGs for unreachable nodes. These are then reported as warnings or errors, depending on importance (e.g. superfluous semicolons are less important than unused branch). The primary goal of REACHABIL-ITYCHECKER is to demonstrate the simplicity of a new checker implementation. With a help of the framework features described in Subsection 2.6, the code of the checker has less than 200 lines including the mentioned error/warning classification and many strings and comments.

Even though it is a very simple checker it was still able to find serious bugs in the kernel. For example a superfluous semicolon can cause unexpected unconditional returns from functions like in the following code: if (cond); return;.

Table 1. STANSE results on the Linux kernel version 2.6.28

| Checker | Automaton | Errors | | | Real/classified error ratio |
		Found	Real	False pos.	
AUTOMATONCHECKER	Pairing	266	65	143	31.3 %
	Pointers	86	48	37	56.5 %
	Deadlocks	35	16	18	47.1 %
LOCKCHECKER		13	6	7	46.2 %
THREADCHECKER		20	9	11	45.0 %
REACHABILITYCHECKER		31	31	0	100.0 %
Overall		451	175	216	47.9 %

4 Results on the Linux Kernel

We have several reasons to choose the Linux kernel for testing STANSE: the kernel is a large and freely available codebase, it fully exercises most of the features of ISO/ANSI C99 and GNU C extensions, it is under constant development (there is a constant income of new bugs), and the absence of bugs is of a great concern.

We applied STANSE, together with the four checkers described in the previous section, to the Linux kernel version 2.6.28. The AUTOMATONCHECKER was configured with three automata describing the following types of errors:

- incorrect pairing of functions (imbalanced locking, reference counting errors)
- bugs in pointer manipulation (null dereference, dangling pointers, etc.)
- deadlocks caused by sleeping inside spinlocks or interrupt handlers

The running time of STANSE on a common desktop machine with two 2.5 GHz cores and 4 GiB of memory was under two hours. The memory usage of the Java process oscillated between 400 and 1000 MiB. The number of errors found by the checkers is presented in Table 1. Let us note that REACHABILITYCHECKER actually found 751 errors, but 720 of them are of low importance (including 696 superfluous semicolons) and they are omitted from our statistics.

We have manually analysed all the found errors and classified them as real errors or false positives (with an exception of 60 errors found by AUTOMATONCHECKER where we are not able to decide in a short time whether it is a false positive or not). Note that the checkers do not produce any false negatives (assuming there is no bug in the checkers' implementation). The reason is that all the checkers implement may analyses, overapproximating the set of error behaviours. The numbers of real errors, false positives and the ratio of real errors to all classified errors can be also found in Table 1. The overall ratio of real errors to all classified errors is not high: 47.9%. However, STANSE in the current version does not have any thorough false positive filtering technique, which may be implemented in future.

More than 70 of the 169 real errors have been reported to kernel developers and fixed in the following kernel releases (the rest have been independently discovered and reported by someone else or the incorrect code disappeared from the kernel before we finished our evaluation of found errors). Some of the reported bugs remained undiscovered for more than seven years (for illustration, see our report at http://lkml.org/lkml/2009/3/11/380).

We have reported another 60 bugs found by STANSE in the subsequent versions of the kernel. This number is increasing every month.

4.1   Important Bugs Found by Stanse

Although checkers currently implemented in STANSE are based on widely known techniques, running them on the Linux kernel helped to uncover several important bugs. In the text below we present two typical bugs discovered by STANSE, each using a different checker.

AutomatonChecker. Many bugs found by the AUTOMATONCHECKER trigger only under specific conditions, however some of them may be visible to the user. Consider this code excerpt taken from the 2.6.27 kernel, drivers/pci/hotplug/p-ciehp_core.c file, set_lock_status function:

```
mutex_lock(&slot->ctrl->crit_sect);
/* has it been >1 sec since our last toggle? */
if ((get_seconds() - slot->last_emi_toggle) < 1)
    return -EINVAL;
```

Note that the call to mutex_lock function is followed by an **if** statement, which returns immediately in the true branch, omitting a call to mutex_unlock. In fact this deadlock could be easily triggered by a user. It is sufficient to write "1" to /sys/bus/pci/slots/.../lock file twice within a second.

ThreadChecker. An example of non-trivial error which could not be found by the AUTOMATONCHECKER. The code described here is from the 2.6.28 kernel, file fs/ecryptfs/messaging.c.

There are three locks in the code, msg_ctx->mux, which is local per context, and two global locks – ecryptfs_daemon_hash_mux and ecryptfs_msg_ctx_lists_mux.

Let us denote lock dependencies as a binary relation where the first component depends on the second. I.e. lock(A) followed by lock(B) means dependency B on A, and we write $A \leftarrow B$.

```
 1  int ecryptfs_process_response (...)
 2  {
 3    ...
 4    mutex_lock(&msg_ctx->mux);
 5    mutex_lock(&ecryptfs_daemon_hash_mux);
 6    ...
 7    mutex_unlock(&ecryptfs_daemon_hash_mux);
 8    ...
 9  unlock:
10    mutex_unlock(&msg_ctx->mux);
```

```
11   out:
12      return rc;
13   }
```

Here the two locks on lines 4 and 5 give msg_ctx->mux ← ecryptfs_daemon_hash_mux.

```
14   static int ecryptfs_send_message_locked (...)
15   {
16      ...
17      mutex_lock(&ecryptfs_msg_ctx_lists_mux);
18      ...
19      mutex_unlock(&ecryptfs_msg_ctx_lists_mux);
20      ...
21   }
22
23   int ecryptfs_send_message (...)
24   {
25      int rc;
26
27      mutex_lock(&ecryptfs_daemon_hash_mux);
28      rc = ecryptfs_send_message_locked (...)
29      mutex_unlock(&ecryptfs_daemon_hash_mux);
30      return rc;
31   }
```

At line 28, function ecryptfs_send_message_locked is called from ecryptfs_send_message, hence the locks at lines 17 and 27 generate lock dependency of ecryptfs_daemon_hash_mux ← ecryptfs_msg_ctx_lists_mux.

```
32   int ecryptfs_wait_for_response (...)
33   {
34      ...
35      mutex_lock(&ecryptfs_msg_ctx_lists_mux);
36      mutex_lock(&msg_ctx->mux);
37      ...
38      mutex_unlock(&msg_ctx->mux);
39      mutex_unlock(&ecryptfs_msg_ctx_lists_mux);
40      return rc;
41   }
```

Finally, this function introduces ecryptfs_msg_ctx_lists_mux ← msg_ctx->mux.

Composing these results together the following circular dependency of these three locks was found:

- msg_ctx->mux ← ecryptfs_daemon_hash_mux
- ecryptfs_daemon_hash_mux ← ecryptfs_msg_ctx_lists_mux
- ecryptfs_msg_ctx_lists_mux ← msg_ctx->mux

This issue was later confirmed as a real bug leading to a deadlock[1].

5 Conclusions and Future Work

STANSE is a free Java-based framework design for simple and efficient implementation of bug-finding algorithms based on static analysis. The framework can process large-scale software projects written in ISO/ANSI C99, together

---

[1] http://lkml.org/lkml/2009/4/14/527

with most the GNU C extensions. STANSE does not currently use any new techniques – its novelty comes from the fact that (to our best knowledge) there is no other open-source framework with comparable applicability and efficiency. We note that more than 130 bugs found by STANSE have been reported to and confirmed by Linux kernel developers already. More information and the tool itself can be found at http://stanse.fi.muni.cz/.

Future Work. We plan to improve the framework in several directions. Firstly we are currently working on C++ support. Furthermore we plan to provide STANSE in the form of an IDE plug-in, e.g. for Eclipse and NetBeans. A lot of work can be done in the area of automatic false alarm filtering and error importance classification. Independently of developing new features, we would like to speed up the framework as well. To this end we intend to replace the current parser written in Java by an optimised parser written in C, to replace the XML format of internal structures by a more succinct representation, to add a support for function summaries, etc.

Acknowledgements. Jan Kučera is the author of the THREADCHECKER. We would like to thank Linux kernel developers, and Cyrill Gorcunov for STANSE alpha testing and useful suggestions. All authors are supported by the research centre Institute for Theoretical Computer Science (ITI), project No. 1M0545.

References

1. Chou, A., Chelf, B., Engler, D., Heinrich, M.: Using meta-level compilation to check FLASH protocol code. ACM SIGOPS Oper. Syst. Rev. 34(5), 59–70 (2000)
2. Engler, D., Chelf, B., Chou, A., Hallem, S.: Checking system rules using system-specific, programmer-written compiler extensions. In: OSDI 2000, pp. 1–16 (2000)
3. Engler, D., Chen, D.Y., Hallem, S., Chou, A., Chelf, B.: Bugs as deviant behavior: A general approach to inferring errors in systems code. ACM SIGOPS Oper. Syst. Rev. 35(5), 57–72 (2001)
4. Hallem, S., Chelf, B., Xie, Y., Engler, D.: A system and language for building system-specific, static analyses. In: PLDI 2002, pp. 69–82. ACM (2002)
5. Hovemeyer, D., Pugh, W.: Finding bugs is easy. In: OOPSLA 2004, pp. 132–136. ACM (2004)
6. Shapiro, M., Horwitz, S.: Fast and accurate flow-insensitive points-to analysis. In: POPL 1997, pp. 1–14. ACM (1997)
7. Steensgaard, B.: Points-to analysis in almost linear time. In: POPL 1996, pp. 32–41. ACM (1996)
8. Voung, J.W., Jhala, R., Lerner, S.: RELAY: static race detection on millions of lines of code. In: ESEC-FSE 2007, pp. 205–214. ACM (2007)
9. CODESONAR, http://www.grammatech.com/products/codesonar/
10. COVERITY, http://www.coverity.com/products/
11. FINDBUGS, http://findbugs.sourceforge.net/
12. KLOCWORK, http://www.klocwork.com/products/
13. SMATCH, http://smatch.sourceforge.net/
14. SPARSE, http://www.kernel.org/pub/software/devel/sparse/
15. UNO, http://spinroot.com/uno/

Introducing the FPGA-Based Hardware Architecture of Systemic Computation (HAoS)

Christos Sakellariou and Peter J. Bentley

Department of Computer Science, University College of London,
Malet Place, London WC1E 6BT, UK
{c.sakellariou,p.bentley}@cs.ucl.ac.uk

Abstract. This paper presents HAoS, the first Hardware Architecture of the bio-inspired computational paradigm known as Systemic Computation (SC). SC was designed to support the modelling of biological processes inherently by defining a massively parallel non-conventional computer architecture and a model of natural behaviour. In this work we describe a novel custom digital design, which addresses the SC architecture parallelism requirement by exploiting the inbuilt parallelism of a Field Programmable Gate Array (FPGA) and by using the highly efficient matching capability of a Ternary Content Addressable Memory (TCAM). Basic processing capabilities are embedded in HAoS, in order to minimize time-demanding data transfers, while the optional use of a CPU provides high-level processing support. We demonstrate a functional simulation-verified prototype, which takes into consideration programmability and scalability. Analysis shows that the proposed architecture provides an effective solution in terms of efficiency versus flexibility trade-off and can potentially outperform prior implementations.

Keywords: Systemic Computation, FPGA, Parallel Architecture, Non-Conventional Computer Architecture, Content Addressable Memory, Natural Computation.

1 Introduction

As conventional silicon-based technologies are about to reach their limits, researchers have drawn inspiration from nature to found new computational paradigms. Such a newly-conceived paradigm is Systemic Computation (SC). SC is designed to be a model of natural behaviour and, at the same time, a model of computation. It incorporates natural characteristics and defines a massively parallel computer architecture that can model natural systems efficiently [1,2].

There are three SC implementations to date. The first two attempts simulate a systemic computer, using conventional CPUs, and provide a satisfactory proof-of-concept but suffer from poor performance [1,2]. The latest attempt successfully maps a part of the model on the parallel resources of a GPU and achieves performance gains up to the order of hundreds [3]. Clearly, the full potential of SC cannot be exploited using conventional hardware.

Z. Kotásek et al. (Eds.): MEMICS 2011, LNCS 7119, pp. 179–190, 2012.
© Springer-Verlag Berlin Heidelberg 2012

Thus, in this paper, an FPGA-based approach is proposed to implement the systemic computer. Section 2 outlines SC and prior implementations. Section 3 summarises our novel custom digital design. In section 4 we demonstrate the verification and evaluation methodology for HAoS. Section 5 concludes the paper.

2   Systemic Computation

2.1   Overview

Systemic computation adopts a holistic analysis approach of systems embracing the significant importance of the interactions of their fundamental elements and their environment. Its intention is to resemble natural computation in order to simulate biological processes effectively. To accomplish this, it follows a set of conventions [1]: (a) everything is a system, (b) systems may comprise or share other nested systems, (c) systems can be transformed but never destroyed or created from nothing, (d) interaction between systems may cause transformation of those systems according to a contextual system, (e) all systems can potentially act as context and interact in some context, (f) the transformation of systems is constrained by the scope of systems, and finally (g) computation is transformation.

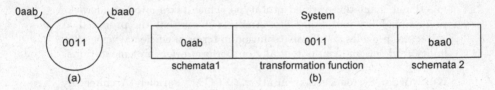

Fig. 1. SC notation and systems representation: (a) Graphical representation of a system in SC (b) The three elements of a system. (Reproduced with permission from [1]).

The interaction of two systems can be described by the systems themselves and a third "contextual" system (which is referred to as context) which denotes how/if the interacting systems are transformed after their interaction. The notions of schemata and transformation function are used in [1] to describe the interaction. Each system comprises of three parts, two schemata and one function (see Fig. 1). Both systems may change after an interaction, which implies circular causality (each system may affect the other). The scope here, as in nature, is an important factor. The scope of a system defines the neighbourhood (which can be other than spatial) in which the system can interact with other systems in a certain way, denoted by the context. Systems are represented as binary strings.

Pairs of systems always interact with a context; these systems constitute a valid triplet. The schemata of the context provide templates for the operand systems to match in order to interact, provided that all three systems belong in the same scope. Thus all computations in SC involve (1) finding valid triplets (context and two matching systems in a shared scope) and (2) updating the two systems according to the transformation function in the context. Full details on SC are provided in [1,2].

2.2 Prior SC Implementations

In [1], Bentley, along with introducing SC, provided a corresponding virtual computer architecture and its first implementation. This prototype included a basic instruction set, an assembly language, a compiler and resulting machine code. However the implementation was merely a simulation of a systemic computer, although it was a satisfactory proof-of-concept.

The second implementation (SCoPE) [2] provides a complete SC platform (language, compiler, virtual machine and visualization tools) which is also an SC simulation, but it is based on a high-level SC language. It is fully programmable and more flexible than the original one. The transformation function set, the string length and the alphabet can be customized by the user for each model simulation in SCoPE. This flexibility comes in expense of execution speed.

In [3], another PC-based implementation is presented, utilizing the inherent parallelism of graphics processors (GPUs) with considerable gains in terms of speed compared to previous attempts. The performance improvement is justified since this is the first implementation with a hardware constituent (GPU cores) and the first step towards a real systemic computer. GPUs are well suited for applications with numerous threads running in parallel over a set of shared data. In [3], the shared data are the systems.

3 The Proposed SC Hardware Architecture

HAoS attempts to satisfy the basic SC requirements, taking into consideration the requirements of a practical implementation: programmability, design friendliness, technology maturity, I/O functionality efficiency, advanced processing features, compiler support and scalability.

HAoS targets an FPGA as this option appears to be the optimal implementation platform among others based on a detailed review and analysis of the literature and available hardware platforms [4]. The conventional underlying architecture of a multi-core processor [5] is capable of just simulating SC, as shown in section 2.2. Conventional network-based platforms (like computer clusters [6], peer-to-peer networks [7] and wireless sensors networks [8]) also rely on the same underlying architecture. However, a network can present characteristics like decentralized and distributed computation and parallelism while simulating asynchrony, self-organization and partial fault-tolerance. Thus, a network with FPGAs as basic building blocks could satisfy a large number of SC requirements by presenting these natural characteristics. Unconventional material (like DNA [9] or quantum [10]) platforms can also provide such characteristics but they are not mature enough yet to provide a practical implementation.

The SC concept dictates that any three systems are eligible to form a valid triplet. A fully parallel implementation would generate a valid triplet of systems, in a random manner, for all contexts, in all scopes during an iteration of an SC program, while all interactions would happen instantaneously, provided that adequate parallel processing resources were available. Resource limitations forbid a practical implementation of this approach on an FPGA. It is apparent that the main two tasks that would ideally be executed in parallel are valid triplet generation and system transformation (the actual data processing).

While one of the assumptions of the SC paradigm is that systems have "local knowledge" storing the system bit representation and the scopes it belongs to in local registers was not adopted but instead, the binary contents of the systems and their scopes are stored in system RAM. This approach was preferred because local knowledge is a feature that cannot be accurately mapped on on-chip logic. The contents of a system could potentially be stored on registers which do not reside on the same area of the chip instead of using a RAM. The use of a RAM in this design is justified by the fact that RAM storage volumes are greater than those provided by registers in modern FPGAs and since no further fabric would need to be consumed for address decoding logic.

Moreover, only a finite number of systems can be stored on a single RAM, which defines a neighbourhood for its systems, while the total number of systems can be spread over multiple RAMs. As a result, a potential failure in one of the RAMs would leave the rest of systems of the program unaffected, providing a limited level of fault-tolerance for the single-FPGA HAoS prototype. The level of fault-tolerance of our single-FPGA configuration can be improved in the application-level, as shown in [11], by combining redundancy (duplicating system instances) with self-maintenance (using self-repairing systems). A multi-FPGA configuration could further improve fault-tolerance by adding redundancy in the hardware-level to address faults that cannot be handled by the application (as a hardware failure of the resources used to store the global scopetable).

One of the main limitations of the software-based implementations was the way valid triplets were generated. The common strategy was to randomly select three systems (one of which acted as context) in a scope and check triplet validity after matching the operand systems with the schemata of the context. A common practice to accelerate this task was to use priority queues that either gave priority to systems that had recently interacted [1] or had not recently interacted [2]. In [3], this task is assigned to the GPU which handles it in parallel resulting in great performance gains.

The present design addresses the valid triplet generation by exploiting the inherent parallelism of a Ternary Content Addressable Memory (TCAM). While traditionally used Random Access Memories (RAMs), when provided with an address return the data stored in this address, CAMs compare their input data with the data which they store and provide all matching addresses in parallel. Moreover, TCAMs have the ability to perform ternary comparisons, meaning that both the input and stored data can include "don't care" bits. This functionality enables a guaranteed match of systems to the schemata of the given context, provided there are such systems in the scope of the context.

HAoS also uses a pseudo-random number generator to randomly identify valid triplets but this operation is not biased by previous interactions. All matching systems have the same interaction probability while, as explained above, the use of the TCAM ensures maximum matching efficiency. While future work will target parallel processing capabilities, true parallel interaction is not supported by HAoS, since writing to the TCAM is limited to one system at a time in order to improve its area and enable ternary comparisons (assuming that parallel interactions would transform the interacting systems simultaneously). A fully asynchronous design might enable the true implementation of the stochastic property, but such an implementation would require that all systems, matching and control circuitry and interconnections would be realized in combinatorial logic which would pose a great area requirement and increase the possibility of timing hazards.

3.1   The SC Architecture

HAoS consists of the SC core (CORE), the Control Unit (CU), the Functional Unit (FU) and a set of configuration and data registers (REG BANK) for communication with the optional CPU (see Fig. 2).

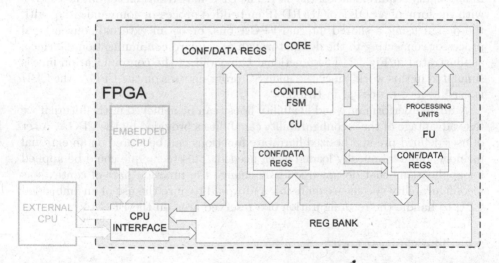

Fig. 2. The SC Hardware Architecture

The CORE contains the optimized logic for the parallel schemata matching and the memory elements. The CU handles the execution sequence of the SC program and the communication with the optional external CPU. The REG BANK provides a control and debug interface between the CPU and the local registers of the SC sub-modules. The FU provides basic local processing functionality.

A set of simple instructions is supported to avoid expensive data transfers between the REG BANK and the CPU.

The prototype implementation includes only one FU, but future implementations can take advantage of the plethora of DSP processing cores which are available on the FPGA, and give the option to be used as a simple ALU each, to provide multiple parallel processing resources. It is noted that only 16-bit signed integer processing is currently supported by the HAoS prototype. The addition of a hardware floating-point unit in future implementations is under investigation. However, floating-point intermediate operations of high-level functions, if required, can be executed from the optional CPU.

The CPU is provided to the system in order to make more complex high-level functions available. This functionality was available only in SCoPE [2], since the other implementations had a fixed instruction set. HAoS increases flexibility by letting the user define new instructions, when this is necessary, in an unrestricted way. The SC compiler, which preserves backwards compatibility with the compiler presented in [1], is written in C and translates SC source code in SC assembly. Apart from the extra usability, the CPU in the prototype design is used to load the SC assembly code into the memory elements of the CORE during initialization or in the case of a hardware reset. A possible enhancement is to provide the option for assembly loading through an external memory card, thus making the CPU link completely optional, depending on the high-level functionality requirements of the user. The CPU may reside either on the FPGA, with the form of a SOFT or HARD IP embedded processor communicating with the design using a shared internal FPGA bus, or be an external conventional processor connecting to the design through a standard communication interface, as illustrated in Fig. 2. The functional behaviour of the communication link is simulated in this work. Since the main SC program runs on the FPGA, the CPU is used as a co-processor in HAoS.

A further performance and flexibility boost can be achieved in the future if we take advantage of the reconfigurability capabilities provided by the FPGA. A set of user defined pre-synthesized hardware functions can be stored on an external memory and dynamically loaded when needed. This technique could be applied for applications that do not frequently change the function part of contexts as reconfigurability speeds are quite low and would require the use of an embedded CPU to handle the reconfiguration of a reserved area on the FPGA.

3.2   The Control Unit

The CU handles the flow of the user-defined SC program. As systems can never be destroyed, the program runs indefinitely, although it halts when all systems become stable and no further interaction is possible. The main control flow for each iteration of the program can be seen in Fig. 3.

Upon a hardware reset, the SC assembly code is loaded into the core. For each iteration of the SC program, four consecutive steps are performed. A scope is randomly selected, and then a valid triplet of systems is randomly chosen, the selected systems are fetched from memory, they interact (the actual computation is performed) and then the outcome of the interaction (the computation results) is written back to memory (the random system selection logic is described in the next section.) At the end of each iteration, the user is granted access to pause execution in order to easily extract debug information. All the optimized low-level SC micro-routines (for scope and memory manipulation) are available to the user, to ensure maximum flexibility.

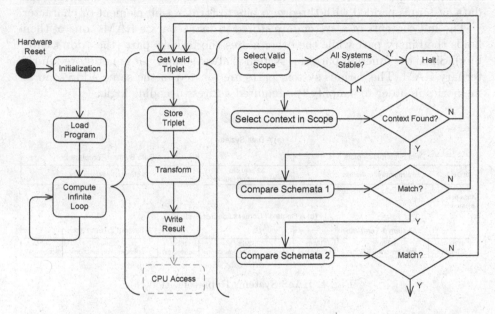

Fig. 3. SC Program Control Flow : HAoS enters an infinite computation loop after the SC program is loaded, which involves finding valid triplets and transforming the selected systems

Various optimizations have been applied in order to improve performance. When the selected context system gives a mismatch, meaning that any of its schemata does not match a system in the scope, it is disabled and becomes an invalid context for this scope to prevent future mismatches (see section 3.3). Moreover, once a scope is selected, if it contains fewer than three systems or no valid contexts, it also is disabled and becomes an invalid scope until a new system is added to it. If all scopes have been disabled, no further transactions can occur and the program halts.

3.3   The SC Core

The CORE is mainly responsible for the efficiency of the design due to the way it handles the task of schemata matching. Its main components are the TCAM, the random selection logic, the system memories, the scopetable memories and the system status registers, as can be seen in Fig. 5.

HAoS supports three types of systems (see Fig. 4): (1) data systems, comprised of two (16-bit) schemata and a zero (32-bit) function part, (2) context systems, comprised of a (32-bit) function and two schemata templates (used for matching with data systems and thus occupying the size of a whole data system, 64-bits,each) and (3) context adapter systems which have the same structure with context systems (but each of their templates can match a data system or a context). Since all the systems have the same size, each bit in a schema of a data system is padded with three zero bits to form a 4-bit element or character.

The full contents of a system are stored in two separate RAMs, one of them holds the binary part while the other stores the ternary part (the "don't care" bits). Since the function part of a system is always binary, it is not stored in the ternary RAM. The various system parts are located in the same address in all memories in order to simplify the required address-decoding logic.

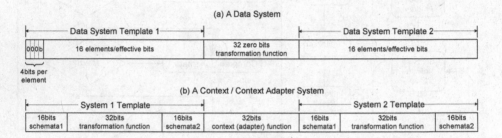

Fig. 4. HAoS Systems Representation

The global scopetable information is stored in three RAM-based structures. One of them stores the systems that belong in each scope at the corresponding to the scope address, the second stores the scopes that each system belongs to at the corresponding to the system address while the third stores a mask for all the invalid contexts in a scope. The first two structures, although effectively storing the same information, provide parallel access to two different aspects of the scopetable (systems in scope and parent scopes of a system).

The TCAM is loaded with the regions of the systems that may be compared during initialization. For data systems, the function part is always zero, so only the binary representation of their two schemata may be compared while for context systems only their function part (which is double the size of a schema) may be compared. This implies that context systems can interact with other context systems or data systems, which greatly enhances functionality since it denotes that context adapting (where context systems can interact with other systems and be changed) is supported (a feature only supported previously in the highly flexible SCoPE implementation). Context adapter systems may not interact with other systems in HAoS. The restriction of comparing only parts of a system is posed by the fact that the TCAM resource requirements scale exponentially with systems capacity (the maximum number of supported systems).

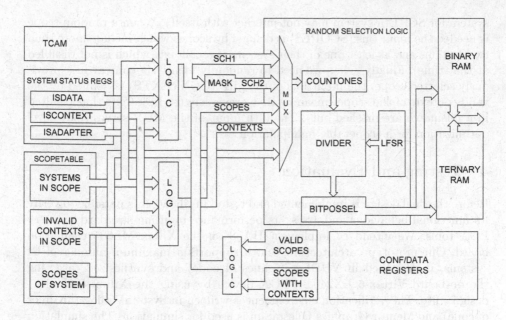

Fig. 5. The SC Core basic building blocks

Thus, by minimizing the size of the TCAM, we maximize the capacity of the prototype. However, as the systems capacity of a single FPGA device is finite, in order to enable further scalability of the HAoS architecture, future work will investigate the use of either a multi-FPGA configuration or an scalable external TCAM.

The random selection logic (RSL) accepts a bus as an input and returns the address of a randomly selected set bit. It consists of a module that counts the set bits of the bus (COUNTONES), a maximal-length Linear Feedback Shift Register (LFSR) for pseudo-random number generation, a combinatorial divider (which also performs integer division when required in the Transform state - see Fig. 3) and a module (BITPOSSEL) that given a bus and the rank of a set bit of this bus (the position of the set bit with rank 2 is 3 in 01001101 - when rank starts from 0 and position 0 is the rightmost one), it returns its position (combining a parallel bit count approach with a branchless selection method). A random number, provided by the LFSR, is divided by the sum of the set bits of the bus. The remainder of this division is used as the rank of the random set bit that is given to BITPOSSEL in order to identify its position.

The function of the RSL (the result of the selection) is controlled by a multiplexer (MUX) which feeds the RSL with one out of five possible input buses (see Fig. 5). When we need to choose a system that matches the first schema of the context, the input bus (SCH1) is generated by combining all the matching systems (the output of the TCAM) with valid SYSTEMS IN SCOPE (which of them are valid depend on the type of the context system). The same bus is used for matching the second schema (SCH2) after masking out the selected system for SCH1 (a system may not interact with itself). When a random scope is needed the input bus (SCOPES) is defined by scopes which include more than two systems and at least one of their systems is a context (which is not disabled at that time). Finally, when we need to randomly identify a context in a previously selected scope, the input bus of the SRL (CONTEXTS) is defined by the valid contexts of the scope (meaning that previously used contexts that resulted in a mismatch are masked out). The fifth input of the MUX serves a low-level optimization for a scopetable manipulation task.

4   Testing and Evaluation

Before the final design is implemented and tested in silicon, it is possible to verify its functional behaviour and assess its performance by using standard industry EDA tools. We intend to implement HAoS on the Xilinx ML605 evaluation board. Our prototype architecture, which supports a maximum number of 64 systems, is described in VHDL (7K lines of code) and synthesized targeting the on-board Virtex-6 LX240T FPGA device by using the Xilinx ISE v13.1 design suite. The verification environment is written in SystemVerilog (5K lines of code) and Mentor Graphics QuestaSim is used for simulation. The simulation experiments are carried on an Intel®Core^{TM}i7 950 CPU with 4 GB of RAM running on 32-bit Windows 7 Ultimate and an nVidia GTX 260 GPU (192 CUDA cores).

Xilinx design tools provide accurate area and timing implementation statistics. Thus, we can present precise performance metrics before downloading our design on the FPGA. The prototype design (excluding the CPU INTERFACE) occupies just 5759 (15%) slices (15487 (10%) slice LUTs and 6019 (1%) slice registers), 143 (23%) I/O blocks, 5 (1%) RAMs and only 1 (0.1%) DSP block (used as a multiplier).

Table 1. A subset of the successfully simulated SC test programs

Systems	Description of the SC Test Program	Functions Used
20	Systems subtract-escape, multiplied & printed	SUBe, MULT, PRINT
24	Systems subtract-escape and recaptured	SUBe, CAPTURE
41	Contexts are transformed to data systems	ADD, SUB, COPY
36	Data systems are transformed to context systems	SUB, COPY, ZERO
33	Part of schemata 1 of a context is changed	ADD, ZERO
12	Fibonacci numbers generator	ADDxce, COPY, PRINT, CAPTURE
4	Optimized incrementing counter	ADDuc
58	A 16-element binary knapsack problem solver based on a genetic algorithm	BINARYMUTATE, CROSSOVER, INIT, OUTPUT

HAoS is divided into two clock domains: the REG BANK, which is connected to the CPU INTERFACE (see Fig. 2) and runs at a higher clock rate (90 MHz) in order to provide faster read/write operations to the CPU, while the rest of the design is clocked at a (6 times) slower rate. Future efforts will include pipelining HAoS in order to achieve higher operating frequencies.

In order to achieve system-level functional coverage closure, a series of 25 SC programs were designed to test and stress the design in various ways. An indicative set of the simulated SC test programs is given in Table 1. It is evident that basic and advanced functionality is supported by HAoS.

The most interesting test case is the genetic algorithm (GA) optimization of the binary knapsack problem (explained in [3]) which is reproduced and simulated as being executed in HAoS. Since [1], [3] and HAoS use the same SC source code, this test program (which has not been optimized for HAoS) is used as a preliminary performance benchmark among the available SC implementations (timing metrics are approximated for the CPU INTERFACE in this work). Experimental simulation results show that for 10000 interactions in the 16-element knapsack problem with 50 systems, the original implementation by [1] requires 33241.2 ms, the GPU-based solution in [3] requires 255.1 ms, while HAoS needs just 55.7 ms, outperforming [1] by a factor of 596 and [3] by a factor of 4.6 (all results are based on the average of 10 repetitions of the experiment). The expected solution is found by HAoS on average after 14.9 ms while the SC program is loaded in 2.67 ms. Timing estimates of the external CPU execution times were acquired by taking the average execution time of each used function (using the high resolution hardware timers of the CPU). These estimates were fed back to the verification environment in order to achieve system-level timing. It was assumed that the CPU INTERFACE (see Fig. 2) can operate at the maximum supported frequency (90MHz) posing a data rate requirement of 700 Mbps on the CPU-FPGA communication link which may be delivered by PCI Express [12] or Gigabit Ethernet [13]. The investigation of the most efficient and practical platform for the CPU INTERFACE and its implementation are subject of future work. Similar results are anticipated for the other test programs.

Table 2. Performance Comparison based on the knapsack SC program

	Sequential	GPU	HAoS
msec (factor)	33241.2 (x596)	255.1 (x4.6)	55.7 (x1)
Solution Found (Weight : 79, Profit: 124)	w:73, p:87	w:75, p:69.7	w:78.7, p:123.5

It is also noted that HAoS outperforms prior implementations in terms of the quality of the obtained results. As seen in Table 2, the correct solution for the knapsack experiment is given for a weight of 79 and a profit of 124. Only HAoS correctly estimates the expected solution given the restricted number of interactions. This high level of efficiency is justified from the effective way of triplet matching and the low-level optimizations of the Control Unit.

5   Conclusion

In this paper, the first hardware architecture specifically designed to support Systemic Computation, HAoS, is presented. The prototype is designed to balance flexibility (combining on-chip and off-chip processing) with efficiency (taking advantage of the efficient parallel comparison capability of a TCAM). Early results based on performance metrics indicate that HAoS could outperform prior implementations.

Acknowledgments. This work was supported by the EPSRC Doctoral Training Centre in VEIV (University College London, UK) and Toumaz UK Limited.

References

1. Bentley, P.J.: Systemic computation: A model of interacting systems with natural characteristics. IJPEDS 22, 103–121 (2007)
2. Le Martelot, E., Bentley, P.J., Lotto, R.B.: A Systemic Computation Platform for the Modelling and Analysis of Processes with Natural Characteristics. In: Proceedings of Genetic and Evolutionary Computation Conference (GECCO 2007), pp. 2809–2816. ACM Press (2007)
3. Rouhipour, M., Bentley, P.J., Shayani, H.: Systemic Computation using Graphics Processors. In: Tempesti, G., Tyrrell, A.M., Miller, J.F. (eds.) ICES 2010. LNCS, vol. 6274, pp. 121–132. Springer, Heidelberg (2010)
4. Sakellariou, C.: Hardware-based Systemic Computation. Thesis (MRes), Department of Computer Science, University College London (2010)
5. Blake, G., Dreslinski, R.G., Mudge, T.: A survey of multicore processors. IEEE Signal Processing Magazine 26, 26–37 (2009)
6. Marcus, E., Stern, H.: Blueprints for High Availability: Designing Resilient Distributed Systems. John Wiley & Sons, Inc. (2000)
7. Milojicic, D.S., Kalogeraki, V., Lukose, R., Nagaraja, K., Pruyne, J., Richard, B., Rollins, S., Xu, Z.: Peer-to-peer computing. Technical Report HPL-2002-57, HP Labs (2002)
8. Akyildiz, I.F., Vuran, M.C.: Wireless sensor networks. John Wiley & Sons, Inc. (2010)
9. Adleman, L.M.: Computing with DNA. Scientific American 279, 34–41 (1998)
10. Kari, L., Rozenberg, G.: The many facets of natural computing. Communications of the ACM 51, 72–83 (2008)
11. Le Martelot, E., Bentley, P.J., Lotto, R.B.: Crash-Proof Systemic Computing: A Demonstration of Native Fault-Tolerance and Self-Maintenance. In: Proceedings of the Fourth IASTED International Conference on Advances in Computer Science and Technology (ACST 2008), pp. 49–55. ACTA Press (2008)
12. Bittner, R.: Bus mastering PCI express in an FPGA. In: Proceeding of the ACM/SIGDA International Symposium on Field Programmable Gate Arrays, pp. 273–276. ACM, New York (2009)
13. Alachiotis, N., Berger, S.A., Stamatakis, A.: Efficient PC-FPGA Communication over Gigabit Ethernet. In: 10th International Conference on Computer and Information Technology, Bradford, pp. 1727–1734 (2010)

A Parallel Compact Hash Table

Steven van der Vegt and Alfons Laarman

Formal Methods and Tools, University of Twente, The Netherlands
s.vandervegt@student.utwente.nl,
a.w.laarman@ewi.utwente.nl

Abstract. We present the first parallel compact hash table algorithm. It delivers high performance and scalability due to its dynamic region-based locking scheme with only a fraction of the memory requirements of a regular hash table.

1 Introduction

During the last decade or so, we are witnessing a shift from ever faster sequential microprocessors towards multi-core processors. This shift is caused by physical limitations on the nanostructures inside the processor chip and is therefore irreversible. Most software systems, however, are still not equipped fully to benefit from the newly available parallelism.

Data structures, like *hash tables*, are crucial building blocks for these systems and many have been parallelized [4,6]. A hash table stores a subset of a large *universe U* of keys and provides the means to lookup individual keys in constant time. It uses a *hash function* to calculate an address h from the unique *key*. The entire key is then stored at its hash or home location in a table (an array of *buckets*): $T[h] \leftarrow key$. Because often $|U| \gg |T|$, multiple keys may have the same hash location. We can handle these so-called *collisions* by calculating alternate hash locations and searching for a key in the list of alternate locations, a process known as *probing*.

In the case that $|U| \leq |T|$, a hash table can be replaced with a *perfect hash function* and a bit array, saving considerable memory. The former ensures that no collisions can occur, hence we can simply turn "on" the bit at the home location of a key, to add it to the set. *Compact hashing* [3] generalizes this concept for the case $|U| > |T|$ by storing only the part of the key that was not used for addressing in T: the *remainder*. The complete key can now be reconstructed from the value in T and the home location of the key. If, due to collisions, the key is not stored at its home location, additional information is needed. Cleary [3] solved this problem with very little overhead by imposing an order on the keys in T and introducing three administration bits per bucket.

The bucket size b of Cleary compact hash tables is thus dependent on U and T as follows: $b = w - m + 3$, with the key size $w = \lceil log_2(|U|) \rceil$ and $m = \lceil log_2(|T|) \rceil$. Assuming that all the buckets in the table can be utilized, the compression ratio obtained is thus close to the information theoretical lower bound of storing a subset of U in a list T, where $b_{optimal} = w - m + 1$ [5]. Note that good compression ratios ($\frac{b}{w}$) are only obtained when m is significant with respect to w.

Z. Kotásek et al. (Eds.): MEMICS 2011, LNCS 7119, pp. 191–204, 2012.

Problem description. Compact hashing has never been parallelized, even though it is ideally suited to be used inside more complex data structures, like *tree tables* [8] and *binary decision diagrams* (BDDs) [2]. Such structures maintain large tables with small pieces of constant-sized data, like pointers, yielding an ideal m and w for compact hashing. But even more interesting than obtaining some (constant-factor) memory reductions, is the ability to store more information in machine-sized words, for efficient parallelization depends crucially on memory alignment and low-level operations on word-sized memory locations [4,7].

Contributions. We present an efficient scheme to parallelize both the Cleary table and the order-preserving bidirectional linear probing (BLP) algorithm that it depends upon. The method is *lockless*, meaning that it does not use operating system locks, thereby providing the performance required for use in high-throughput environments, like in BDDs, and avoiding memory overhead.

Our algorithm guarantees read/write exclusion, but not on the lowest level of buckets, as in [4,7], nor on fixed-size regions in the table as in *region-based/striped* locking, but instead on the logical level of a *cluster*: a maximal subarray $T[i \ldots j]$ such that $\forall x : i \leq x \leq j \implies T[x].occ$,where $T[x].occ$ denotes a filled bucket. We call this novel method: *dynamic region-based locking* (DRL).

2   Background

In the current section, we explain the Cleary table and the BLP algorithm it uses. Finally, we discuss some parallelization approaches that have been used before for hash tables and the issues that arise when applying them to the Cleary table.

For this discussion, the distinction between *open-addressing* and *chained* hash tables is an important one. With open addressing, the probing for alternate locations is done inside the existing table as is done in BLP and hence also in Cleary tables. While *chained* or *closed-addressing* hash tables resolve collisions by maintaining (concurrent) linked lists at each location in the table.

2.1   Bidirectional Linear Probing

Linear probing (LP) is the simplest form of open addressing: alternate hash locations in the table are calculated by adding one to the current location. While this probing technique provides good spatial locality, it is known for producing larger clusters, i.e., increasing the average probing distance [4].

BLP [1,9] mitigates the downside of LP, by enforcing a global order on the keys in the buckets using a *monotonic hash function*: if $k_1 < k_2$ then $hash(k_1) \leq hash(k_2)$. Therefore, the look-up of a key k boils down to: compare the k to the bucket at the home location h, if $T[h] > k$, probe left linearly ($h' \leftarrow h - 1$), until $T[h'] = k$. If k is not present in the table, the probe sequence stops at either an *empty* bucket, denoted by $\neg T[h'].occ$, or when $T[h'] < k$. If $T[h] < k$, do the reverse.

To maintain order during an insert of a key, the BLP algorithm needs to move part of a cluster to the left or the right in the table, thereby making space for the new key at the correct (in-order) location. This move is usually done with pair-wise swaps, starting from the empty bucket at one end of the cluster. Therefore, this is referred to as the *swapping* operation. For algorithms and a more detailed explanation, please refer to [9].

2.2   A Compact Hash Table Using the Cleary Algorithm

As explained in Sec. 1, Cleary's compact hash table [3] stores only the remainder of a key in T. With the use of the sorting property of the BLP algorithm and 3 additional *administration* bits per bucket, the home location h of the remainder can be reconstructed, even for colliding entries that are not stored at their home location. The *rem* function is the complement of the monotonic hashing function and calculates the remainder, e.g., $rem(x) = x\%10$ and $hash(x) = x/10$.[1] A *group* h is a sequence of successive remainders in T with the same home location h. All adjacent groups in T form a cluster, as defined in Sec. 1, which by definition is enclosed by empty buckets.

The first administration bit *occ* is used to indicate occupied buckets. The *virgin* bit is set on a bucket h to indicate the existence of the related group h in T. And finally, the *change* bit marks the last (right-most) remainder of a group, such that the next bucket is empty or the start of another group.

Fig. 1 shows the Cleary table with $|T| = 10$ that uses the example *hash* and *rem* functions from above. A group h is indicated with g_h. Statically, keys can be reconstructed by multiplying the group number by 10, and adding the remainder: $key(j) = group(T[j]) \times 10 + T[j] = hash^{-1}(group(T[j])) + T[j]$. For example, bucket 6 stores remainder 8 and $group(6) = 4$, therefore $key(6) = 4 \times 10 + 8 = 48$.

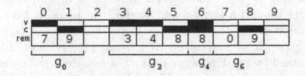

Fig. 1. Example Cleary table with 10 buckets containing 8 remainders, 2 clusters and 4 groups, representing the keys: 7,9,33,34,38,48,60,69

The algorithms maintain the following invariants [3]: the amount of *change* and *virgin* bits within a cluster is always equal, and, when a virgin bit is set on a bucket, this bucket is always occupied.

The FIND function in Alg. 1a makes use of these invariants as follows: it counts the number of *virgin* bits between the home location h and the left end

---

[1] To increase the performance of the hash function, it is common practice to apply an invertible randomization function to the key before hashing it [1,3,5]. Throughout this paper, we assume keys to be randomized.

```
1: procedure VCOUNT-LEFT(j)           Require: (∃i : ¬T[i].occ) ∧ ¬FIND(k)
2:      c ← 0            ▷ count variable    1: procedure PUT(k)
3:      while T[j].occ do                     2:      h ← hash(k)
4:          c ← c + T[j].virgin              3:      (j, c) ← VCOUNT-LEFT(h)
5:          j ← j − 1                         4:      T[j] ← rem(k)
6:      return j, c                          5:      T[j].occ ← 1
7: procedure FIND(k)                         6:      T[j].change ← 0
8:      j ← hash(k)                          7:      while c ≠ 0 do
9:      if ¬T[j].virgin then                 8:          if T[h].virgin ∧ c = 1∧
10:         return NOT_FOUND   ▷ false        9:              T[j + 1] > rem(k) then
11:     (j, c) ← VCOUNT-LEFT(j)             10:              return
12:     j ← j + 1                           11:          c ← c − T[j + 1].change
13:     while c ≠ 0 ∧ T[j].occ do          12:          SWAP(T[j + 1], T[j])
14:         if c = 1 ∧ T[j] = rem(k) then  13:          j ← j + 1
15:             return FOUND    ▷ true      14:      if T[h].virgin then
16:         c ← c − T[j].change             15:          T[j − 1].change ← 0
17:         j ← j + 1                       16:      T[j].change ← 1
18:     return NOT_FOUND     ▷ false        17:      T[h].virgin ← 1
```

Alg. 1. Functions for finding (a) and inserting (b) a key in a Cleary table

of the cluster in c (see VCOUNT-LEFT). Since the last encountered *virgin* bit corresponds to the left-most group, the group h can now be located by counting c *change* bits to the right (l.13-17). The first iteration where $c = 1$ marks that start of group h. Hence, the algorithm starts comparing the remainders in $T[j]$ with $rem(k)$ at l.14, and returns *FOUND* when they are equal. Once c becomes 0 again, the group h did not contain the key, and *NOT_FOUND* is returned at l.18.

The PUT function in Alg. 1b inserts the remainder of k in the empty bucket left of the cluster around h at l.4-6 and swaps it in place at l.7-13 (SWAP only swaps the remainder and the *change* bit). In this case, *in place* means two things: within group h as guaranteed by l.7 and l.8, and sorted by remainder value as guaranteed by l.9. Furthermore, PUT guarantees the correct setting of the administration bits. First, the *occ* bit is always set for every inserted element at l.5. Also, before return, the *virgin* bit is always set for $T[h]$ (see l.8 and l.17).

To understand the correct setting of the *change* bits, we introduce an invariant: at l.8, $group(T[j + 1]) \leq h$. Consequently, a return at l.10, means that the remainder is not swapped to the end of group h, therefore the *change* bits do not require updating. On the other hand, if the **while** loop terminates normally, the remainer is swapped to the end of group h, therefore the *change* bit needs to be set (l.16). If group h already existed ($T[h].virgin =$ true), the previous last remainder of the group needs to have its *change* bit unset (l.15).

We illustrate PUT with an example. Inserting the key 43 into the table of Fig. 1 gives a $h = hash(43) = 4$ and $rem(43) = 3$. Searching for the empty bucket left of the cluster at l.3, results in $j = 2$ and $c = 2$, since there are two *virgin* bits in buckets 3 and 4. The remainder is initially inserted in $T[2]$ (l.4-6). At l.12 the remainder in bucket 2 is swapped with bucket 3 (the *virgin* bit remains unchanged). These steps are repeated until j points to bucket 5. Then, at l.11 c becomes 1, indicating $group(T[j+1]) = h$. In the next iteration $(j' = j - 1)$, the condition at l.8-9 holds, meaning that the remainder is at its correct location: at the start of g_4.

If instead, we were inserting the key 49, c would have become 0, ending the **while** loop with $j = 6$ (l.7), after swapping the remainder 9 to bucket 6. Because g_4 already existed, the previous *change* bit (now on $T[5]$) is unset by l.14-15. Finally, the *change* bit at bucket 6 is set by l.16.

To make groups grow symmetrically around their home locations and keep probing sequence shorter, it is important that the PUT function periodically also starts inserting remainders from the right of the cluster (not shown in the algorithm). Our experimental results confirm that a random choice between the two insert directions yields the same probe distances as reportedly obtained by the optimal replacement algorithms in [1].

2.3   Related Work on Parallel Hash Tables

In this subsection, we recapitulate some relevant, existing approaches to parallelize hash tables. With relevant, we mean parallel hash tables that can efficiently store smaller pieces of data (remember, from the introduction, that the key size w should be significant with respect to m for compact hashing to be effective). Furthermore, the scalability should be good for high-throughput systems like inside BDDs.

Many parallel hash table implementations are based on chaining. More advanced approaches even introduce more pointers per bucket, for example: *split-ordered lists* [6, Sec. 13.3], which: "move[s] the buckets among the [keys], instead of moving the [keys] among the buckets". While these kind of hash tables lend themselves well for maintaining small sets in parallel settings like graphical user interfaces, they are less suited for our goals for two reasons: (1) the pointers require relatively much additional memory compared to the small bucket sizes that are so typical for compact hashing and (2) the pointers increase the *memory working set*, which is disastrous for scalability on modern computer systems with steep memory hierarchies [7,4].

Slightly more relevant to our cause is the use of operating system locks to make access to a hash table (chained or open addressing) concurrent. One lock can be used for the entire table, but this is hardly scalable. Alternatively, one lock can be used per bucket, but this uses too much memory (we measured 56 bytes for POSIX locking structures, this excludes any memory allocated by the constructor). A decent middle way is to use one lock for a group of buckets. The well-known *striped* hash table [6, Sec. 13.2.2], does this for chained tables. To employ the same idea for an open-addressing table, it does not make sense to 'stripe' the locks over the table buckets. Preferably, we group subsequent buckets into one region, so that only one lock needs to be taken for multiple probes. We dub this method "region-based locking" (RBL).

Lockless hash tables avoid the use of operating system locks entirely. Instead, atomic instructions are used to change the status of buckets ("locking" in parentheses). A lockless hash table (LHT) is presented in [7], based on ideas from [4]. It uses open addressing with LP and even modifies the probe sequence to loop over cache lines ("walking the line") to lower the memory working set and achieve higher scalability. For maximum scalability, only individual buckets are "locked" using one additional bit; the only memory overhead that is required.

None of the above-mentioned methods are suitable for *ordered hash tables*, like BLP and Cleary tables. First the regions in RBL are fixed, while the clusters in ordered tables can be at the boundary of a region. While this could be solved with more complicated locking mechanism, it would negatively affect the performance of RBL, which is already meager compared to the lockless approaches (see Sec. 4). The lockless approach, in turn, also fails for ordered hash tables since it is much harder to "lock" pairs of buckets that are swapped atomically. And even if it would be technically possible to efficiently perform an atomic pairwise swap, it would severely increase the amount of (expensive) atomic operations per insert (Sec. 3.2 discusses the complexity of the swapping operations).

In [9], we introduced a lockless algorithm for BLP that "locks" only the cluster during swapping operation. FIND operations do not require this exclusive access, for an ongoing PUT operation can only cause false negatives that can be mitigated by another *exclusive* FIND operation. However, this method is not suitable for the Cleary table, since its FIND function is *probe-sensitive*, because it counts the *virgin* and *change* bits during probing. Therefore, it can cause false positives in case of ongoing swapping operations. The current paper is an answer to the future work of [9].

3   Dynamic Region-Based Locking

In the current section, we first present *dynamic region-based locking* (DRL): a locking strategy that is compatible with the access patterns of both the BLP algorithm with its swapping property and the Cleary table with its probe-sensitive lookup strategy. We limit our scope to a procedure that combines the FIND and PUT functions, described in the previous section, into the FIND-OR-PUT function, which searches the table for a key k and inserts k if not found. The reason for this choice is twofold: first, it covers all issues of parallelizing the individual operations, and second, the FIND-OR-PUT operation is sufficient to implement advanced tasks like *model checking* [7,8].

Additionally, in Sec. 3.2, we show that DRL only slightly increases the number of memory accesses for both BLP and PCT. From this and the limited number of atomic operations that it requires, we conclude that its scalability is likely as good as LHT's. We end with a correctness proof of DRL in Sec. 3.3.

3.1   Parallel FIND-OR-PUT Algorithm

We generalize the lockless BLP algorithm from [9] to accommodate Cleary compact hashing with its *probe-sensitive* FIND operation. It uses one extra bit field per bucket (*lock*) to provide light-weight mutual exclusion. This method has limited memory overhead and does not require a context switch and additional synchronization points like operating system locks.

The atomic functions TRY-LOCK and UNLOCK control this bit field and have the following specifications: TRY-LOCK requires an empty and unlocked bucket and guarantees an empty, locked bucket or otherwise fails. UNLOCK accepts multiple buckets and ensures all are unlocked upon return (each atomically, the multiple arguments are merely syntactic sugar). These functions can be implemented using the processor's CAS(a, b, c) operation, which updates a word-sized memory location at a with c atomically, if and only if the condition b holds for location a [6, Ch. 5.8]. CAS returns the initial value at location a, used to evaluate the condition.

Alg. 2 shows the dynamic locking scheme for the FIND-OR-PUT algorithm. First, at l.3, the algorithm tries a non-exclusive write using CAS, which succeeds if the home location h is empty and unlocked ($\neg lock \wedge \neg occ$). The success of the operation can be determined from the return value *old* of CAS (see l.4). If a lock or full bucket was detected, the algorithm is restarted at l.7.

From l.10 onwards, the algorithm tries to acquire exclusive access to the cluster around $T[h]$. Note that $T[h]$ is occupied. At l.10 and l.11, the first empty location left of and right of h are found in T. If both can be locked, the algorithm enters a local *critical section* (*CS*) after l.16, else it restarts at l.13 or l.16 (after releasing all taken locks). In the *CS*, the algorithm can now safely perform exclusive reads and exclusive writes on the cluster (l.17 and l.20).

DRL is suitable in combination with the FIND and PUT operations of both BLP and the Cleary table. If we are implementing the BLP algorithm using this locking scheme, then FIND at l.8 can perform a non-exclusive read (concurrent to any ongoing write operations). The possibility of a false negative is mitigated by an upcoming exclusive read at l.17. For the Cleary algorithm, however, the non-exclusive read needs to be dropped because the probe-sensitive lookup mechanism might yield a false positive due to ongoing swapping operations.

```
 1: procedure FIND-OR-PUT(k)              12:    if ¬TRY-LOCK(T[left]) then
 2:     h ← hash(k)      ▷ non-excl. write: 13:        return FIND-OR-PUT(k)
 3:     old ← CAS(T[h], ¬lock ∧ ¬occ, k)  14:    if ¬TRY-LOCK(T[right]) then
 4:     if ¬old.occ ∧ ¬old.lock then      15:        UNLOCK(T[left])
 5:         return INSERTED               16:        return FIND-OR-PUT(k)
 6:     else if old.lock then
 7:         return FIND-OR-PUT(k)         17:    if FIND(k) then  ▷ exclusive read
 8:     if FIND(k) then  ▷ non-excl. read 18:        UNLOCK(T[left], T[right])
 9:         return FOUND                  19:        return FOUND
10:     left ← CL-LEFT(h)                 20:    PUT(k)           ▷ exclusive write
11:     right ← CL-RIGHT(h)               21:    UNLOCK(T[left], T[right])
                                          22:    return INSERTED
```

Alg. 2. Concurrent bidirectional linear find-or-put algorithm

3.2 Complexity and Scalability

Two questions come to mind when studying the DRL: (1) What is the added complexity compared to the sequential BLP or Cleary algorithm? (2) What scalability can we expect from such an algorithm. Below, we discuss these matters.

For *ordered hash tables*, like BLP and Cleary tables, the cluster size L depends on the load factor α, as follows: $L = (\alpha - 1)^{-2} - 1$ [1], where $\alpha = n/|T|$ and n the number of inserted keys. Since DRL probes to the empty buckets at both ends of the cluster, it requires $(\alpha - 1)^{-2} + 1$ bucket accesses. When implementing the Cleary table using DRL, this is the complexity for the FIND-OR-PUT operation independent whether an insert occurred or not, because in both cases it "locks" the entire cluster. Note that we do not count the bucket accesses of the called FIND and the PUT operations, since, in theory, these could be done simultaneously by the CL-LEFT and CL-RIGHT operations. In practice, this seems unnecessary, because the cluster will be cache hot after locking it.

The sequential Cleary FIND and PUT algorithm have to probe to one end of the cluster to count the virgin and change bits, hence require $\frac{1}{2}(\alpha - 1)^{-2} + \frac{1}{2}$ bucket accesses (again assuming that we can count both in one pass or that the second pass is cached and therefore insignificant). We conclude that Cleary+DRL (with one worker thread) is only twice as slow as the original Cleary algorithm.

For BLP+DRL the story changes, but the outcome is the same. The sequential BLP algorithm does not have to probe to the end of the cluster and is empirically shown to be much faster than LP [1]. However, DRL+BLP is correct with non-exclusive reads as long as an unsuccessful FIND operation is followed by an exclusive FIND to mitigate false negatives, as is done in Alg. 2. But false negatives are rare, so again the parallel FIND operation is not much slower than the sequential one. The same holds for the PUT operation, since the sequential version on average needs to swap half of an entire cluster and the parallel version "locks" the whole cluster.

Scalability of DRL can be argued to come from three causes: first, the complexity (in memory access) of the parallel algorithm is the same the sequential versions, as shown above, second, the number of (expensive) atomic operations used is low, DRL uses two at most, and third, the memory accesses are all consecutive. We analyze the third cause in some more detail.

To mitigate the effect of slow memories, caching is important for modern multi-core systems. Each memory access causes a fixed region of memory, known as a cache line, to be loaded into the CPU's cache. If it is written to, the entire line is invalidated and has to be reload on all cores that use it; an operation which is several orders of magnitude more expensive than other operations using in-cache data. We have shown before that highly scalable hashing algorithms can be obtained by lowering the number of cache lines that are accessed: the *memory working set* [7].

The open-addressing tables discussed in this paper exhibit only consecutive memory accesses. And while it seems that the amount of buckets probed in the Cleary algorithm is high, typically few cache lines are accessed. For example, there are 26 bucket accesses on average for $\alpha = 0.8$, while on average only

$\lceil 26/64 \rceil + 26/64 = 1.41$ cache lines are accessed, assuming a bucket size of 1 byte and a cache line size of 64 byte. When α grows to 0.85, we get 1.71 cache line accesses on average, and when $\alpha = .9$, 3.59 accesses. Note finally that with buckets of 1 byte, the cleary algorithm can store keys of more than 32 bit for large tables, e.g, if $m = 28$, then $w = b + m - 3 = 8 + 28 - 3 = 33$, while non-compacting hash table requires five bytes per bucket to store as many data. In conclusion, we can expect Cleary+DRL to perform and scale good until load factors of 0.8 and competitive performance to that of [7].

3.3 Proof of Correctness

To prove correctness, we show that Alg. 2 is *linearizable*, i.e., its effects appear instantaneously to the rest of the system [6, Ch. 3.6]. Here, we do this in a constructive way: first, we construct all possible local schedules that Alg. 2 allows, then we show by contradiction that any interleaving of the schedules of two workers always respects a certain critical section (*CS*) of the algorithm, and finally, we generalize this for more workers. From the fact that *CS* is the only place where writes occur, we can conclude linearizability.[2] We assume that all lines in the code can be executed as atomic steps.

If the home location of a key k is empty, correctness follows from the properties of the atomic CAS operation at l.3. For every other table accesses (l.17 and l.20), we prove that never two workers can be in their *CS* for the same cluster.

The '$\rightarrow$' operator is used to denote the *happens-before relation* between those steps [6]. For example, 'CL-RIGHT$_i(\overline{x}) \rightarrow$ TRY-LOCK$_i(x)$' means that a Worker i always first executes CL-RIGHT writing to the variable x (l.11), and subsequently calls TRY-LOCK using (reading) the variable x. We omit the subscript i, if it is clear from the context which worker we are talking about. We concern ourselves with the following local happens-before order: CAS$(h) \rightsquigarrow$ CL-LEFT$(\overline{l}) \rightarrow$ CL-RIGHT$(\overline{r}) \rightarrow$ TRY-LOCK$(l) \rightsquigarrow$ TRY-LOCK$(r) \rightsquigarrow (occ(l) \oplus occ(r))$, where $occ(x)$ signifies a fill of a bucket $(T[x].occ \leftarrow 1)$ and $\rightsquigarrow$ indicates a happens-before relation dependent on a condition. Depending on the replacement end (left or right), PUT fills one of the buckets at the end of the cluster, hence the exclusive-or: $\oplus$. Furthermore, we write l_i, r_i and h_i for: the *left* variable, the *right* variable and the home-location $h_i = hash(k)$, all local to a Worker i.

Lemma 1. *Alg. 2 ensures that when two workers try to enter their CS for the same cluster, then:* $l_i = l_j \vee r_i = l_j \vee l_i = r_j \vee r_i = r_j$.

Proof. Assume Worker W_i is in its *CS*, and Worker W_j is about to enter the *CS* for the same cluster. Since W_i is in its *CS*, we have $T[l_i].lock$ and $T[r_i].lock$. W_i is going to perform the step $occ(l_i)$ or $occ(r_i)$. Note that these operations might influence the clusters, as two clusters separated by only one empty bucket, may become one upon filling the bucket.

---

[2] For completeness sake, we should also mention that we only allow for false positives to occur in non-exclusive reads and that unsuccessful non-exclusive reads are always followed by a read operation in the *CS*, i.e., an exclusive read.

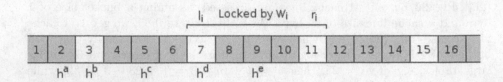

Fig. 2. Several clusters and empty positions. The cluster 8-10 is locked by worker W_i. Location marked with h^a to h^e potential home locations for worker W_j.

Worker W_j has yet to enter its CS, executing the steps: $\text{CAS}(h_j) \rightarrow \text{CL-LEFT}(\bar{l}_j)$ $\rightarrow \text{CL-RIGHT}(\bar{r}_j)$. With a generalizable example, Fig. 2 illustrates five non-trivial cases that we consider, where W_j starts with a h_j respective to the cluster l_i, r_i. Clusters in T are colored gray and we assume that they are separated by one empty bucket (white), because more empty buckets makes the resulting cases only more trivial. There are several representative home-locations marked with h^a to h^e (e.g., choosing a different location within the same cluster leaves the results of the CL-LEFT and CL-RIGHT operations unaffected). Locations on the right of r_i follow from symmetry. Below, we consider the outcome of all the cases for h_j. We use the fact that there are no empty buckets between l_j and r_j.

$h_j = h^a$: Because $T[h_j].occ$, $\text{CAS}(h_j)$ fails. W_j performs the steps CL-LEFT$(\bar{l}_j)$ $\rightarrow$ CL-RIGHT$(\bar{r}_j)$. Since $l_j = 1 < r_j = 3 < l_i$, Lemma 1 is vacuously true.

$h_j = h^b$: This location is unoccupied and not locked, so the $\text{CAS}(h_j)$ succeeds and the algorithm returns never reaching CS, making Lemma 1 vacuously true.

$h_j = h^c$: This location is occupied so $\text{CAS}(h_j)$ fails. Next, the step CL-LEFT$(\bar{l}_j)$ results in $l_j = 3$. The result r_j of CL-RIGHT is dependent on the state of W_i. If W_i has not already performed any occ or did perform $occ(11)$, then $r_j = 7$. If W_i has executed $occ(7)$, then $r_j = 11$. So, $r_j = 7 = l_i \vee r_j = 11 = r_i$.

$h_j = h^d$: The success of the $\text{CAS}(h_j)$ depends on the state of W_i. If W_i has not performed any steps, then $\text{CAS}(h_j)$ restarts the algorithm at l.7. If W_i has performed $occ(7)$, then W_j continues with CL-LEFT$(\bar{l}_j)$ and CL-RIGHT$(\bar{r}_j)$, resulting in $l_j = 3, r_j = 11 = r_i$. If W_i has performed step $occ(11)$, then $l_j = 7 = l_i, r_j = 15$.

$h_j = h^e$: Since h^e is occupied, $\text{CAS}(h_j)$ fails again. W_j continues with the CL-LEFT$(\bar{l}_j)$ and CL-RIGHT$(\bar{r}_j)$. The result depends on if W_i has executed $occ(7)$ or $occ(11)$. We distinguish five interleavings:

1: CL-LEFT$(\bar{l}_j) \rightarrow$ CL-RIGHT$(\bar{r}_j) \rightarrow (occ_i(7) \oplus occ_i(11)) \Rightarrow l_j = 7, r_j = 11 = r_i$
2: CL-LEFT$(\bar{l}_j) \rightarrow occ_i(7) \rightarrow$ CL-RIGHT$(r_j) \Rightarrow l_j = 7 = l_i, r_j = 11 = r_i$
3: CL-LEFT$(\bar{l}_j) \rightarrow occ_i(11) \rightarrow$ CL-RIGHT$(r_j) \Rightarrow l_j = 7 = l_i, r_j = 15$
4: $occ_i(7) \rightarrow$ CL-LEFT$(\bar{l}_j) \rightarrow$ CL-RIGHT$(r_j) \Rightarrow l_j = 3, r_j = 11 = r_i$
5: $occ_i(11) \rightarrow$ CL-LEFT$(\bar{l}_j) \rightarrow$ CL-RIGHT$(r_j) \Rightarrow l_j = 7 = l_i, r_j = 15$

Thus, under the above assumption: $l_i = l_j \vee r_i = l_j \vee l_i = r_j \vee r_i = r_j$. □

Theorem 1. *No two workers can be in their CS at the same time and work on the same cluster such that $l_i \leq l_j \leq r_i \vee l_i \leq r_j \leq r_i \vee (l_j \leq l_i \wedge r_j \geq r_i)$.*

Proof. By contradiction, assume the opposite: both W_i and W_j reach their CS and $l_i \leq l_j \leq r_i \vee l_i \leq r_j \leq r_i \vee (l_j \leq l_i \wedge r_j \geq r_i)$. Without loss of generality because of symmetry, we assume again W_i to have entered its CS first. The steps for W_j to arrive in its CS are:
CAS$(h_j) \rightarrow$ CL-LEFT$(l_j) \rightarrow$ CL-RIGHT$(r_j) \rightarrow$ TRY-LOCK$(l_j) \rightarrow$ TRY-LOCK(r_j).
The remaining step for W_i is: $occ(l_i) \oplus occ(r_i)$
W_i hash performed TRY-LOCK$(l_i) \rightarrow$ TRY-LOCK(r_i), thus we have $T[l_i].lock \wedge$ $T[r_i].lock$. According to Lemma 1 that at least one of the locations l_j and r_j equals either l_i or r_i. Therefore, W_j will always fail with either TRY-LOCK(l_j) or TRY-LOCK(r_j). This conclusively proves mutual exclusion for two workers. Since additional workers cannot influence W_j in such a way that Lemma 1 is invalidated, Theorem 1 also holds for $N > 2$ workers.   □

Absence of deadlocks (infinite restarts at l.7, l.13 and l.16), follows from the fact that all "locks" are always released before a restart or a return. Furthermore, we have absence of livelocks, because workers first "lock" the left side of a cluster. The one which locks the right side first, wins. With a fair scheduler the algorithm is also starvation-free, because each worker eventually finished its CS in a finite number of steps. From this, we conclude that Alg. 2 is linearizable.

4   Experiments

In the current section, we show an empirical evaluation of the Parallel Cleary Table (PCT), i.e. Cleary+DRL, by comparing its absolute performance and scalability with that of BLP+DRL, LHT and RBL. In our experiments, several parameters have been fixed as follows: $m = 28$, $b = 16$ for PCT, while for the non-compacting tables $b = 64$, and finally $\alpha = 0.9$. These parameters reflect best the goals we had in mind for this work, since all tables can store pointers larger than 32 bits. Furthermore, the load factor and bucket size for PCT is higher than the values discussed in Sec. 3.2, creating a healthy bias against this algorithm. Additionally, we investigated the influence of different load factors on all tables.

We used the following benchmark setup. All tables were implemented in the C language using pthreads.[3] For RBL, we determined the optimal size of the regions by finding the size that yielded the lowest parallel runtime. For table of 2^{28} buckets, this turned out to be 2^{13}. The benchmarks were run on Linux servers with 4 AMD Opteron(tm) 8356 CPUs (16 cores total) and 64GB memory. The maximum key size w that all tables can store in our configuration is 40: for PCT we have $w = b + m - 4 = 16 + 28 - 4 = 40$, and for BLP, LHT and RBL we have $w = 64 - 2 = 62$ (2 for the *lock* and *occ* bit). Therefore, we fed the tables with 40 bit keys, generated with a pseudo random number generator.

Table 1 gives the runtimes of all hash tables for different read/write ratios and load factor of 90%. Beside the runtimes with 1, 2, 4, 8, and 16 cores (T_N for $N \in \{1, 2, 4, 8, 16\}$), we included the runtimes of the sequential versions of the algorithms T_{seq}, i.e., the algorithm run without any locks and atomic

---

[3] Available at: http://fmt.cs.utwente.nl/tools/ltsmin/memics-2011

Table 1. Runtimes of BLP, RBL, LHT and PCT with r/w ratios 0:1, 3:1 and 9:1

Alg.	LHT			RBL			BLP			PCT		
r/w ratio	0:1	0:3	0:9	0:1	0:3	0:9	0:1	0:3	0:9	0:1	0:3	0:9
T_{seq}	77.5	242.4	569.2	76.7	239.9	563.2	71.8	279.1	676.0	54.5	368.9	1050.
T_1	81.6	255.2	599.2	145.9	565.4	1404.	97.5	302.0	726.3	77.3	565.9	1543.
T_2	51.6	157.6	371.0	85.0	327.6	813.4	60.8	188.8	443.9	44.4	317.7	863.9
T_4	26.5	77.9	184.0	46.2	170.2	424.9	31.3	94.0	219.1	23.4	159.7	431.9
T_8	13.9	39.6	92.9	24.0	89.4	219.2	16.5	47.8	110.3	11.5	79.7	216.0
T_{16}	7.7	21.1	48.8	13.5	48.6	120.5	9.4	25.5	57.2	6.0	41.6	112.9

instructions. From this, we can deduce the overhead from the parallelization. Comparing the runs with a r/w ratio of 0:1, we see that the sequential variants have more or less the same runtime (PCT is slightly faster, due to its compacter table). Only the lockless algorithms show little overhead when we compare T_{seq} to T_1, while DRL shows that the POSIX mutexes slow the algorithm down by a factor of two. The same trend is reflected in the values for T_N with $N > 1$.

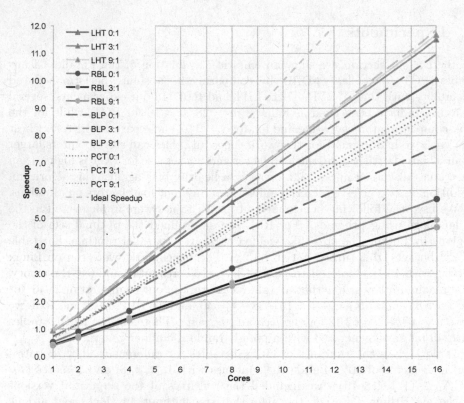

Fig. 3. Speedups of BLP, RBL, LHT and PCT with r/w ratios 0:1, 3:1 and 9:1

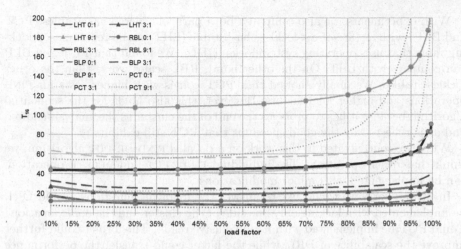

Fig. 4. 16-core runtimes of BLP, RBL, LHT and PCT

If we now focus our attention to the higher r/w ratios, we see that reads are much more expensive for PCT. This was expected, since non-exclusive reads in DRL are not allowed for PCT as explained in the previous section. To investigate the influence of the r/w ratio, we plotted the absolute speedups ($S_N = T_{seq}/T_N$) of the presented runs in Fig. 3. The lightweight locking mechanism of DRL delivers good scalability for PCT and BLP, almost matching those of LHT. While PCT speedups are insensitive to the r/w ratio, since the algorithm always performs the same locking steps for both read and write operations, BLP shows much better speedups for higher r/w ratios. Finally, we see that RBL is no competition to the lockless algorithms.

To investigate the effects of the load factor, we measured the 16-core runtimes of all algorithms for different load factors. To obtain different load factors we modified the number of keys inserted and not the hash table size, therefore we plotted the normalized runtimes T^{norm} in Fig. 4 ($T^{norm} = T/\alpha$, where $\alpha = n/|T|$ is the load factor and n the number of keys inserted). Due to the open-addressing nature of the hash tables presented here, the asymptotic behavior is expected for α close to 100% (the probe sequences grow larger as the table fills up). However, this effect is more pronounced for PCT, again because of the read-write exclusion, and for RBL, because more locks have to be taken once the probe distance grows.

5   Discussion and Conclusions

We have introduced DRL: an efficient lockless mechanism to parallelize BLP and Cleary compact hash tables efficiently. We have shown, analytically and empirically, that these Parallel Cleary Tables (PCT) scale well up to load factors of at least 80%. This is acceptable, since the compression ratio, obtained by compact hashing, can be far below this value.

With experiments, we also compared both parallel ordered hash tables (PCT and BLP) with a state-of-art lockless hash table (LHT) and a region-based locking table that uses operating system locks (RBL). We found that PCT and BLP can compete with LHT. On the other hand, RBL scales worse than the other lockless tables. We finally showed that PCT comes with higher costs for FIND operations and higher load factors. However, this also holds for the sequential algorithm because it has to probe to the end of the cluster as the analysis showed and as is reflected by the good speedups that PCT still exhibits.

While we concentrated in this work on a parallel FIND-OR-PUT algorithm, we think that other operations, like individual FIND, PUT and DELETE operation, can be implemented with minor modifications.

In future work, we would like to answer the following questions: Could DRL be implemented with locking only one side of the cluster and the home location? Could PCT be implemented with non-exclusive reads? The former could further improve the scalability of DRL, while the latter could transfer the performance figures of parallel BLP to those of PCT.

Acknowledgements. We thank Jaco van de Pol for providing useful comments on this work.

References

1. Amble, O., Knuth, D.E.: Ordered Hash Tables. The Computer Journal 17(2), 135–142 (1974)
2. Bryant, R.E.: Graph-Based Algorithms for Boolean Function Manipulation. IEEE Transactions on Computers 35, 677–691 (1986)
3. Cleary, J.G.: Compact Hash Tables Using Bidirectional Linear Probing. IEEE Transactions on Computers C-33(9), 828–834 (1984)
4. Click, C.: A Lock-Free Hash Table. Talk at JavaOne (2007),
   http://www.azulsystems.com/events/javaone_2007/2007_LockFreeHash.pdf
5. Geldenhuys, J., Valmari, A.: A Nearly Memory-Optimal Data Structure for Sets and Mappings. In: Ball, T., Rajamani, S.K. (eds.) SPIN 2003. LNCS, vol. 2648, pp. 136–150. Springer, Heidelberg (2003)
6. Herlihy, M., Shavit, N.: The Art of Multiprocessor Programming. M. Kaufmann (2008)
7. Laarman, A.W., van de Pol, J.C., Weber, M.: Boosting Multi-Core Reachability Performance with Shared Hash Tables. In: Sharygina, N., Bloem, R. (eds.) FMCAD 2010, pp. 247–255. IEEE Computer Society (2010)
8. Laarman, A., van de Pol, J., Weber, M.: Parallel Recursive State Compression for Free. In: Groce, A., Musuvathi, M. (eds.) SPIN Workshops 2011. LNCS, vol. 6823, pp. 38–56. Springer, Heidelberg (2011)
9. van der Vegt, S.: A Concurrent Bidirectional Linear Probing Algorithm. In: Heijnen, C., Koppelman, H. (eds.) 15th Twente Student Conference on Information Technology, Enschede, The Netherlands, Enschede. TSConIT, vol. 15, pp. 269–276. Twente University Press (2011),
   http://referaat.cs.utwente.nl/TSConIT/download.php?id=981

Four Authorization Protocols
for an Electronic Payment System

Roman Žilka[1], Vashek Matyáš[1], and Libor Kyncl[2]

[1] Faculty of Informatics, Masaryk University, Brno, Czech Republic
{zilka,matyas}@fi.muni.cz
[2] Faculty of Law, Masaryk University, Brno, Czech Republic
libor.kyncl@law.muni.cz

Abstract. Over the recent years the Czech law has become quite liberal towards electronic payment systems dealing with low-value goods ("micropayments") [1]. As of today, few businesses make use of the new legal facilities. This paper concerns a project aiming to support proliferation of the micropayment-based operations by creating a feature-rich, secure payment system with an open specification. More precisely, the key focus here will be payment authorization: as payments are carried out by an electronic device on a customer's behalf, there is a clear need for prevention of its abuse in case of theft. We introduce four original authorization protocols – each suited to a different environment – that prescribe the behavior of all relevant communicating devices and hopefully allow for secure and sound authorization.

Keywords: authorization, PIN, payment system, payment scheme, micropayments, security, privacy, Payment System Act.

1   Motivation and Setting

1.1   The Original Payment System

In legal terms a *payment system* (PS) is a funds transfer system with formal and standardised arrangements and common rules for processing, clearing and/or settlement of payment transactions [2]. Vaguely put, a PS defines an infrastructure for buying and selling services and goods, be it a tangible or electronic variety. A PS specification defines, among other items, a *payment scheme*: a set of communication protocols all system components must follow in order to attain the PS goals. This includes the format of data structures passed during communication.

In 2008 our team at the Faculty of Informatics, Masaryk University, Brno and the Y Soft Corporation, an industry partner, started a project whose aim is to develop a PS [4] which is to be secure, highly scalable, feature-rich and suitable for low-cost payments. Moreover, its specification is to be open, which then makes the PS unique. Figure 1 depicts the operation of the PS in a nutshell and marks the chronological order in which events take place. It also introduces the three

Z. Kotásek et al. (Eds.): MEMICS 2011, LNCS 7119, pp. 205–214, 2012.

main classes of actors: *customers* who buy items (event group III in Fig. 1) from *vendors* for units of digital cash – *cheques*. Cheques collected by vendors can be exchanged ("redeemed") for actual money at the *broker* (group IV) who controls a certain portion of customers' financial resources placed in payment accounts of sorts. Inscribed in the cheque is the precise value, the debtor (customer) and recipient (vendor) of money, as well as an identifier which makes the cheque substantially unique among all others.

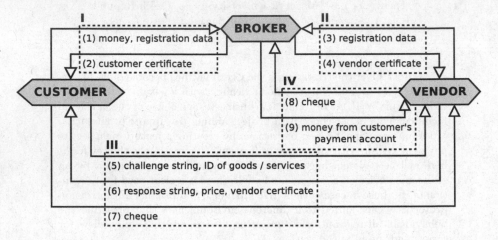

Fig. 1. A simplistic view of the payment system

In the electronic world of the payment scheme the broker is impersonated by a form of terminals or servers that are, by default, present only in a few designated locations, such as the broker's headquarters and branch offices. Vendors are impersonated by payment terminals situated at selling points. Payment terminals can make a remote connection to the broker terminal. Customers are represented by portable smart hardware *tokens* (customer tokens, CTs) that produce the (digitally signed) cheques. CTs are equipped with a display and the capacity to communicate with the broker and vendor terminals, but have to be physically brought to them. Any modifications to the software and contents of memory of the token can only be made by the token itself or by a broker terminal.

In one instance of the PS there are many customers and vendors, but only one broker who serves as a trusted third party to the former two groups. The broker registers a customer or a vendor in the system by accepting selected personal or corporate data from them and issuing a *customer certificate* or a *vendor certificate*, respectively (groups I and II in Fig. 1). Certificates are digitally signed by the broker and contain a public key of the holder, among other items. We assume the broker's public key to be known to all customers and vendors. Certificates also identify the debtor and recipient of money in a cheque.

1.2   Motivation for Payment Authorization

At some point during the development of the payment scheme we started carefully re-considering the cases of a customer finding out that she has been charged by the broker for wrongful transactions and trying to reclaim them. Here "wrongful transactions" may refer both to whole transactions and to incorrect values of transactions. Generally speaking, there are four groups of causes for such an occurrence: incorrect execution of a payment transaction, CT abuse by a thief, error made by the customer and cheating on part of the customer. Incorrect execution encompasses all possible problems that arise upon execution of the transaction itself and afterwards during its further processing. These problems may originate within the CT, at the vendor or at the broker.

According to the Czech law, in a PS which handles electronic money the way our system does, the customer is liable for loss of her money (actual or alleged) in any of these four cases ([1], art. 116, part 3). That is highly unfavorable for the customer, whose payment account would be open to free abuse by thieves. The customer thus asks that the broker provide a means of making sure that a purchase operation cannot result in a valid cheque, unless a secret held by the customer (not her CT, that is) is supplied. Providing such a mandatory parameter of a transaction is called *authorization* of a transaction by a customer. As the broker proceeds to implement authorization in the payment scheme, he announces to all vendors that cheques produced during unauthorized transactions will not be redeemed. It must be recognizable for the broker and the vendors whether authorization was carried out by the customer properly or not. Please note that a PS based on "electronic money" (as per [1]) is not legally obliged to support authorization. In fact, not so many existing systems do.

The law has much more to say on the whole topic and aims to define clearly who is to blame in the various non-standard situations the broker, the vendor and the customer can potentially find themselves in. Among other items, the law states that it is actually the broker who covers payments carried out using a stolen CT by a thief, but only if the customer had properly protected the PIN (i.e., had not written it down on the CT, had not told it to anyone etc.) and if she notifies the broker of the CT theft. However, if the customer claims that she had protected the PIN, the broker either has to believe her, or insist that the customer actually had not handled the PIN properly and prove this fact true directly to the customer, or at the financial arbitrator, or at the court – whichever necessary. Also, the broker becomes fully responsible for the thief's spendings only after the customer reports the CT loss – before that happens, it is the customer who pays for the thief, up to a limit of €150. That keeps the customer somewhat motivated to take good care of her CT.

On the other hand, in case the customer reclaims a transaction without a theft being involved, then the broker is again obliged to pay back for the transaction, if the customer proves that she has not lost the CT and claims that she has protected the PIN properly. This leaves the system vulnerable to a new set of abuse vectors. Please refer to [1] for full details on the legal environment.

The rest of the paper will only deal with transactions where authorization exists and is mandatory. For the sake of completeness let us add that in transactions where no authorization is implemented at all the law rids the broker of the obligation to pay back to the customer for all reclaimed transactions by default – the customer herself covers all transactions in that case. Our PS will possibly feature authorization-free transactions as well, but we have not yet decided firmly on the details.

1.3   Basic Requirements

According to a business decision made by Y Soft, we limit ourselves to authorization based on *PINs* – short decimal digit strings. We take it for granted that a means of manual PIN input ("PINpad" henceforth) will be available to the customer to carry out authorization at all selling points.

In each one of our authorization protocol (AP) designs we seek three qualities that together ensure the AP's *soundness*, i.e., security and proper functioning:

- *C-Dependence*: The sole possession of a CT is not enough to create a valid piece of digital currency (e.g., a "cheque with authorization", a cheque accompanied by another data structure, etc.). The correct PIN is a mandatory parameter of the purchase procedure. Only the legitimate customer (and possibly broker) is able to supply the correct PIN. For each purchase the expected correct PIN may be different.
- *B-Verifiability*: From the aforementioned piece of currency it must be recognizable for the broker whether the entity that issued the piece deemed authorization to have taken place correctly or not. This does not imply C-dependence, but together with C-dependence gives the broker a trustworthy means of telling authorized transactions from unauthorized ones.
- *V-Verifiability*: As with B-verifiability, but this time the said fact must be recognizable to the vendor.

2   Payment Authorization Protocols

2.1   Protocol 1: A Trusted PINpad

Key prerequisites:

- (i) Integrity of the CT is uncompromised, i.e., it operates as the broker intended and can be trusted in this sense by the customer and vendor.
- (ii) The CT and the PINpad share a secure communication channel (this implies, above all, that the vendor cannot eavesdrop on or interfere with the communication).
- (iii) The PINpad itself does not leak PINs outside the channel it shares with the CT.

– (iv) The PINpad is physically perfectly separated from the actual eyes and fingers of every person but the legitimate customer.

Under such circumstances, it is safe to pre-equip the customer with a single PIN to authorize all transactions. Authorization takes place just before step 7 of the payment scheme, as shown in Fig. 1. The CT knows the same PIN and unless it is supplied through the PINpad, the CT refuses to issue the cheque. Upon receiving and validating a PIN, the CT inserts a pre-defined tag into the cheque structure, signs the now-complete cheque and sends it to the vendor.

The AP is sound:

– C-Dependence: The CT refuses to hand over the (tagged) cheque to the vendor, unless the legitimate customer had previously input the correct PIN. No other person knows the PIN. The CT operates correctly, so its holder can trust it.
– B-Verifiability: The broker recognizes an authorized transaction by checking for the presence of the tag in the cheque.
– V-Verifiability: The same procedure.

An advantage of this AP is its low overhead: only a single PIN has to be given to a customer. This handover can take place in a secure environment (such as the broker's quarters) before any actual transaction. At the same time, the PIN is a single point of failure and because a human must memorize it, it must be short, which makes guessing not entirely impossible. Moreover, prerequisites (ii), (iii) and (iv) may be hard to realize.

2.2   Protocol 2: Customer Token Not Involved

This and the subsequent APs do not rely on the difficult prerequisites (ii), (iii) and (iv). As a consequence, the single-PIN strategy applied in the AP #1 does not work anymore: only the very first transaction of a customer would satisfy C-dependence. Transaction-specific single-use PINs are necessary then and we cannot rely on the customer remembering a number of them at once or learning them one after another at any reasonable pace. Single-use PINs are a specific variety of one-time passwords – a well-studied sub-field of IT security (see [3] and many others). Our protocols take heed of general recommendations; practical details, however, are not within the rather theoretical scope of this paper.

Key prerequisites:

– (v) The vendor has a stable means of communication with the broker.
– (vi) The (legitimate) customer carries a mobile phone. The broker can make use of that to contact her anytime; the broker-phone channel is considered as private. The customer is in exclusive, full control of her phone.

Figure 2 lists[1] the steps of the AP #2. While reading it, please bear in mind the structure of the cheque as given in Sect. 1.1. The protocol takes over immediately after step 7 as seen in Fig. 1. The CT does not appear in it at all. The vendor and the customer make use of the trusted third party – the broker, who generates a fresh PIN for each transaction.

1.	$V \to B$	$REQ = \mathbb{S}_V(cheque)$
2.	B	$\mathbb{V}(cert_C,\ cert_V,\ cheque);\ \mathbb{V}_{cert_V}(REQ)$
3.	B	checks that $cheque$ is fresh
4.	B	generates random PIN and $salt$; stores pair $(PIN, cheque)$
5.	B	$HPIN = \mathbb{F}(PIN, salt)$
6.	$B \to V$	$RESP = \mathbb{S}_B(cheque,\ HPIN,\ salt)$
7. $B \to$ C-Tel		PIN; phone number known by $cert_C$ in $cheque$
8.	$C \to$ pad	PIN
9.	pad $\to V$	PIN
10.	V	$\mathbb{V}(RESP)$; checks that $\mathbb{F}(PIN, salt) = HPIN$
11.	V	stores $RESP$ and pair $(cheque, PIN)$

Fig. 2. Authorization protocol #2 – a model run

The AP is sound:

– C-Dependence: The PIN is random for each transaction and is sent privately to the legitimate owner of the CT. The broker announces that he will refuse to redeem the cheque unless the PIN is submitted along with it. Matching PINs with cheques is possible on part of the broker (see steps 2–4 in Fig. 2). The broker knows whose phone number to send the PIN to by matching the serial number of the customer certificate stored in the cheque against a local customer phone number database. The vendor can only learn the correct PIN from the legitimate holder of the certificate.

– B-Verifiability: Follows from C-dependence.

– V-Verifiability: The broker sends a hash of the correct single-use PIN to the vendor as a response to the vendor's original request. The hash does not reveal the secret PIN to the vendor, yet allows him to verify whether the customer attempts to authorize the transaction using the correct PIN.

---

[1] For the sake of saving space we do not reflect the possible transmission errors and attacks in any of the protocol listings, although checks are present in their completeness. We put 'V' = vendor terminal, 'B' = broker terminal, 'CT' = customer token, 'C' = customer herself (the physical person), 'C-Tel' = customer's mobile phone, 'pad' = PINpad, '$cert_C$' = customer certificate, '$cert_V$' = vendor certificate, $\mathbb{S}_A(msg)$ = message and its signature made by the party A, $\mathbb{V}_{cert_A}(msg_1, msg_2, \dots)$ = verification of signatures on messages using the public key found in the $cert_A$, $\mathbb{V}(msg_1, msg_2, \dots)$ = verification of signatures on messages (using potentially different public keys), $\mathbb{E}_K(msg)$ = message encrypted by the symmetric key K, $\mathbb{F}(msg)$ = message processed by a slow one-way function.

If so, the vendor can be sure that the customer-provided PIN will allow for redemption of the current cheque.

Aside from soundness, the protocol takes measures to protect the PS from secondary attacks and errors. Above all, the threat of PIN-distribution infrastructure abuse (e.g., spamming, DoS) is countered by steps 2 and 3 as seen in Fig. 2. Still, abuse of this nature is possible: for example, in cooperation with a vendor, a thief could use a stolen CT to spam its owner's phone with PINs.

The AP #2 is advantageous over the AP #1 by allowing for slightly longer PINs (approx. 10 digits). That reduces the probability of a successful guess and makes brute-force attack on $HPIN$ infeasible within a reasonable time limit (please note that $\mathbb{F}$ is a slow function). Moreover, the PIN is different every time – once the customer has decided to use it, it would not matter if it were literally publicized. The mechanism is also immune to human forgetfulness.

A noteworthy disadvantage, on the other hand, is the protocol's very high overhead in communication and computation. This would be even greater if the protocol included the vendor's confirmation of accepting the hashed PIN from the broker. By omitting this step we force the broker to accept (and respond) only once to every single cheque. This, in return, triggers the need to dismiss a cheque and create another one to re-purchase the same goods in case the broker's response to the vendor gets lost or PIN delivery to the customer fails. Comfort of use is lower as well – the customer has to carry her mobile phone with her and copy a PIN from it during every transaction.

2.3   Protocol 3: Pre-distributed PINs

Key prerequisites:

- Prerequisite (i).
- (vii) The customer carries an item which can store PINs in hundreds; for the sake of simplicity and conformance to expected practice we will assume that it is a mobile phone. The customer is in exclusive, full control of this phone.
- (viii) New broker-produced random PINs are generated in batches – ordered sets ("PIN lists"). A copy of the PIN list is uploaded to the customer's mobile phone and another copy on her CT. Both these transfers are considered as private.
- (ix) From her own initiative the customer seeks out a broker terminal to receive new PINs whenever she deems it necessary.
- (x) The PIN list on a customer's CT and the list in her mobile phone are both immutable, except for the option to mark one or more PINs as 'used'. These marks are permanent for a given list.

In the AP #3 single-use PINs are delivered to the customer not only after a payment protocol run has begun, but beforehand in groups. The protocol does without a secure, reliable PINpad, but makes use of the CT. The typical run of the AP is depicted in Fig. 3. In terms of Fig. 1 it starts immediately after step 6 and is followed immediately by step 7.

1.	CT	all standard cheque components P_1, P_2, ... prepared
2.	CT	let PIN_1 = the last PIN marked as 'used'
3.	CT	let PIN_2 = the first PIN not marked as 'used'
4.	CT	$cheque = \mathbb{S}_C(PIN_2, P_1, P_2, \ldots)$
5.	CT	marks PIN_2 as 'used'
6.	CT	indicates on its display PIN_1
7.	C $\rightarrow$ pad	PIN_C = PIN from phone which follows the one on display
8.	pad $\rightarrow$ CT	PIN_C
9.	CT	if $PIN_C \neq PIN_2$, discards $cheque$ and terminates

Fig. 3. Authorization protocol #3 – a model run

The AP is sound:

- C-Dependence: The broker-generated PINs are random, so we can assume they will not be guessed. The broker will only redeem cheques that bear a valid signature and contain a PIN. A CT produces such cheque only if the correct single-use PIN is supplied. Only the legitimate customer knows this PIN. Furthermore, the CT only starts accepting a PIN as input after it has marked the first unused PIN as used and bound it irreversibly to the cheque that is to be handed over once the current transaction is authorized. This bound PIN can thus only authorize the current transaction and no other. Even if a malicious third party takes control of the PINpad, learns the PIN as it is input by the customer, prevents the PIN from reaching the CT, terminates the current transaction, later takes a hold of the CT and initiates a new transaction with it, the stolen PIN will be useless.
- B-Verifiability: A cheque bearing a valid signature is a sufficient proof.
- V-Verifiability: Analogous to B-verifiability.

Positives of this AP include ease of deployment, simplicity, absence of interaction with the broker during a transaction and feasibility of long and varying PINs. The foremost negative facet is the customer's and vendor's reliance on the integrity of the CT, as seen in the AP #1. Borrowed from the AP #2 is the trait of the customer having to carry around her PIN list. The prerequisite (ix) may feel somewhat inconvenient.

2.4   Protocol 4: On-Demand PIN List Delivery

Key prerequisites:

- Prerequisites (i), (v), (vi), (vii), (viii), (x).
- (xi) The broker and the CT share a secret symmetric key SK_{BC}.

The core ideas of the AP #4 copy those of the previous protocol. Here, however, the PIN list is sent to the customer's phone always over the mobile network (in the previous protocol the means of transport was unspecified), and the CT downloads its list via a vendor-broker channel during a transaction. Both these

1.	CT → V	a new PIN list request $REQ = \mathbb{S}_C(nonce, \text{cert}_C)$
2.	V → B	$V\text{-}REQ = \mathbb{S}_V(REQ, \text{cert}_V)$
3.	B	$\mathbb{V}_{\text{cert}_V}(V\text{-}REQ)$; $\mathbb{V}(\text{cert}_C, \text{cert}_V, REQ)$
4.	B	checks that request with pair $(nonce, \text{cert}_C)$ is fresh
5.	B	generates new random PIN list L; $RESP = \mathbb{S}_B(L, nonce)$
6. B → C-Tel		L
7.	C-Tel	adds L to current working PIN list
8.	B → V	$V\text{-}RESP = \mathbb{E}_{SK_{BC}}(\text{"PINLIST"}, RESP)$
9.	V → CT	$V\text{-}RESP$
10.	CT	$\mathbb{V}(RESP)$; checks $nonce$ in $RESP$
11.	CT	adds L to current working PIN list

Fig. 4. PIN list transfer sub-protocol for the authorization protocol #4 – a model run

list updates are triggered by a CT request, which occurs whenever the number of unused PINs on the CT has got too small. We deliberately avoid stating what "too small" is. If the number of unused PINs is sufficient at the beginning of a transaction, the procedure in Fig. 3 applies as AP with no changes. PIN list transfer comprises inserting steps given in Fig. 4 in between steps 1 and 2 of the protocol in Fig. 3.

The AP is sound:

- C-Dependence: The AP #3 is C-dependent. Even if the PIN list distribution sub-protocol in Fig. 4 is included, C-dependence will not be flawed – the PIN list is delivered only to the legitimate customer's phone (by a safe route) and to her CT (encrypted by SK_{BC}). The CT makes use of a random nonce to tell a fresh list from one replayed by an attacker.
- B-Verifiability: The AP #3 is B-verifiable.
- V-Verifiability: The AP #3 is V-verifiable.

The PIN list delivery infrastructure is susceptible to abuse in ways analogous to those discussed in Sect. 2.2 (spamming, DoS attacks). Similar measures are taken to counter such abuse.

This last AP can be viewed as a comfortable variation on the third one: the PIN list is delivered to the customer automatically when necessary, and she is not asked to regularly bring her CT (and mobile phone, if need be) to a broker terminal – an existing on-site communication infrastructure of the vendor is employed instead. This comfort brings about a range of negative traits almost equivalent to a sum of those of the second and third protocol: above all, integrity of the CT is assumed uncompromised, and a single run of the authorization sub-protocol is lengthy if new PINs need to be obtained from the broker. That, however, is expected to happen rarely. Because of that, in reality not every vendor needs to be connected to the broker constantly.

3 Conclusions

In this paper we have introduced in detail four novel PIN-based authorization protocols intended for our payment system. Each AP is suited for a different configuration of the PS and we clearly state the expected initial conditions per AP. Major prerequisites include an uncompromised customer token (in the APs #1, #3, #4), a secure, reliable PINpad (in the AP #1), and a ready vendor-broker communication channel (in the AP #2 and partially #4). Our aspiration with this paper is to seek critique from specialists in the fields of electronic security, protocol design, payment systems and possibly commercial and financial law. We have explored the general legal context of PSs and plan on performing a similar analysis of the APs themselves once their format is finalized.

Acknowledgements. Last but not least, we thank Ondřej Krajíček (Y Soft) and Andriy Stetsko (Masaryk Uni.) for their assistance and insight. We also thank the anonymous reviewers for their comments and suggestions.

References

1. Act No. 284/2009 Sb., Payment System Act, as amended
2. Directive 2007/64/EC of the European Parliament and of the Council of 13, on payment services in the internal market amending Directives 97/7/EC, 2002/65/EC, 2005/60/EC and 2006/48/EC and repealing Directive 97/5/EC, as amended (November 2007)
3. Menezes, A.J., van Oorschot, P.C., Vanstone, S.A.: Handbook of Applied Cryptography. CRC Press (2001)
4. Žilka, R., Tuček, P., Matyáš, V., Stetsko, A.: Otevřené mikroplatební schéma pro rozsáhlé infrastruktury. In: Rudolf, V. (ed.) Sborník příspěvků z 36. konference EurOpen.CZ. pp. 63–80. EurOpen.CZ, Plzeň, Czech Republic (May 2010), ISBN 978-80-86583-19-8, http://www.europen.cz/Anot/36/eo-1-10.pdf

Author Index